Television Musicals

Television Musicals

*Plots, Critiques, Casts and
Credits for 222 Shows
Written for and Presented on
Television, 1944–1996*

by
Joan Baxter

McFarland & Company, Inc., Publishers
Jefferson, North Carolina, and London

British Library Cataloguing-in-Publication data are available

Library of Congress Cataloguing-in-Publication Data

Baxter, Joan, 1925–
    Television musicals : plots, critiques, casts and credits for 222
shows written for and presented on television, 1944–1996 / by Joan
Baxter.
        p.   cm.
    Includes bibliographical references and index.
    ISBN 0-7864-0286-5 (library binding : 50# alkaline paper) ∞
    1. Television musicals—United States—Catalogs.   2. Television
musicals—United States—Plots, themes, etc.   I. Title.
ML2080.B39   1997
016.79145'6—dc21   97-13655
                                                                            CIP
                                                                            MN

Manufactured in the United States of America

*McFarland & Company, Inc., Publishers
    Box 611, Jefferson, North Carolina 28640*

To lovers of musicals everywhere

ACKNOWLEDGMENTS

I owe a great deal to the many people who assisted with this book by finding and providing information and photographs.

Thanks to Elizabeth W. Adkins and Alissa Berman of Kraft Foods Archives, director Kirk Browning, director Jon Jory and Wanda Snyder of the Actors Theatre of Louisville, actor Bradford Dillman, and composers Richard Adler, Steve Allen, Leonard Kastle, Albert Hague, and Fred Karlin for kindly digging out and filling in program information. Ronnie Pugh and Alan Stoker of the Country Music Foundation, Anthony Shanks of ABC's music department, and Tim Pickney, assistant to Fred Ebb, also supplied valuable pieces to fill gaps.

Ann Limongello of Capital Cities/ABC, Karl Koss of the General Electric Co., Ellen Hoch of the Hallmark Hall of Fame, and Gary Faircloth of East Carolina University Department of Theater Arts were most helpful and generous with photographs and supporting information. Ron and Howard Mandelbaum of Photofest also provided cheerful assistance in the picture department.

Ken Mandelbaum, Richard C. Lynch, Dave Jasen, and Don Stubblebine contributed their knowledge of musicals to answer some knotty questions, and Dave's listings of television sheet music were useful beginnings.

Most grateful thanks to Jane Klain for her interest, enthusiasm, and skill in tracking the minutiae of almost-lost musicals.

Special thanks to Joseph K. Albertson and Jim Baxter for providing a variety of source materials, innumerable bits and pages of information, and much moral support, and to Derek Hulse for additional assistance.

Although this book has different coverage, the books of authors George W. Woolery, Vincent Terrace, William Torbert Leonard, and Ken Bloom supplied much detail not available elsewhere for those shows of mutual interest.

Libraries played a major role in my research, and the gracious assistance of Thomas Nixon and other reference librarians and staff members at the University of North Carolina–Chapel Hill's Davis Library helped me through, as did librarian Diane

Pettit at the UNC Music Library, the staff at the North Carolina Collection of the Wilson Library, and the reference staff of the Chapel Hill Public Library.

A final overdue tip of the hat to Basil Rathbone and Cyril Ritchard, whose consummate theatricality enlivened many a television musical, and whose delectable hijinks made my studies fun.

CONTENTS

Acknowledgments vii
Preface 1
Introduction 3

THE MUSICALS

PREFACE

There is something special, something magical, about musicals. They are a unique form of entertainment, romantic and funny and exhilarating. The combination of words, music, color, and motion appeals to the ear and eye, and at its best fully involves the audience.

A "musical" as traditionally performed on the stage is a story with songs that are part of the story. The story has a beginning, middle and end; the songs help establish characters, move the plot along, intensify emotions and, above all, create appropriate moods. Generally musicals are thought of as light and cheerful entertainment, but serious subjects, even tragedy, can be the basis for a musical. Stories for musicals may be original, or may be adaptations of books or non-musical plays. Lyrics are original, but sometimes incorporate lines from source materials. Music is almost always original, though a few musicals have adapted classical music for songs. Musicals have been called light opera, operetta, musical comedy or sometimes plays with music. In operas most all dialogue is sung; otherwise the differences are mostly a matter of

definition or interpretation. Musicals on television have the same characteristics as stage or movie musicals but may be done in ways more suited to the small screen.

This book is an effort to provide information about original musicals written for and presented on television. Included are one-shot musical specials of any length; musical episodes from usually non-musical series; animated musical specials of interest to adults as well as children; and operas and related works commissioned for television. Made-for-television movies that are musicals are also covered. Some of the works listed have only one or two songs but are significant in television musical history. Not included are variety shows, which do not have a plot (and which are well-documented in Terrace's *Television Specials*); revues, which sometimes have a unifying theme but only occasional original music; and most children's animated musical specials of 30 minutes or less (which are well-documented in Woolery's *Animated Specials*). Broadway musicals adapted for television, even with different casts, are not included unless they were

1

completely new versions. For example, the Broadway version of *Peter Pan* starring Mary Martin was on stage before being shown on television and is therefore not covered here, but the 1976 *Peter Pan* had new words and music and is included. For information on shows and movies transferred to television, see Leonard's *Stage to Screen to Television*.

Are television musicals worth remembering? I think so. Of course some were better than others; the majority of stage and movie musicals were flops as well, and only a few stand out. Some critics have commented that songs from television musicals were forgettable, but few songs from any kind of musical succeed out of their story context, unless they receive repeated exposure to the public through an original cast album or recordings by pop singers. Regardless of critical opinion, there are some "hits" among our television musicals. As you will see, critics were not kind to many of the musicals listed herein, but it has been observed that critics are not always equipped to judge both drama and music. Sometimes, too, as with Broadway shows and movies, the music was good but a show lacked a coherent book or had a poorly chosen cast.

Other potential problems were unique to the medium. Actors lacking experience with television did not always do well. Furthermore, with a few exceptions (Rodgers and Hammerstein took nine months to develop *Cinderella*), television productions were written with shorter deadlines and less time was allowed for rehearsal. Despite all these possible drawbacks, there have been some fine musicals presented on television, and the real shame is that relatively few have been preserved for us to view again.

There is no easy way to locate all the musicals that have been done on television. Sorting out which are original works is a problem. For many shows, only meager information about the contents has been found. In the interest of broad coverage, shows have been included if they appear to have been musicals, but there may well be others which have not been recognized. In the earliest years, most programs were presented "live" and could not be "previewed" by the media, and reviews afterwards were not common. With live shows, little thought was given to preserving program contents. If they were filmed at all, it was by means of kinescopes (recordings made by filming TV monitors), many of which were later thrown away. Information about early television programs is poorly catalogued and sometimes inaccurate. I have endeavored to correct errors, expand coverage, and reconstruct missing information.

My primary goal in writing this book was to provide as much information as could be found about original television musicals (especially those heretofore not documented) and to identify their subjects, composers, lyricists, songs and performers. I can only hope that despite some gaps, my efforts have produced a useful reference work for those who love musicals.

INTRODUCTION

In more than fifty years of commercial television there have been many original musical productions. Some well-known authors, composers and lyricists have contributed their talents to these musicals.

When television began, little thought was given to program content. Equipment was being tested and improved. Productions were limited to a few people and basic sets; cameras lacked mobility; extremely bright lights were needed for an adequate picture. On the receiving end, television screens were small, and pictures lacked definition.

By the early 1930s, at least a dozen experimental stations were operating around the country. These stations used a variety of programs: scenes from plays, vaudeville skits, pantomimes, musical numbers, even film clips. Programs were short and broadcasts irregular. Program logs from that period give us inklings of musical offerings: CBS in New York had a "tele-musical" in 1931, followed shortly by a series, *Ned Wayburn's Musical Comedy*. Chicago offered a musical comedy, *Their Television Honeymoon*, in 1931. NBC gave its

first regular television demonstration in 1936 and followed this with several years of original and adapted programs; musical performances ranged from comedy skits to opera segments.

At the end of the decade, many people still believed there was no future in television. Radio people did not want the competition of television and tried to preserve their empires by discouraging talent from going to the new medium. Technical people were still concerned with improving the equipment. Only a few visionaries were interested in doing musicals, and for the time being, their visions would have to wait.

In 1940, in a dispute over royalties, the American Society of Composers, Authors and Publishers (ASCAP) banned broadcast of its entire catalog of music, which discouraged thoughts of musical productions. Broadcast Music Incorporated was quickly organized and signed up songwriters to fill the gap, which partially solved that problem, and the ASCAP matter was resolved in 1941. But Pearl Harbor changed priorities. Television development slowed to a crawl during World War II. Materials and personnel were diverted to military and government needs. Even though some stations now had commercial licenses, potential sponsors were unable to make products available, and most were not interested in the still-limited audience of television. Programs were curtailed or halted, except for public service and patriotic shows. Stations gradually resumed broadcasting, and an occasional musical was scheduled, but details are limited. The first fully documented, full-length original musical written for television was *The Boys from Boise*, seen on DuMont in 1944 (see listings).

Even after the war, government restrictions continued to delay assignment of television frequencies and manufacture of equipment. Further, the postwar economy got off to a slow start, and materials for the manufacture of television sets were not readily available. When production did resume, sales skyrocketed, and broadcasters searched for program materials to fill their expanding schedules. Networks were gradually built by use of coaxial cables connecting major cities (though coast-to-coast broadcasting was not achieved until 1951).

Yet an obstacle remained in the path of television musicals. In February 1945, the American Federation of Musicians had ordered its members not to appear on live television. Though some programs were done with recordings or *a cappella*, without live musicians, production of musicals seemed doomed. The ban was ended in 1948, and musical variety shows soon became a staple of early television.

Since networks originated programs from New York City, it is not surprising that Broadway stage productions soon became fodder for television, though usually as excerpts or condensations. Some stage musicals were also adapted for television broadcast, but not without difficulties. Early studios were small, so musicals had to be done with principals and chorus in the studio and the orchestra in another room following a monitor. Scenery had to be minimal in these crowded quarters. Furthermore, stage musicals, with their large casts and elaborate costumes and sets, were expensive to produce; early television, with little income, had to do with less.

Time limitations were another problem. Used to working with stage productions (whose running times were flexible) or films (which could be edited afterwards), writers and composers struggled with television's strict requirements. With live productions, running times could vary considerably even with carefully planned sequences.

Aside from the practical problems, each medium has its own unique qualities. Hollywood producers of the '30s were still struggling to learn how best to adapt a stage play to film; television producers now had to learn most effective ways to show plays on television. They soon realized that television was an intimate medium, putting the performer face-to-face with the viewer. Panoramic scenes did not work well; close-ups were important, and facial expressions became significant. Improved lenses and mobile and multiple cameras enhanced television shots. Entire production crews learned as they worked.

In 1947, the Kraft Theatre began its many years of dramatic programs. Philco, Goodyear, Alcoa, U.S. Steel, and other sponsors soon followed with similar anthology series. At first most dramas were adapted from novels or plays, but sponsors late turned to original works. Among the many serious dramas and comedies there were occasional musical offerings. *Omnibus*, which began in 1952, offered a wide range of cultural segments including music, drama, dance, and documentaries. In 1954 NBC began airing 90-minute "spectaculars" on Saturday and Sunday evenings. These shows were in color and included musical revues, adaptations of stage musicals, variety shows, and original musicals. The first "spectacular" was an original musical, *Satins and Spurs* with Betty Hutton, broadcast September 12, 1954. This production was not well received, but the specials continued under the title of *Producer's Showcase*. Their showing in March 1955 of *Peter Pan* with Mary Martin was probably the best known of the NBC specials. CBS soon followed with its own 90-minute specials, which included Rodgers and Hammerstein's *Cinderella* in 1957. ABC tried to bring back the "specials" with their *ABC Stage 67*, but this lasted for only one season. The DuMont network, which had had a continuing struggle to survive, went out of business in 1956. Meanwhile, NBC had formed a resident opera company in 1949 and commissioned composer Gian Carlo Menotti to write an original opera. Menotti's *Amahl and the Night Visitors* was performed for Christmas 1951. Other operas were commissioned and shown through the 1950s and early 1960s. CBS offered as specials a cantata, an oratorio, a Biblical spectacular and a number of operas.

As costs escalated, filmed shows replaced live television, sponsors became less willing to experiment, and ratings began to control commercial television offerings. By the mid-1960s, live programs could be videotaped, but there were fewer musicals to be preserved. A Ford Foundation grant brought new operas to public television in the early 1970s, and there were occasional musicals on the networks, but specials were largely "star" musical performances and variety shows.

Today's television is very different from what was available in earlier years, with innumerable channels and an endless variety of program offerings. But for original musicals, the best we can hope for is probably a holiday special now and then.

A Guide to the Entries

Shows are listed alphabetically by show title. Listings also contain all or some of the items described below.

All entries begin with the title of the show, the running time (with commercials), and a description identifying the type of show (primarily Musical, Animated Musical, Opera, or Drama with Music). Any alternate titles are noted in the comments and cross-referenced in the listing. If the show was broadcast as part of a series or special such as *Shower of Stars* or *Lincoln-Mercury Startime*, the title of that series or special follows the show descriptor.

Broadcasting information follows, providing the date, time and network of the first television performance. Time is Eastern Standard or Daylight time. Programs may have been broadcast at other times by stations carrying more than one network. In some cases, too, broadcast may have been delayed by other events. PBS show times vary locally. Syndicated shows may not have specific dates. Repeat showings are not listed.

Following the broadcast data are credits for the producer, director, lyricist, composer and others contributing to show production. "Writer" means author of the book for the show; if the story was adapted from a book, short story or play, the source is identified in the comments on the work. Likewise, if music is based on works of a classical composer, that information is supplied in the commentary.

Information on vocal recordings, videotapes, and sheet music follows the credits. If a show was ever recorded, or a videotape issued, this information is listed even though the recording or video may not be currently available. If songs were published, the name of the publisher and the number of songs published is provided; the number in parentheses following the publisher's name indicates the number of songs published. In some cases, vocal selections or complete scores were published.

The cast list for each show is compiled from all available sources and is as complete as possible.

Complete song listings are given when available. Sometimes only "highlights" were found, and in a few cases no song titles were located. Sources for this information include videos, recordings, sheet music, *TV Guide* listings and reviews. Some composers were contacted for song lists. Because operas are sung through, they do not have separate song listings.

Information about stories was gathered from a variety of sources. If a video was available, it was viewed and the story summarized. Otherwise, source materials (books, plays and short stories) were consulted, and information from *TV Guide* listings and reviews used to reconstruct the storylines. In some cases, detailed plot information simply could not be found; inaccuracies may exist in these write-ups.

Miscellaneous information following the story outline includes the source of the story and, where applicable, the music; any "firsts" that the work represents; and notes about composers, lyricists, and actors. If a show was nominated for or received awards, that information is also noted. In the case of Emmy awards, the nomination is probably more significant than the award itself. Award categories have changed over the years but generally lump together several kinds of shows (e.g., "best musical, variety or comedy special"). Julie Andrews was nominated for *Cinderella*, but in the category "Actress— best single performance (lead or support)." Without separate categories for musicals, voters appear to lean toward the serious dramatic works or comedies, so a nomination for a musical is noteworthy indeed.

Availability of reviews varied over the years, as publications began and discontinued their television reviews at different times. If no reviews were found contemporary with the shows, video guides were searched for pertinent comments. Dates of reviews are included whenever possible. (Some reviews were available only through secondary sources that did not furnish dates.)

Where to Find More Information

For anyone wanting to do further research on the musicals listed here, the following information may prove helpful:

a. In an up-to-date check of the Schwann catalogs, I found only a handful of audio recordings (in any format) to be currently available. Some LPs can be found through auction lists or in used record stores.

b. The majority of videos mentioned in the text are no longer available, but local rental outlets may still have some in stock.

c. Sheet music publishers have often been bought out, merged or gone out of business. Music may or

may not be available from successors. The most likely sources are used music sales.

d. Sponsors of the earlier shows do not, for the most part, have records of these shows. The few companies having archives advise that their records are generally incomplete.

e. Sources listed below have films and tapes for on-site viewing, including kinescopes not otherwise available:

> Museums of Television and Radio (New York City and Los Angeles)
> Library of Congress
> UCLA Film and Television Archive

There are many other film archives, but not many include television, and some that do specialize in news and special events coverage.

These comments are not meant to discourage researchers. While the information gaps at times proved so disheartening that I thought of calling this book *Lost Musicals*, I believe the information can still be found somewhere, perhaps in private collections.

THE MUSICALS

1. *The Accused* 30 minutes. Opera. *Camera Three*. Broadcast May 7, 1961 (Sunday, 10:30–11:00 A.M.) CBS

Executive Producer Merrill Brockway; *Director* John Desmond; *Librettist* Sheppard Kerman; *Composer* John Strauss; *Conductor* Julius Rudel; *Set Designer* Neil De Luck.

Cast: Patricia Neway

Story: A woman condemned to death in the Salem witch trials faces her accusers; she charges them with wanting to destroy all that is good and free in the human soul.

Camera Three was a Sunday-morning fixture on CBS. The show had a wide variety of programs in the arts and sciences, including concerts, dramas and interviews. This show was a one-woman drama; none of the persecutors appear, and murmurs of the courtroom crowd are conveyed by the orchestra. Neway appeared in many television operas, and played the Abbess in Broadway's *The Sound of Music.*

Review: *Musical America* (July 1961): Critic Michael Sorrino wrote that Neway's acting, in a role that required great emotional range, "became unrestrained to the point of embarrassment," sacrificing "tonal quality, musicianship and enunciation for 'acting.'" Sorrino noted that while a good score might have improved the situation, the best this work had to offer was "a grab-bag assortment of Wozzeck-like intensity and neo-romantic clichés," with a pretentious libretto. Sorrino's praise was reserved for technical matters: "Sets, lighting and camera work were excellent."

2. *Ace Hits the Big Time* 60 minutes. Musical. *CBS Schoolbreak Special*. Broadcast April 2, 1985 (Tuesday, 4:00–5:00 P.M.) CBS

Producer Martin Tahse; *Director* Robert C. Thompson; *Writer* Linda Elstad; *Lyricist* Harriet Schock; *Composer* Misha Segal.

Cast: Rob Stone, Julie Akin, Karen Petrasek, Kelly Britt, Tony Longo, Anthony Barrile, James Le Gros, Lance Slaughter

Songs: Not found.

Story: Horace "Ace" Hobart, a 16-year-old from New Jersey, tries to adjust to his move to Marshall High in Manhattan. His fantasies about his new life and his actual confrontations with street gangs (the Piranhas and the Purple Falcons) make up the story.

3. *The Adventures of Huck Finn*
60 minutes. Musical. *U.S. Steel Hour.*
Broadcast November 20, 1957 (Wednesday, 10:00–11:00 P.M.) CBS

Director Elliott Silverstein; *Writer* Ann Croswell; *Lyricists/Composers* Frank Luther, Ann Croswell, Lee Pockriss.

Cast: Jack Carson, Basil Rathbone, Jimmy Boyd, Florence Henderson, Earle Hyman, Karlen Wolfe

Songs: "Loafin' on the Water," "My Friend Huckleberry Finn," "The Boasting Song," "The Time Has Come to Say Goodbye," "We'll All Shout Together in the Mornin'," "Storm Come A-Risin'," "Funny But Likeable," "Too Wonderful for Me," "You Are One to Wander."

Story: Huck Finn and his friend Jim, a runaway slave, are traveling down the Mississippi River on a raft when they meet two scoundrels who call themselves King and Duke. Jim is completely taken in by their fakery, but Huck goes along with their lies and swindles until they try to bilk the Wilks sisters by posing as long-lost relatives. Huck knows it is wrong for the crooks to take the money, so he steals it back and hides it in a coffin. When he is satisfied that the money will be returned to the sisters, Huck runs off.

Based on the book by Mark Twain (1885). Rathbone in his autobiography commented on the making of this show, alluding to the frantic atmosphere and inadequacies of time for preparation and rehearsal. Composer Frank Luther wrote a large number of children's songs for records.

Reviews: *Variety* (Nov. 27, 1957): "Emerged as a vapid piece lacking the color, satire and inspiration of the original. ... Huck and Jim are of secondary importance ... Carson and Rathbone

had a Smithfield day hamming up their parts, played it broad and loud. ... Luther's score added little...."

Time (Dec. 2, 1957): "They changed it all around and they put the wrong people in it. ... To see Rathbone & Carson was like a showboat, not a raft.... They made [Huck] slushy romantical over Mary Jane Wilks and had her batting her eyes and singing love songs at him."

4. *The Adventures of Marco Polo*
90 minutes. Musical. *Max Liebman Presents.* Broadcast April 14, 1956 (Saturday, 9:00– 10:30 P.M.) NBC

Producer/Director Max Liebman; *Assistant Producer* Bill Hobin; *Writers* William Friedberg, Neil Simon; *Lyricist* Edward Eager; *Music* Clay Warnick, Mel Pahl; *Conductor* Charles Sanford; *Orchestrator* Irwin Kostal; *Choreographer* James Starbuck; *Set Designer/Art Director* Frederick Fox; *Costume Designer* Paul du Pont; *Record* LP Columbia ML 5111; *Sheet Music* Mason Music (3).

Cast: Alfred Drake, Doretta Morrow, Beatrice Kraft, Arnold Moss, George Mitchell, Paul Ukena, Harold Vermilyea, Ray Drakeley

Songs: "Beyond the Sunset," "The Tartar Song," "You'll Be Seeing Me," "The Garden of Imagining," "Market Day," "Who, Me?," "Xanadu," "Uneasy Lies the Head," "Population," "Worlds," "Silver Bells," "Is It You?"

Story: The adventures of Italian explorer Marco Polo as recorded in his journal take him from Venice to the mysterious lands of the East. He visits the opulent court of Kublai Khan in China, the exotic realm of the ruler of Tibet and the mysterious kingdom of Persia, with many bazaars and entertainments (as well as a love story) along the way.

The composers adapted the music of Russian composer Rimsky-Korsakov for their songs. Alfred Drake, who played Marco, had starred on Broadway in *Oklahoma!*, *Kiss Me Kate*, *Kismet* and many other musicals and dramas.

Review: *Variety* (April 18, 1956): "Max Liebman brought in a lush, lusty and tasty dish. It was a sumptuous production, romantic in the right places, a tongue-in-cheek romp in others." *Variety* deemed Alfred Drake to be a "solid sender," and found good songs and a "nifty book."

5. *Aladdin* 90 minutes. Musical. *Du Pont Show of the Month.* Broadcast February 21, 1958 (Friday, 7:30– 9:00 P.M.) CBS

Producer Richard Lewine; *Director* Ralph Nelson; *Writer* S. J. Perelman; *Lyricist/Composer* Cole Porter; *Musical Director* Robert Emmett Dolan; *Orchestrator* Joe Glover; *Choreographer* Rod Alexander; *Costume Designer* Irene Sharaff; *Scenic Designer* Robert Makell; *Record* LP Columbia CL 1117; *Sheet Music* Buxton Hill (4).

Cast: Anna Maria Alberghetti, Cyril Ritchard, Dennis King, Sal Mineo, Basil Rathbone, Una Merkel, George Hall, Howard Morris, Geoffrey Holder, Alexander Clark, John McCurry

Songs: "Come to the Supermarket," "Wouldn't It Be Fun," "Make Way for the Emperor," "Aladdin," "Trust Your Destiny to a Star," "I Adore You," "Opportunity Knocks But Once," "No Wonder Taxes Are High."

Story: The magician narrates the story. At the supermarket in Peking, Aladdin sees Princess Ming Chu, daughter of Emperor Chang. When her skirt accidentally catches fire, Aladdin rushes to put out the flame. The princess thanks him, they exchange glances and are smitten. Magician Sui Generis spots Aladdin and develops a scheme in which the Astrologer catches Aladdin and tells him he will be visited by a long-lost relative; the Magician poses as the uncle, and after visiting with Aladdin's mother, takes the boy to a distant cave to try to retrieve a magic lamp, planning to kill Aladdin afterwards. But the cave closes up with Aladdin—and the lamp—inside. Given up for dead, Aladdin accidentally summons the Genie of the Lamp and at his wish is transported home. He asks the Genie for a meeting with the Princess, who is pining for him, and she and Aladdin declare their love. Aladdin then visits the Emperor to request his daughter's hand, and promises to perform some magic to show he is worthy. Meanwhile the Magician has learned of Aladdin's return, obtains the magic lamp by trading new lamps for old, replaces the Emperor with himself and puts the Emperor and Aladdin in the dungeon. When Aladdin's pickpocket neighbor appears in the cell, Aladdin asks him to steal back the lamp, and order is restored. Aladdin and the Princess are wed and live happily ever after.

Aladdin was Porter's first original work for television and, as it turned out, his last musical. The last song he wrote was for the Emperor, "Wouldn't It Be Fun" (not to be famous, not to be rich), which some felt reflected Porter's view of his life. This song does not appear on the kinescope. The lavish production cost $500,000.

Reviews: Stephen Citron (*Noël and Cole*): "Unfortunately it shows very little of the wit that Cole generally brought to fairy tales or fantasy. Perelman's script moved the hero into ancient China and owed more to slapstick than to his usual vitriolic wit, while Cole's music ... did not even seem to try for the kind of elegant East-West fusion ... of which Cole was entirely capable."

Time (March 3, 1958): "The story had everything but taste. Cyril Ritchard's sporadic drollery clashed with the eager droolings of the teenager's rage, Sal Mineo, whose Aladdin only maddened."

Variety (Feb. 26, 1958): "Dull as it was opulent. ...Sal Mineo's Aladdin didn't particularly enhance matters ... still a tough kid of the street. ...Serviceable score."

New York Times (Jack Gould, Feb. 22, 1958): "A pretentious ordeal. ... Mineo hopelessly out of place, ... The book was a routine and labored operation. Mr. Porter was similarly uninspired."

6. *Aladdin* 60 minutes. Musical. Broadcast December 6, 1967 (Wednesday, 7:30–8:30 P.M.) CBS

Executive Producer Richard R. Rector; *Producer* Ethel Burns; *Director* Nick Havinga; *Writer/Stager* Jim Eilers; *Songs* Jim Eiler/Jeanne Bargy; *Arranger* Richard Hayman; *Decor* A. E. Klein.

Cast: Fred Grades, Will B. Able, Don Liberto, Avril Gentles, Vicki Morales, David Lile, Robert Dagny, Graziella

Songs: "Flying My Kite," "Magician Chant," "Lovely Morning in China," "I Am a Genie," "Aladdin," "Fatima Dance," "The Journey," "Tea Time."

Story: A poor tailor's son falls in love with and tries to win the Emperor's daughter. He is aided in his courtship by the Genie of the magic lamp, and despite the opposition of a wicked magician, finally wins his fair lady.

Produced by New York's Prince Street Players, Limited, this show was staged in the traditional style of the Chinese theater. The Prince Street Players also presented *Pinocchio*, *Jack and the Beanstalk* and *The Emperor's New Clothes* for TV.

Review: *Variety* (Dec. 13, 1967): "This new production was an entertaining one. ... Pleasant songs by Jim Eiler/Jeanne Bargy, attractive trappings by A. E. Klein, pert performances by the Prince Street Players in their fourth production."

7. *Alice in Wonderland* or *"What's a Nice Kid Like You Doing in a Place Like This?"* 60 minutes. Animated Musical Broadcast March 30, 1966 (Wednesday, 8:00–9:00 P.M.) ABC

Executive Producers William Hanna, Joseph Barbera; *Producer/Director* Alex Lovy; *Writer* Bill Dana; *Lyricist* Lee Adams; *Composer* Charles Strouse; *Music Director* Hoyt Curtin; *Arranger* Marty Paich; *Record* LP HBR 2051 (Demo, different cast); *Video* Worldvision; *Sheet Music* Edwin H. Morris.

Cast (voices): Sammy Davis, Jr., Hedda Hopper, Zsa Zsa Gabor, Harvey Korman, Bill Dana, Howard Morris, Alan Reed, Mel Blanc, Janet Waldo, Doris Drew, Allan Melvin, Daws Butler, Don Messick

Songs: "Life's a Game," "Today's a Wonderful Day," "They'll Never Split Us Apart," "I'm Home," "What's a Nice Kid Like You Doing in a Place Like This?"

Story: In a modern-day spoof of the classic story, Alice and her dog Fluff visit Wonderland. They meet the usual characters but with some cartoon character traits and witty dialogue. Characters include Hedda Hatter and Humphrey Dumpty.

Bill Dana played the White Knight using his José Jiminez voice. Composer/lyricist Strouse and Adams wrote a number of Broadway musicals including *Bye Bye Birdie*. This show was nominated for an Emmy for music arranging.

Reviews: *Variety* (April 6, 1966): "The stab at hip humor didn't even come close. The stuff consisted of showbiz allusions, some home sampler (camp) philosophy, and pedestrian puns. ... Voiceover celebs parodied only themselves. The results were strictly ho-hum."

8. *Alice in Wonderland Part I* 2 hours. Musical. Broadcast December 9, 1985 (Monday, 8:00–10:00 P.M.) CBS (See also *Alice in Wonderland Part II*, broadcast December 10, 1985)

Producer Irwin Allen; *Director* Harry Harris; *Writer* Paul Zindel; *Lyricist/Composer* Steve Allen; *Conductor/Score* Morton Stevens; *Costume Designer* Paul Zastupnevich; *Choreographer* Miriam Nelson; *Video* Warner Home Video; *Music* Columbia (Vocal Selections).

Cast: Sheila Allen, Steve Allen, Scott Baio, Ernest Borgnine, Beau Bridges, Lloyd Bridges, Red Buttons, Sid Caesar, Carol Channing, Imogene Coca, Sammy Davis, Jr., Patrick Duffy, George Gobel, Eydie Gorme, Natalie Gregory, Merv Griffin, Sherman Hemsley, Ann Jillian, Arte Johnson, Harvey Korman, Steve Lawrence, Karl Malden, Roddy McDowall, Jayne Meadows, Donna Mills, Pat Morita, Robert Morley, Anthony Newley, Donald O'Connor, Louis Nye, Martha Raye, Telly Savalas, John Stamos, Ringo Starr, Sally Struthers, Jack Warden, Jonathan Winters, Shelley Winters, Charles Dougherty, Billy Braver, Ernie Orsatti, Scotch Byerly, Robert Axelrod, Michael Chieffo, Jeffrey Winner, John Walter Davis, James Joseph Galante, Selma Archerd, George Savalas, Candace Savalas, Troy Jordan, Tom McLoughlin, Patrick Culliton, Laura Carlson, Kristi Lynes, Desiree Szabo, Barbie Alison, Janie Walton, Dee Brantlinger, Don Matheson

Songs: "I Hate Dogs and Cats," "Laugh," "Father William," "Off with Their Heads!," "I Didn't, You Did," "Nonsense," "There's No Way Home," "There's Something to Say for Hatred," "Why Do People Act as If They're Crazy?"

Story: Alice, sitting on the bank of a stream with her sister, sees a white rabbit hustling by. Following it, she falls down a rabbit hole and finds herself in a room with many doors. With magical potions she grows smaller, then bigger, then smaller again; she finally leaves through a hole and falls into a pool of her own tears where birds and a mouse swim by. Off to the rabbit's house she goes, but drinks another potion and becomes too big to leave the house and scares the animals. She eats a cake, gets smaller, and goes on her way. She meets the Caterpillar and the Cheshire Cat (who disappears). She visits the Duchess' house, takes the crying baby and it turns into a pig. She stops at the Mad Hatter's tea party, then finds her way into a formal garden where white roses are being painted red for the Queen of Hearts. Alice plays their strange game of croquet, meets the Griffin and the Mock Turtle, then attends a trial. She finally says "You're nothing but a pack of cards!" and awakens back home.

This lavish production was a four-hour spectacle shown on two successive

Steve Allen

nights. Producer Irwin Allen, best known for his sci-fi and disaster pictures, showed a change of pace here (but perhaps his background accounted for the major role of the Jabberwock in *Part II*). The show followed Lewis Carroll's books of 1865 and 1871 fairly closely. Writer Zindel is a Pulitzer Prize-winning playwright. Sheila Allen, who played Alice's mother, is Irwin Allen's wife. Steve Allen (no relation) wrote the songs (and many more, not used); he also appeared as the Gentleman in the Paper Suit. His wife Jayne Meadows played the Queen of Hearts. Steve was an Emmy and Grammy winner for earlier work. Talented Natalie Gregory, who played Alice, was about the right age, and her acting, singing and dancing were excellent. Especially noteworthy was the tap

Left to right: Pat Morita, Steve Allen, Merv Griffin, Natalie Gregory, and Patrick Duffy in *Alice in Wonderland Part II* **(1985). Courtesy of Steve Allen.**

dance routine with the Caterpillar (Sammy Davis, Jr.).

Reviews: *New York Times* (Dec. 9, 1985): Critic John J. O'Conner was pleased to find that most of Carroll's characters and situations had "a chance to strut their stuff.... And Mr. Allen's penchant for special effects adds a number of embellishments.... Some songs, especially the ballads, are quite lovely.... Most are merely serviceable...."

    Variety (Dec. 18, 1985): "Charm of the original has been all but demolished except for the delightful talented and winning Natalie Gregory as Alice...." *Variety* called Steve Allen's songs "banal, simplistic ditties."

9. *Alice in Wonderland Part II* 2 hours. Musical. Broadcast December 10, 1985 (Tuesday, 8:00–10:00 P.M.) CBS

Producer Irwin Allen; *Director* Harry Harris; *Writer* Paul Zindel; *Lyricist/*

Composer Steve Allen; *Conductor/Score* Morton Stevens; *Costume Designer* Paul Zastupnevich; *Choreographer* Miriam Nelson; *Video* Warner Home Video; *Music* Columbia (Vocal Selections).

Cast: See *Alice in Wonderland Part I* where entire cast is listed. Although this part is a different story, some characters appear in both parts.

Songs: "How Do You Do, Shake Hands," "Can You Do Addition?," "The Lion and the Unicorn," "Emotions," "The Walrus and the Carpenter," "Hush-A-Bye Lady," "Jam Tomorrow," "To the Looking-Glass World," "We Are Dancing," "Alice."

Story: Alice finds herself on the other side of the mirror, reading a book about the Jabberwock. She says she is not afraid, but when the monster comes, along with a violent storm, she screams and knocks over the chessmen. She picks them up and finds the little creatures talking. The owl in a picture tells her that in Looking Glass Land everything is backwards and beginnings are endings. Alice finds herself in a garden with talking flowers. The Red Queen enters and tells Alice she can become a queen when she gets to the eighth square. Alice lands on a train with strange characters, journeys on to meet Tweedledum and Tweedledee, and has a chat with the White Queen. The Jabberwock pushes Humpty Dumpty off the wall. After more adventures, Alice reaches the eighth square and finds a crown on her head. The Red Queen and the White Queen quiz her on her suitability. She enters a house marked "Queen Alice" and finds everything ready for a party. While everyone is making merry, a present is delivered for Alice. She opens it and out pops the Jabberwock. There is great fighting and running and screaming by everybody. Alice runs, finds herself by the mirror and climbs through, the Jabberwock hot on her trail. She realizes she must conquer her fear, tells the Jabberwock she doesn't believe in him, and he disappears.

This part is based on Lewis Carroll's *Through the Looking Glass*. The video is titled *Alice Through the Looking Glass*.

Reviews: See *Part I*

10. *Alice Through the Looking Glass*
90 minutes. Musical. Broadcast November 6, 1966 (Sunday, 7:30–9:00 P.M.) NBC

Producers Alan Handley, Bob Wynn; *Director* Alan Handley; *Associate Producer/Art Editor* E. Jay Krause; *Writer* Albert Simmons; *Lyricist* Elsie Simmons; *Composer* Moose Charlap; *Musical Director* Harper MacKay; *Choreographer* Tony Charmoli; *Vocal Arranger* Don Costa; *Costumes* Bob Mackey, Ray

Aghayan; *Makeup* Claude Thompson; *Record* LP RCA LOC 1130; *Video* Sultan Entertainment.

Cast: Roy Castle, Robert Coote, Jimmy Durante, Nanette Fabray, Judi Rolin, Jack Palance, Agnes Moorehead, Richard Denning, Ricardo Montalban, Tom Smothers, Dick Smothers, Iris Adrian, Mary Esther Denver, Shannon Hale, Jackie Joseph, Clara Taft, George Simmons, Donna Walsh

Songs: "Through the Looking Glass," "Keep on the Grass," "I Wasn't Meant to Be a Queen," "Some Summer Day," "Jabberwock Song," "The Backwards Alphabet," "Who Are You?," "'Twas Brillig," "There Are Two Sides to Everything," "Come Out, Come Out, Wherever You Are," "Alice Is Coming to Tea."

Story: Alice's family is having a party for grownups, and her father suggests that Alice set up the chessmen in the library. She finds herself going through the mirror with the Red King, and they discuss his two sides. Alice meets the inept White Queen, who warns Alice of the Jabberwock, but Alice calls out the Jabberwock and says she is not afraid. The royals agree to send Alice to the castle to make her a Queen. The Jabberwock appears, and frightens Alice. She finds a door that leads her to a garden with talking flowers; Lester, the royal jester, joins Alice, and dancers perform. Everyone disappears and Alice finds herself with the White King, who gives her good advice. Alice then runs into some witches, Tweedledum and Tweedledee and Humpty Dumpty, with the kings and queens, the Jabberwock and the jester making appearances along the way. The kings and queens thank Alice for defeating the Jabberwock, and the knights, after a spectacular dance, ride out to finish the creature off. The others crown Alice queen, but when the Jabberwock is brought in he breaks loose and chases Alice back to her mirror library where she and Lester go through the mirror. Her father finds her asleep in the chair, holding a jester doll.

Based on the 1871 book. Though not all of Lewis Carroll's characters appear in this version of *Through the Looking Glass*, much of the original nonsense is used in dialogue and songs. It appear this production was done in a large auditorium with an audience who laughed in the right places and applauded the dancing. The music was lively and the scenes colorful. The show won an Emmy for costume design and was nominated for makeup. The Original Cast recording was nominated for a Grammy for best children's recording.

Review: *Variety* (Nov. 9, 1966): "Bold coloring, star performances, broad comic value ... capable performances ... buoyant production numbers ... generally unimpressive music and lyrics."

11. *All About Me*   60 minutes. Animated/Live Musical. *NBC Children's Theatre*. Broadcast January 13, 1973 (Saturday, 1:00–2:00 P.M.) NBC

Executive Producer George Heinemann; *Producer* C. C. Ryder; *Director* Bill Ackerman; *Writers* Will Ito, Ric Gonzalez, Bill Ackerman, Cal Howards, Roy Freeman; *Lyricist/Composer* C. C. Ryder; *Lyrics "Skin Song"* Roy Freeman.

Cast (voices): Sterling Holloway, Peter Halton

Songs: "All About Me," "Feet Are Neat," "Heart Song," "Skin Song," "The Medulla Do."

Story: Scott, a young boy, falls asleep in class and dreams he is touring his own body. Scott learns all about his organs and body functions through the explanations of Colonel Corpuscle.

12. *Amahl and the Night Visitors* 60 minutes. Opera. *Hallmark Hall of Fame*. Broadcast December 24, 1951 (Monday, 9:30–10:30 P.M.) NBC

Producer Samuel Chotzinoff; *Director* Kirk Browning; *Librettist/Composer* Gian Carlo Menotti; *Conductor* Thomas Schippers; *Choreographer* John Butler; *Settings and Costumes* Eugene Berman; *Record* LP RCA LPM 1701, also CD; *Video* Worldvision (later cast); *Music* G. Schirmer (Score).

Cast: Chet Allen, Rosemary Kuhlmann, Andrew McKinley, Leon Lishner, David Aiken, Francis Monachino, Melissa Hayden, Glen Tetley, Nicholas Magallanes, NBC Opera Company

Story: Amahl, a crippled shepherd boy, sits outside the hut playing his pipe and watching the bright night sky, lit by the Star of the East. His mother calls him inside; he pleads to stay out and tells her about the sky, but she doesn't believe him. After weeping about their poverty, she sends Amahl to bed. Hearing the sounds of the Three Kings, Amahl goes to the window, then answers a knock at the door. Again his mother doesn't believe him, but after she sees the Kings, she invites them in to rest, and sends Amahl to other shepherds requesting food. The others bring donations and dance for the Kings; the Kings show off their gifts for the Christ Child, then sleep. Amahl's mother decides to steal the gold but is caught by the Kings' page. Amahl defends her. He then gives his crutch to the Kings as a gift for the Child, and miraculously finds he can now walk. He asks if he can go with the Kings to visit the Child, and his mother lets him go.

Amahl was the first opera written for television. NBC commissioned Menotti to write an original opera as early as 1949. In 1951, however, NBC was still waiting. Menotti felt a new

Rosemary Kuhlmann and Chet Allen in *Amahl and the Night Visitors* **(1951). Courtesy Hallmark Hall of Fame.**

kind of opera was needed for television. He delivered *Amahl* on December 1, 1951. Menotti said he was inspired by a painting of Hieronymus Bosch, "The Adoration of the Magi," and recalled his own childhood in Italy where the Three Kings brought Christmas gifts.

NBC did not have a sponsor for the show until the last minute. Hallmark realized that the December 24 production would not sell Christmas cards, but decided to thank viewers who had already purchased cards. Sarah Churchill delivered the Hallmark message. The show won a Peabody award for outstanding entertainment (musical) and was nominated for an Emmy for best original music. The show was repeated for numerous Christmases, and later versions have been made.

Although *Amahl* was the first opera commissioned for television, NBC radio had commissioned Menotti's *Old Maid and the Thief* for radio, and broadcast its premiere in 1939. This opera was adapted for and presented on television in 1949.

Reviews: There were some quibbles over the scenery, but the show was otherwise well-received. In a review titled "Three Kings in 50 Minutes," *Time* commented that this was a "simple Menotti mix of melodrama and pathos ... a production of care and quality." They noted that this was the largest TV hookup (35 stations) NBC had ever lined up for an opera.

Musical America (Quaintance Eaton, Jan. 1, 1952): "As television, this work succeeded where others failed or were less impressive, and chiefly because of inspired direction."

New York Times (Olin Downes, Dec. 30, 1951): "A work that few indeed could have seen and heard last night save through blurred eyes and with emotions that were not easy to conceal ... a tender and exquisite ... A throbbing personal communication ..."

13. *Androcles and the Lion* 90 minutes. Musical. Broadcast November 15, 1967 (Wednesday, 7:30–9:00 P.M.) NBC

Producer Marc Merson; *Associate Producer* James S. Stanley; *Director* Joe Layton; *Writer* Peter Stone; *Lyricist/Composer* Richard Rodgers; *Music Director* Jay Blackton; *Orchestrator* Robert Russell Bennett; *Choreographer* David Baker; *Art Director* Tom John; *Costumes* Theoni Aldredge; *Record* LP RCA LOC 1141; *Sheet Music* Williamson Music (4).

Cast: Noël Coward, Norman Wisdom, Ed Ames, Inga Swenson, Brian Bedford, John Cullum, Clifford David,

William Hickey, Kurt Kasznar, Patricia Routledge, George Mathews, Geoffrey Holder, Bill Starr, George Reeder, William Redfield

Songs: "Velvet Paws," "Gladiators' Ballet," "Follow in Our Footsteps," "The Emperor's Thumb," "Strangers," "No More Waiting," "A Fine Young Man," "The Arena Pantomime," "Strength Is My Weakness," "Don't Be Afraid of an Animal."

Story: Androcles is a Greek tailor who has become a Christian. While traveling through an African jungle with his wife, he meets a lion with a sore paw and removes from it a large thorn. Later Androcles is rounded up with other Christians and taken to Rome to be fed to the lions. Androcles finds himself confronting the jungle lion he helped, and the lion spares his life. The Emperor is so amazed he pardons all the prisoners.

This is a musical version of George Bernard Shaw's play. Richard Rodgers said that since he could choose his own lyricist he chose himself, but he felt the down didn't come off well. He observed that Noël Coward played Julius Caesar as "a wickedly charming Coward."

Reviews: *Boston Herald-Traveler* (Eleanor Robert): "What a joy this adaptation was! ... Excellent television fare—handsomely choreographed—laced with wit and humor—yet getting its message across."

Variety (Nov. 22, 1967): "Disappointing televersion of the Shaw play ... insufficient in music or conception to make it really work. ... Staging appeared constricted and boxed in. ... Lilting songs ... Coward and Wisdom good."

New York Times (Jack Gould, Nov. 16, 1967): "Wavered disconcertingly in its indecision whether to be serious or to have fun."

New York Daily News (Ben Gross): "Proved that on television, at least, martyrdom and musical comedy do not mix. Rodgers' music, as always, had a fetching quality.... The book was a workmanlike job."

14. *Around the World with Nellie Bly* 60 minutes. Musical. *Chevy Show.* Broadcast January 3, 1960 (Sunday, 9:00–10:00 P.M.) NBC

Director Barry Shear; *Writers* Sid Herzig, Norman Lessing; *Lyricist/Composer* Jack Brooks; *Conductor* Paul Weston; *Choreographer* Tony Charmoli.

Cast: Janet Blair, Cornel Wilde, Addison Richards, Jerome Cowan

Songs: "Sewing Ballet," "Ricksha," "Ship's Concert," "It Never Was You," "No More Women."

Story: Looking for a new challenge, investigative reporter Nellie Bly of the *New York World* decides to go around the world, trying to beat the 80-day record of Jules Verne's fictional character Phileas Fogg. World publisher Joseph Pulitzer encourages the trip, and Nellie's reports of her adventures help the paper's circulation as readers follow her journey. A handsome rival reporter woos and eventually wins her, as she encounters an Apache tribe, visits a harem in Arabia and takes a ricksha ride in Hong Kong, among other adventures. Nellie does beat the record, in 72 days, 6 hours and 11 minutes.

Real-life reporter Nellie Bly (real name Elizabeth Cochrane) really did achieve fame for her trip around the world, as well as for earlier exposés of conditions in asylums, sweatshops, jails and the legislature, and she was probably the best-known woman journalist of her time. The romance in the story is, however, fiction. Nellie married a

New York businessman and retired from journalism for a time.

Cornel Wilde played five different characters in this production. Thirty Hollywood old-timers were used in cameos, causing critics to compare the show with the film version of *Around the World in 80 Days*.

Review: *Variety* (Jan. 13, 1960): "A curious hodge-podge. Miss Blair's charm and voice are such that there was little she could do wrong ... [but] production lacked smoothness and cohesion."

15. *Art Carney Meets Peter and the Wolf* 60 minutes. Musical. Broadcast November 30, 1958 (Sunday, 5:00–6:00 P.M.) ABC

Executive Producer John B. Green; *Producer* Burt Shevelove; *Director* Dick Feldman; *Writer* A. J. Russell; *Lyricists* Ogden Nash, Sheldon Harnick; *Composer/Conductor* Paul Weston.

Cast: Art Carney, Bil and Cora Baird Puppets

Songs: "Magical Morning," "You Can't Catch Me," "Wolf's Lament," "Turpitude," "Her," "Be Glad There's a Hole in Your Head."

Story: The wolf, with sympathy from Carney, tries to prove he's not such a bad sort after all, and denies all the crimes blamed on him in Mother Goose tales. Scenes include an aria of the nearsighted, love-smitten hound, the teardrenched wolf's lament that everybody is against him, and a vaudeville skit with Carney and two rabbits trying to convince the wolf that he too can be in show business.

This production intertwined Prokofiev's original "Peter and the Wolf" story and music with original songs and dialogue depicting other aspects of "wolfness."

Review: *Variety* (Dec. 3, 1958): "Subtlety, wit, charm and artistry, and music ... of a high order." This review went on to say that while the book may have been less inspired than the score, "it was more than compensated for by the cleverness of Ogden Nash's lyrics and the brilliance of Carney and the assorted marionettes."

16. *Art Carney Meets the Sorcerer's Apprentice*   60 minutes. Musical. Broadcast April 5, 1959 (Sunday, 5:00–6:00 P.M.) ABC

Executive Producer John B. Green; *Producer* Burt Shevelove; *Director* Seymour Robbie; *Writer* A. J. Russell; *Lyricist* Ogden Nash; *Composer/Conductor* Paul Weston.

Cast: Art Carney, Bil and Cora Baird Puppets

Songs: "Hail to Thee Macbeth."

Story: Cicero, a second-rate carnival magician, borrows the power of a sorcerer and conjures up an evil genie, Lialalmallee, who had previously served Nero, Napoleon and Cleopatra, and wants to do things for Cicero "in a grand manner." The magician realizes that this genie is a menace, and after his apprentice rabbits invite the genie to make a small war, Cicero with the aid of three witches riddles his way into getting rid of the evil genie.
Music from "The Sorcerer's Apprentice" by Paul Dukas provided some of the background, but there was additional music by Paul Weston and songs with Ogden Nash lyrics.

Reviews: *New York Times* (Jack Gould, April 6, 1959): "A distinct disappointment. ... The story moved rather tediously and never quite achieved either the enchantment or the suspense that seemed necessary."
Variety (April 8, 1959): There was much that was imaginative and fun, but ... this one tried a little too hard, was frequently contrived and overshot its mark.... Carney, the puppets and lyrics were almost always in a delightful and witty vein."

17. *Autumn in New York*   30 minutes. Musical. *Schlitz Playhouse of Stars* Broadcast May 16, 1952 (Friday, 9:00–9:30 P.M.) CBS

Producer/Director Bill Brown; *Writer* Arnold Schulman; *Composer* Vernon Duke; *Choreographer* Bob Heigel.

Cast: Polly Bergen, Skip Homeier, Donald Briggs

Songs: "Autumn in New York" and other Vernon Duke songs (not specified)

Story: A girl wants to use the $1000 her fiancé has saved toward a house to take a trip to Paris.

Review: *Variety* (May 21, 1952): "Schlitz furnished solid proof last Friday night that live tele still has a number of kicks in store for viewers. ... Bright, fresh story ... with several of Vernon Duke's top standard tunes ... [a] sparkling half hour."

18. *Babes in Toyland*   3 hours. Musical. Broadcast December 19, 1986 (Friday, 8:00–11:00 P.M.) NBC

Producers Tony Ford, Neil T. Maffeo; *Director* Clive Donner; *Writer* Paul Zindel; *Lyricist/Composer* Leslie Bricusse; *Conductor* Ian Fraser; *Choreographer* Eleanor Fazan; *Art Director* Helmut Gassner; *Costume Designer* Evangeline Harrison; *Video* Orion.

Cast: Drew Barrymore, Richard Mulligan, Eileen Brennan, Keanu Reeves, Jill Schoelen, Googy Gress, Pat Morita, Walter Buschoff, Rolf Knie, Gaston Haeni, Shari Weiser, Pipo Sosman, Chad Carlson, Elizabeth Schott, Mona Lee Goss, Herbert Heidt, Ray Samberg, Wanda Burke, Jean Leroy, Veronica Loomis, John Kanarowski, Tony Barton

Songs: "Toyland," "The Girl of the Year," "March of the Toys," "Monsterpiece," "Cin-cin-nat-i," "(If You Can See) The Eyes and Mind of a Child," "May We Wish You the Happiest (Christmas, Marriage, Birthday) Anyone Ever Knew."

Story: On Christmas Eve, Lisa Piper is home alone while a blizzard descends on Cincinnati. When the television and telephone go out because of the storm, Lisa rushes out to the toy store where her sister Mary and Mary's boyfriend Jack work. The store is run by mean Barnaby Barnacle. After some harassment, Mary, Jack and their friend George all quit. As Jack is driving them home, Lisa (perched on her new sled) slides out of the vehicle and crashes into a tree. When she comes to, she is in the magical make-believe Toyland, where Mary Contrary is about to marry the evil Barnaby. Lisa stops the wedding. Barnaby and his two goons steal all of the cookies from the cookie factory, then accuse Jack of the theft and he is jailed. Mary, Lisa and Georgie get him out and they go to the cookie factory to find out where the cookies went. Jack falls through a tunnel into Barnaby's cave, inhabited by his legion of trolls. The children seek out the Toymaster for help. After many battles between the good and evil factions, Barnaby, his goons and his hateful trolls are driven out of Toyland, and Mary marries Jack. Lisa is taken home by Santa in his sleigh and is back with her family for Christmas.

This Toyland tale was a stage production with music by Victor Herbert, book and lyrics by Glenn MacDonough, in 1903. Film versions in 1934 and 1961 and earlier television versions of the story varied somewhat in the details, but all had used the Victor Herbert music and are therefore not included in this book as original musicals. This show, however, retained only two Victor Herbert songs ("Toyland" and "March of the Toys"). Other songs were written by Leslie Bricusse. This production was filmed in Munich.

19. *The Bachelor* 90 minutes. Musical. *Sunday Spectacular.* Broadcast July 15, 1956 (Sunday, 7:30–9:00 P.M.) NBC

Producer/Director Joseph Cates; *Writers* Arnie Rosen, Coleman Jacoby; *Lyricists/Composers* Steve Allen, Ervin Drake; *Musical Director* Ted Raph; *Choreographer* Carol Haney; *Set Designer* Burr Smidt; *Record* See below; *Sheet Music* Rosemeadow (2).

Cast: Hal March, Jayne Mansfield, Carol Haney, Julie Wilson, Georgann Johnson, Harry Holcombe, Renzo Cesana. Raymond Bramley, Peter Gennaro, Frank Derbas

Songs: "This Could Be the Start of Something Big," "My Little Black Book," "Rogue Male," "The Girl in the Gray Flannel Suit," "Three Cheers and a Tiger," "Slave Girl," "I'm a One-Man Woman," "I'm Simply Starved," "Impossible," "The Natives Are Restless Tonight."

Story: Thirty-seven year-old advertising account executive Larry Blaine keeps three beautiful girls on the string: Leslie, a talented ad copywriter, Frances, a spoiled heiress, and Robin, a not-too-bright model. His efforts to keep them apart make for comic adventures, but his secretary Marion decides to teach him a lesson. She schedules dates with all three girls at the same time and place so they find out about Larry's social life. Furious, they tell Larry he must choose one of them. He realizes that none of them would make a good wife, and that Marion has the qualities he really wants.

This was one of the better-received NBC spectaculars; reviewers made special note of Carol Haney's song and dance numbers. Haney had earlier been acclaimed for her "Hernando's Hideaway" dance number in *The Pajama Game* on Broadway. Composer/lyricist Steve Allen had just begun his prime-time *Steve Allen Show* and was still doing *The Tonight Show* part-time. Composer/lyricist Ervin Drake wrote for Broadway. Hal March had acted in many comedy shows and was then host of *The $64,000 Question*. Nat King Cole had a best-selling record of "Impossible"; Steve Lawrence and Eydie Gorme sang "This Could Be the Start of Something Big."

Reviews: *Variety* (July 18, 1956): "... March carries tunes nicely, handles lines excellently. Haney as secretary is bright and witty. ... Engaging score, literate lyrics and tunes have merit."

Newsweek (July 30, 1956): "Bright and entertaining.... Amiable inconsequential book. ... Steve Allen's music both clever and hummable. ... Hal March even better as a comedian and crooner than as a quiz master."

20. *The Ballad of Smokey the Bear*

60 minutes. Animated Musical. Broadcast November 24, 1966 (Thursday, 7:30–8:30 P.M.) NBC

Producers Arthur Rankin, Jr., Jules Bass; *Director* Takeo Nakamura; *Writer* Joseph Schrank; *Lyricist/Composer* Johnny Marks; *Video* Videocraft International; *Sheet Music* St. Nicholas Music (8).

Cast (voices): James Cagney (narrator), Barry Pearl, William Marine, Herbert Duncan, Rose Marie Jun, George Petrie, Bryna Raeburn

Songs: "Ballad of Smokey the Bear," "All Together," "Tell It to a Turtle," "Curiosity," "Delilah," "Anyone Can Move a Mountain," "Don't Wait," "Serenade of the Trees."

Story: A young bear cub frolics in the woods with his animal friends until the woods suffer a forest fire in which the cub is burned and loses his mother. The subsequently withdrawn bear grows up in fear of fire. As an adult, he finds an escaped gorilla starting small brushfires, and helps capture the gorilla. A brave new Smokey, with his ranger hat, becomes a reminder to all to prevent forest fires.

This was a Thanksgiving musical presentation. Johnny Marks, who wrote the songs, is best known for his Christmas music, including "Rudolph, the Red-Nosed Reindeer."

The original Smokey Bear, a cartoon character drawn for the U. S. Forest Service by Albert Staale in 1944, became the Forest Service trademark. In 1950 a black bear cub rescued from a fire was donated to the Washington D.C. Zoo, becoming a living symbol of Smokey Bear. (Note: Despite recent publicity saying the name is "Smokey Bear," the character was known as "Smokey the Bear" for many years.) Steve Nelson and Jack Rollins, who wrote "Frosty the Snowman" and "Peter Cottontail," wrote a 1952 song called "Smokey the Bear."

21. *The Bear Who Slept Through Christmas* 30 minutes. Animated Musical. Broadcast December 17, 1973 (Monday, 8:00–8:30 P.M.) NBC

Executive Producer Norman Sedawie; *Producers* David H. De Patie, Friz Freleng; *Directors* Hawley Pratt, Gerry Chiniquy; *Writers* Larry Spiegel, John Barrett; *Lyricist/Composer* Doug Goodwin; *Record* See below; *Video* Family Home Entertainment.

Cast (voices): Casey Kasem (narrator), Tommy Smothers, Barbara Feldon, Arte Johnson, Robert Holt, Kelly Lange, Michael Bell, Caryn Paperny

Songs: "Where Can I Find Christmas?" "Merry Christmas to You," "Christmas Is for Everyone."

Story: Theodore Edward Bear works in a honey factory which closes down for the hibernation season, but he doesn't want to sleep. He wants to stay awake and find Christmas. He has read that there is a place called "Christmas" where you hear beautiful music and find gifts, and that a human with a red suit and a white beard is in charge. Theodore searches far and wide for a place called Christmas and ends up in the city. He thinks he has found Christmas in a toy store, but he is locked in with unsold toys. Escaping from the store, he meets the man in a red suit, who tells him Christmas is how you feel inside. Theodore ends up as a present for a little girl who loves him.

Based on the story by John Barrett. Johnny Mathis recorded two of these songs on his album "Christmas Eve with Johnny Mathis," 1986.

Review: *Variety* (Jan. 2, 1974): "An ordinary half-hour cartoon. It had standard elements of holiday fare, but didn't amount to much in entertainment terms."

22. *Beatrice* Opera. Broadcast October 23, 1959 (Friday)

Director Burt Blackwell; *Lyricist* Marcia Nardi; *Composer* Lee Hoiby; *Conductor* Moritz Bomhard; *Set Designer* George Tuell.

Cast: Audrey Nossaman, Louisville musicians and singers

Story: A ravaged nun takes refuge in bordellos. She later returns to the convent in her old age and meets a saintly prioress in whom she recognizes herself as she might have been. She dies absolved of shame.

This opera, based on Maeterlinck's "Soeur Beatrice," was commissioned for the opening of a new radio and television center for the University of Louisville, Kentucky, and the town. The opera had its world premiere on station WAVE-TV. Composer Hoiby has had many operatic commissions and is also a concert pianist.

Review: *Musical America* (William Mootz, Nov. 15, 1959): "[Hoiby] presented Louisville with a score of unfailing lyricism, and the city's musicians and singers made of it a handsome, exciting show. ... A work of mounting power and emotional perspective."

23. *A Bell for Adano* 90 minutes. Musical. *Ford Star Jubilee.* Broadcast June 2, 1956 (Saturday, 9:30–11:00 P.M.) CBS

Producer Arthur Schwartz; *Director* Paul Nickell; *Writer* Robert Buckner; *Lyricist* Howard Dietz; *Composer* Arthur Schwartz; *Conductor* David Rose; *Record* LP Blue Pear BP 1019; *Sheet Music* Chappell (2).

Cast: Anna Maria Alberghetti, Edwin Steffe, Barry Sullivan, Frank Yaconelli, James Howell, Marie Siletti, Lisa

Fusaro, Naomi Stevens, Michael Vallon, Paul Picerni, John Dennis, Recs Ford, Charles La Lerre, Edwin Firestone, Herbert Patterson, Jay Novello, Ernest Sarracino, Frank Puglia, Hugh Sanders

Songs: "A Bell for Adano," "Fish," "Okay, Mister Major," "I'm Part of You."

Story: American Army Major Joppolo is assigned as occupation officer in the Italian village of Adano. An idealist, he hopes to educate the people in the principles of democracy. The town has many problems including hunger and red tape. The major is taken advantage of by some of the inhabitants, and falls in love with a local girl. He and his men help the residents and ultimately retrieve the town bell which had been taken by the Germans.

This story is based on the 1944 Pulitzer Prize–winning novel by John Hersey. The background was filmed in Italy. Composer Schwartz had previously written the music for the TV production *High Tor*, and the team of Dietz and Schwartz had written a number of Broadway musicals. This story had earlier been done as a stage play and a 1945 movie. As a child, Anna Maria Alberghetti sang for GIs in her native Italy.

Review: *Variety* (June 6, 1956): "Some of the season's most inventive and elaborate sets in an imaginative production … [but] a lot of warmth and humanity of the novel were sacrificed to give a carnival atmosphere." In short, the reviewer found the production too colorful for a war-ravaged town. He observed that Alberghetti sang adequately but didn't suit the background. The singing of the village characters was better received, adding warmth and bringing the story to life.

24. *The Borrowers*   90 minutes. Musical. *Hallmark Hall of Fame.* Broadcast December 14, 1973 (Friday, 8:30–10:00 P.M.) NBC

Executive Producer Duane C. Bogie; *Producers* Walt De Faria, Warren L. Lockhart; *Director* Walter C. Miller; *Writer* Jay Presson Allen; *Lyricist/Composer* Rod McKuen; *Music Director* Billy Byers; *Art Director* Bill Zaharuk; *Special Effects* Doug Trumbull; *Record* LP Stanyan SRQ 4014; *Video* See below.

Cast: Eddie Albert, Tammy Grimes, Dame Judith Anderson, Karen Pearson, Dennis Larson, Beatrice Straight, Barnard Hughes, Murray Westgate, Danny McIlravey

Songs: "This Is Our House," "Isn't It Something."

Songs performed by Rod McKuen and Shelby Flint. There are also many orchestral themes.

Story: A family of little people barely six inches high lives beneath the floor of a Victorian mansion. They survive by "borrowing" from the house residents, and they have two rules: They must not borrow things that will be missed, and they must never be seen by humans. Family members are Pod Clock, his wife Homily Clock, and their daughter Arietty. They live comfortably, but Arietty wants to see what is in the world beyond. The family is discovered by an eight-year-old boy visiting the mansion. Arietty makes friends with the boy, and her family is appalled. The boy tries to help them with gifts of furniture and furnishings, but the residents, thinking they have mice, destroy the Clocks' home and let loose a ferret upon them. The ferret is killed at the last minute, and the family escapes.

From the novel by Mary Norton. The show was nominated for Emmys for outstanding children's special, direc-

A tiny Tammy Grimes in *The Borrowers* (1973). Courtesy Hallmark Hall of Fame.

tion, art direction, set decoration and costume design; Dame Judith Anderson was nominated for best performer in a children's program. The show also won a Peabody award for "Outstanding Youth and Children's Program." While this *Hallmark* version is not available on video, a more recent BBC production and a sequel are.

Reviews: *New York Times* (Howard Thompson, Dec. 15, 1973): "Care and taste pervaded *The Borrowers*' 90 minutes.... Yet until the suspenseful climax ... the program seemed extremely tippy toe.... Underscored by some tinkly music by Rod McKuen."

Variety (Dec. 19, 1953): "Had great charm and imagination almost all the way. ... Then climax sank clashingly into action-adventure frame with horror and morbidity."

25. *A Bouquet for Millie*   30 minutes. Musical. *Lux Video Theatre.* Broadcast December 17, 1953 (Thursday, 9:00–9:30 P.M.) CBS

Writer Joseph Cochran; *Lyricist* Taylor Williams; *Composer* Albert Selden.

Cast: Marge and Gower Champion

Story: A rough-and-tumble husband is sentenced to bring a bouquet of flowers to his wife for ten straight days, as an apology for having hit her. He is embarrassed by his task, and is teased by his colleagues, but he fulfills his requirement. On the eleventh day his wife anxiously waits to see whether he will continue the practice; he argues with himself but finally decides he will get the flowers. He arrives at the florist's shop too late and finds it closed. When he arrives home empty-handed, his wife is ready to move out, but the florist arrives with a bouquet and explains that the husband did try but arrived too late. The episode includes a dream ballet and songs.

Review: *Variety* (Dec. 23, 1953): "If there's to be a future for original musi-comedy on TV, it will have to be made of stronger stuff. ... It was a flimsy yarn tied together by an uninspired score. Its only assets were its stars."

26. *The Box Supper* 30 minutes. Musical. *Nash Airflyte Theatre.* Broad-cast October 19, 1950 (Thursday, 10:30–11:00 P.M.) CBS

Producer/Director Marc Daniels; *Writers* Ted Mabley, Otis Clements.

Cast: Marguerite Piazza, Dorothy Peterson, David Brooks, William Brower, Wallace House, Ellen Martin, William Gaxton (host)

Songs: Not found.

Story: Two young men, one from Princeton and one hometown boy, com-pete to win the bid for a box supper of a young and pretty schoolteacher at the church social.

Review: *Variety* (Oct. 25, 1950): "An original folk opera ... made for a pleas-ant half hour viewing." The reviewer found both book and music largely unmemorable with one or two catchy exceptions. However, "with a standout cast and some fine staging ... the show emerged as good professional enter-tainment."

27. *The Boys from Boise* 2 hours. Musical. Broadcast September 28, 1944 (Thursday) DuMont

Producer Sam Medoff; *Director* Ray Nel-son; *Lyricist/Composer/Conductor* Sam Medoff; *Writers* Sam Medoff, Ray Nel-son, Constance Smith; Costumes by Brooks.

Cast: Audrey Sperling, Turner twins (Judy & Cecile), Jules Racine, Jr., Jack O'Brien, Don Saxon, Gwen Davis, Nina Orla, Dolores Wilson, Adrian Storms, Elizabeth Dewing, Joan Charl-ton, Bette Bugbee, Jedi Charles, Frosty Webb, Joan Pederson, Allan Keith, Jacqueline Soans, Betty Carroll, Sylvia Opert

Songs: "Girls of the 8-to-the Bar-X Ranch," "I'll Take the Trail to You," "Sunset Trail," "That Certain Light in Your Eyes," "Chiki Chiquita," "Thou-sand Mile Shirt," "It's a Mystery to Me," "Broken-Hearted Blues," "Come Up and See Me Sometime," "You Put Your Brand on My Heart," "Rodeo," "Western Omelet," "I'm Just a Home-body," "Star-Spangled Serenade."

Story: Showgirls stranded in Boise take jobs as cowgirls on a ranch to raise fare to return home. The ranch is owned by a villainess who controls the mort-gage and runs a band of rustlers. The ranch manager is an undercover FBI agent after the bad gal. His girlfriend comes home from an eastern music school to take over his duties when he gets drafted.

Review: *Billboard* (Oct. 7, 1944): found this "first full-fledged show" a "worthy experiment." They pointed out the problems of trying to do a full-scale musical with a large cast in the then-primitive television facilities but noted, "Direction was smooth all the way ... the answer was in the preparation. ... Important and expensive first."

28. *Break of Day* 30 minutes. Opera. *Directions '61.* Broadcast April 2, 1961 (Sunday) ABC

Executive Producer (series) Sid Darion; *Producer (series)* Wiler Hance; *Director* William Ayres; *Librettist* Leo Brady; *Composer* George Thaddeus Jones; *Con-ductor* Glenn Osser.

Cast: Roald Rutan, Mildred Allen, Loren Driscoll, Elaine Bonazzi

Story: A Roman soldier is accused of stealing Jesus' body when the tomb is found to be empty.

Review: *New York Times* (Eric Salzman, April 3, 1961): "Story ought to have had more strength than this weak and incongruous little tale, all plastered over with a padding and patchwork score."

29. Burlesque 60 minutes. Musical. *Shower of Stars.* Broadcast March 17, 1955 (Thursday, 8:30–9:30 P.M.) CBS

Producer Nat Perrin; *Director* Seymour Burns; *Writers* Morton Fyne, David Friedkin; *Music Director* David Rose.

Cast: Jack Oakie, Joan Blondell, Dan Dailey, Jimmy Burke, James Gleason, Dick Foran, Marilyn Maxwell, Helen Stanley, Jack Benny

Songs: "Don't Bring Lulu," "Daughter of Rosie O'Grady," "You Forgot," "Wedding March," "You're an Old Smoothie."

Story: A second-rate hoofer and his performer wife try to make the big time; their ups and downs are portrayed.

Another case of overworked material this show was said to be a musical version of the 1927 Broadway play by George Manker Watters and Arthur Hopkins. A 1929 movie musical, *Dance of Life,* and a 1937 film *Swing High, Swing Low, not* a musical, were based on the play. More significantly, the 1948 movie *When My Baby Smiles at Me* was a musical version of the same story starring Dan Dailey and Betty Grable, and using some of the same old standard songs. The television show may have been a musical, but it appears to have had little new to offer. (The play was also restaged on Broadway in 1946 and done on television in 1949.)

Review: *Variety* (March 25, 1955): "A hardy perennial of the the-atre … [in TV version] only the framework remained, but it came off as an acceptable replica if not memorable.… A good staging with zestful movement. David Rose's music was a strong plus."

30. Cabeza de Vaca 60 minutes. Cantata. Broadcast June 10, 1962 (Sunday, 10:00–11:00 A.M.) CBS

Librettist Allan Dowling; *Composer* George Antheil; *Choral Director* Johannes Somary; *Music* Templeton Publishing/Shawnee Press (Score).

Cast: Ron Holgate, Rudolf Petrack, Bruce Zaharides, AmorArtis Chorale

Story: Álvar Núñez Cabeza de Vaca, a Spanish explorer, sets out in 1527 as treasurer of an expedition to conquer and colonize Florida. The expedition marches overland and tries to reach Mexico but many men are lost. Cabeza de Vaca leads the survivors to an island off the Texas coast, where they are captured by Indians. Several years later Cabeza de Vaca and three others escape and make their way through the Southwest. Their suffering, Cabeza de Vaca's discovery of his healing powers and the transformation of the quest from a material to a spiritual one are portrayed.

This production had its world premiere on CBS in observance of Whitsuntide, replacing the regular Sunday morning features. The production was illustrated by André Girard drawings and is based on Cabeza de Vaca's letters to King Charles V of Spain. The work was performed posthumously (the composer died in 1959).

Reviews: *New York Times* (Howard Klein, June 11, 1962): "Most of the music has a subdued, liturgical quality.... Melodic lines are simple and strong, and the orchestration solid and non-sensational. The choral writing is clear and moving."

31. *The Cage* 30 minutes. Opera. *The Catholic Hour.* Broadcast May 10, 1959 (Sunday afternoon) NBC

Executive Producer (series) Martin H. Work; *Producer (series)* Richard J. Walsh; *Librettist* Leo Brady; *Composer* George Thaddeus Jones.

Cast: Catholic University students

Story: Henry, tired of his job as an elevator operator, and even more tired of the demands of his deaf and widowed mother, starts looking at travel brochures and dreams of escaping his "cage." When almost ready to undertake his travel, he gives up his plans so that his sister can leave the "cage" to marry.

Commissioned by the National Council of Catholic Men for *The Catholic Hour*, this was one of four operas presented.

Reviews: *Musical America* (Charles Crowder, May 1959): "The libretto by Leo Brady is terse, poignant and distinctive.... In combination with Mr. Jones' score, the details of which dramatize each line as well as the over-all situation, the result is ... unbelievable completeness...."

32. *The Canterville Ghost* 60 minutes. Musical. *ABC Stage 67.* Broadcast November 2, 1966 (Wednesday, 10:00–11:00 P.M.) ABC

Director/Writer Burt Shevelove; *Lyricist* Sheldon Harnick; *Composer* Jerry Bock; *Record* LP Blue Pear BP 1019.

Cast: Michael Redgrave, Douglas Fairbanks, Jr., Natalie Schafer, Mark Coleano, David Charkham, Tippy Walker, Peter Noone

Songs: "Canterville Hall," "Vengeance," "Undertow," "You're Super," "I Worry— If You Never Try," "Overhead," "Rattletrap," "Peace."

Story: An American family renting an old English mansion disturbs the 300-year-old ghost of Sir Simon, under a curse to roam the castle. The ghost tries to scare the family away, but the young children are more curious than frightened by the inept tricks. The ghost's problems are finally resolved so he can rest in peace. There is also a romance between the daughter and a young duke.

This drama is based on the classic short story by Oscar Wilde, written in 1887. The show was taped on location in Kent, England. The musical team of Bock and Harnick had written Broadway musicals *Fiorello* and *Fiddler on the Roof*, and had just opened *The Apple Tree* on Broadway. Peter Noone was leader of the rock group Herman's Hermits, but had earlier studied acting.

Reviews: *Variety* (Nov. 9, 1966): "A spiritless, soggy effort.... They updated everything but the quality. Completely gone were the charm and delight of the original. ... Lyrics and music were forgettable."

New York Times (Jack Gould, Nov. 3, 1966): "Incoherent mishmash. ... Not a single player who could carry a tune. ... Score better left unrendered."

33. *Charles Dickens' David Copperfield* 2 hours. Animated Musical. Broadcast December 10, 1993 (Friday, 8:00–10:00 P.M.) NBC

Producer Jacques Pettigrew; *Director*

Michael Redgrave tries his best to frighten Douglas Fairbanks, Jr., in *The Canterville Ghost* **(1966). © 1996 Capital Cities/ABC.**

Don Arioli; *Writers* Judith & Garfield Reeves-Stevens; *Songs* Al Kasha, Joel Hirschhorn; *Video* Goodtimes Home Video.

Cast (voices): Julian Lennon, Sheena Easton, Kelly LeBrock, Michael York, Howie Mandel, Joseph Marcell, Andrea Martin

Songs: "I Hate Boys," "I'll Be Your Hero," "Welcome to My Warehouse," "Is There Anyone to Guide Me?," "Something's Gonna Turn Up," "Street

Smart," "Everybody Is a Big Cheese," "A Family Christmas."

Story: The story opens with young David being born to the Widow Copperfield. Aunt Betsy Trotwood, hurrying to see her new niece, is disappointed to find the baby is a boy. As David grows, he teaches himself to play the harpsichord and writes a song for his mother. He loves to read and act out adventure stories. Mr. Murdstone, owner of a cheese factory, has designs on the widow, and when he marries her he has her change her will in his favor, then takes David to London to work in his cheese factory. David briefly meets the Duke who owns the factory and his daughter Agnes. David boards with the Micawber family, who treat him well, but his behavior at work causes David and his friend Mealy to be confined to the tower. David escapes with Agnes' help, Murdstone and Grimby chase them, but they finally get to Dover to Aunt Betsy's house. After many more complications, Mr. Murdstone and his partner Grimby are arrested and David regains his heritage.

In this animated version of the Dickens story of 1849–50, David and his family are cats, and other characters are other animals. The show was produced in Canada and France. The songwriters won Oscars for their songs "The Morning After" and "We May Never Love Like This Again."

Review: *Los Angeles Times* (Charles Solomon, Dec. 10, 1993): "Ill-conceived and sloppily executed. ... Teleplay sanitizes and trivializes Dickens' attack on child exploitation and other social problems.... A number of sappy rock songs."

34. *A Charlie Brown Christmas*
30 minutes. Animated Feature. Broadcast December 9, 1965 (Thursday, 8:00–8:30 P.M.) CBS

Executive Producer Lee Mendelson; *Producers* Lee Mendelson, Bill Melendez; *Director* Bill Melendez; *Writer* Charles M. Schulz; *Lyricist/Composer* Vince Guaraldi; *Record* LP Fantasy 8431; *Video* Hi-Tops Video; *Sheet Music* Next Day Music, S & J Music.

Cast (voices): Peter Robbins, Tracy Stratford, Christopher Shea, Chris Doran, Sally Dryer, Kathy Steinberg, Ann Altieri

Songs: "Christmas Time Is Here," "Hark the Herald Angels Sing."

Story: Charlie Brown is depressed over the commercialism of Christmas, especially when he finds Snoopy decorating his doghouse for a contest. Lucy suggests that Charlie Brown direct the church play, but he doesn't get much cooperation. He goes out to look for a tree and finds a scraggly pine, but the others make fun of him and his tree. Charlie Brown asks whether anyone knows the true spirit of Christmas. Linus quotes the gospel of Luke, reciting the passage where the angels appear to the shepherds and Charlie Brown understands. He takes his tree with him as he departs, but leaves it behind when an ornament from Snoopy's doghouse makes it droop. The others decorate the tree, which becomes beautiful.

Wanting to get away from the usual cartoon music, Schulz and Mendelson asked San Francisco composer-musician Vince Guaraldi to develop a jazz-oriented score for the show. He came up with the "Linus and Lucy" theme, which delighted Schulz and Mendelson. Although the other music is not named after characters, it is uniquely identified with the "Peanuts" gang and marks the feature as adult fare. The music has been much requested, and the soundtrack album has sold well. Various Christmas carols are interwoven with the jazz score. Network executives didn't have much hope for this quiet little special, but the show was not only well-received by critics and the public, but also won a Peabody award for "distinguished and meritorious public service," and an Emmy for outstanding children's program.

A Charlie Brown Christmas is the second most frequently aired network animated Christmas special (after *Rudolph*).

Guaraldi went on to compose and perform all the music for the first 16 "Peanuts" TV specials before his untimely death. Schulz and collaborators have to date produced 40 Peanuts "specials" for television and movies. This show was the first time the Peanuts characters were heard.

Reviews: *Variety* (Dec. 15, 1965): "A simple show ... voices oddly right. ... What made the show fascinating and haunting was its intentional sketchiness, an artifice that allowed each viewer to fill in the details."

Mick Martin and Marsha Porter, *Video Movie Guide*: "Adorable seasonal special, which should be required viewing for anybody concerned about losing the Christmas spirit. Vince Guaraldi's jazz themes are a highlight."

35. *A Child Is Born* 30 minutes. Opera. *General Electric Theater*. Broadcast December 25, 1955 (Sunday, 9:00–9:30 P.M.) CBS

Producer Mort Abrams; *Director* Don Medford; *Lyricist* Maxwell Anderson; *Composer/Conductor/Orchestrator* Bernard Herrmann; *Choral Director* Roger Wagner; *Record* 10" LP General Electric C55.

Cast: Nadine Conner, Theodor Uppman, Robert Middleton, Harve Presnell, Roger Wagner Chorale

Story: In Bethlehem, an innkeeper and his wife are preparing dinner for the prefect and his officers, and the prefect has ordered that there be no other guests at the inn. The innkeeper's wife is sad because she has lost a child and cannot have more, but she sings as she works. She and her husband discuss the oppression of the occupying soldiers, but agree they must make the best of the situation and make a living. During the evening, Joseph and Mary knock at the door; the innkeeper tells them he cannot have guests, but the wife suggests they find shelter in the stable, and they gratefully accept. The wife feels that there is something new and strange in the air, something that will change the world. Later, when the guests have gone, the innkeeper and his wife hear the shepherds and wise men coming and offer them lodging, but they are bound for the stable to see the child. While the innkeeper, his wife and the servant girls are discussing the significance of the child's birth, they are interrupted by Dismas, a thief, who saw the child and asks if the child is for him. The wife says the baby is for every man alive, and says they must go to him, as he is alone. They head for the stables, each preparing to offer a small gift.

Stephen Vincent Benét originally wrote this verse play for a *Cavalcade of America* radio broadcast in 1942. It is a story of the Nativity from the viewpoint of the innkeeper's wife. This version has also been called a musical play. Herrmann and Anderson had written a musical version of "A Christmas Carol" the previous year.

Review: Steven C. Smith *A Heart at Fire's Center:* "Despite stilted dialogue and a stiff performance by Robert Middleton as the innkeeper, *A Child Is Born* is filled with affecting moments: Herrmann's gentle theme for the Virgin

Mary ... his solemn plagal setting of the wife's vision ... the soft choral hymn of the wandering shepherds."

36. *A Christmas Carol*   60 minutes. Musical. *Shower of Stars.* Broadcast December 23, 1954 (Thursday, 8:30–9:30 P.M.) CBS

Producer/Director Ralph Levy; *Writer/ Lyricist* Maxwell Anderson; *Composer/ Conductor* Bernard Herrmann; *Assoc. Conductor* Victor Bay; *Choreographer* Donald Saddler; *Set Designer* Edward Boyle; *Costumes* Kate Drain Lawson; *Makeup* Karl Herlinger; *Vocal Supervisor* Roger Wagner; *Record* LP Unicorn RHS 850; *Video* Classic TV.

Cast: Fredric March, Basil Rathbone, Bob Sweeney, Queenie Leonard, Craig Hill, Christopher Cook, Ray Middleton, Sally Fraser, Peter Miles, Janine Perreau, Bonnie Franklin, Judy Franklin, Roger Wagner Chorale; Hosts: William Lundigan, Mary Costa; Voices: William Olvis, Marilynn Horne, David Venesty

Songs: "On This Darkest Day of Winter," "Dear God of Christmas and the New Year," "Santa Claus," "Marley's Ghost," "What Shall I Give My Lad/Girl for Christmas?" "A Very Merry Christmas."

Orchestra: "Humbug!," "The Journey into Christmas Past," "The Dream Ends," "Scrooge Rejoins the Human Race," "A Happy Ending."

Story: As a streetlamp is lit, carolers, accompanied by a flute and boy soprano, sing along the street where shops are decorated for Christmas. A bookshop shows Dickens' "A Christmas Carol" (and a customer leafing though the book shows us credits for the show). While people are cheerfully greeting one another and bustling about the streets, Scrooge is in his office. He grumpily turns down two men requesting donations, says "Bah, Humbug" when his cheerful nephew wishes him a "Merry Christmas," and grudgingly gives Bob Cratchit Christmas Day off. Muttering to himself, Scrooge locks up the office and goes home to a supper of gruel and tea. While writing in his ledger, he is visited by Marley's ghost, who bemoans his fate and promises Scrooge the same or worse. In bed, Scrooge is visited by the Ghost of Christmas Past (a woman who resembles his former girlfriend Belle) and he is taken to Fezziwig's Christmas party to see the good feelings there and to see a later conversation where Belle tells him his love of gold has hardened him and she will no longer see him. The jolly Ghost of Christmas Present (who looks like Scrooge's nephew) entertains Scrooge with magic tricks, then takes him to visit the Cratchit family. Scrooge next finds himself visiting the tombstones of himself and Tiny Tim. A new man the next morning, Scrooge runs to the street, donates to the charity, decorates the office sign, knocks at his nephew's door and tells him he'll be back, goes to the Cratchits' house and tells Bob he's giving him a raise, and joins the Cratchits for Christmas dinner, all the while smiling and laughing.

Based on Charles Dickens' "A Christmas Carol" (1843), this program was shown on two subsequent Christmases. The music was nominated for an Emmy for best original music. Tasteful commercials had the carolers (Roger Wagner Chorale) singing "The Spirit of Christmas," written especially for the show. Some of the songs were sung by off-stage singers. The music was well done but perhaps would not appeal to all, as some songs were operetta-like, others operatic. Dialogue followed the book for the most part; omissions were probably due to time limits.

Author Anderson had written stage plays such as *High Tor* (to be a TV musical two years later) and a number of topical and historical dramas. Composer Herrmann wrote many outstanding film scores, including that of *Citizen Kane*. Rathbone, who here played Marley's ghost, played Scrooge two years later in *The Stingiest Man in Town*.

Reviews: *Variety:* (Dec. 26, 1954): The critic remarked that although Dickens supplied the masterful script, he "did not dictate the flavor and poetry of Anderson's lyrics or his stunning conception of the absorbing, no-waste-motion libretto...." The music, according to this review, was "truly majestic."

Steven C. Smith, *A Heart at Fire's Center:* "Too many of Anderson's lyrics are simple to the point of laziness. ... But at least two songs stand apart from the mostly forgettable score: *On This Darkest Day of Winter* ... and *Dear God of Christmas* ... Herrmann's underscoring is even more evocative."

Time (Jan. 3, 1955): "Fredric March harrumphed and hammed as Scrooge, Basil Rathbone clanked and groaned as Marley's ghost, and although there were occasional tuneful moments, most Dickens fanciers recoiled from the sight of the Spirit-of-Christmas-Present (Ray Middleton) bursting into operetta-like arias."

37. *Cinderella*   90 minutes. Musical. Broadcast March 31, 1957 (Sunday, 8:00–9:30 P.M.) CBS

Producer Richard Lewine; *Assistant to the Producer* Paul Davis; *Director* Ralph Nelson; *Associate Director* Rowland Vance; *Writer/Lyricist* Oscar Hammerstein II; *Composer* Richard Rodgers; *Musical Director* Alfredo Antonini; *Orchestrator* Robert Russell Bennett;

Choreographer Jonathan Lucas; *Settings and Costumes* William and Jean Eckart; *Set Decorator* Gene Callahan; *Lighting* Robert Barry; *Record* LP Columbia OS 2005 (also CD, CS); *Sheet Music* Williamson Music (8).

Cast: Julie Andrews, Jon Cypher, Howard Lindsay, Dorothy Stickney, Ilka Chase, Alice Ghostley, Kaye Ballard, Bob Penn, George Hall, Iggie Wolfington, Edith Adams and 20 dancers

Songs: "The Prince Is Giving a Ball," "Ten Minutes Ago," "In My Own Little Corner," "Stepsisters' Lament," "Your Majesties," "Do I Love You Because You're Beautiful?" "Fol de Rol and Fiddle de Dee," "Impossible/It's Possible," "A Lovely Night," "When You're Driving Through the Moonlight."

Orchestral music: "March," ("Where Is Cinderella?"), "Gavotte," "Waltz for a Ball."

Story: As the Prince's ball is being announced throughout the kingdom, Cinderella, her stepmother and stepsisters come home from shopping (Cinderella carrying all the packages). Despite the family's many demands, she remains cheerful and helpful. The stepmother coaches the sisters on how to appeal to the Prince at the ball. When the stepmother and sisters have left for the ball, Cinderella retreats to her corner and wishes she could go to the ball. Her Godmother comes in, but tells her such dreams are impossible. Cinderella keeps wishing so hard that the Godmother, who has some magical powers, finally creates the coach, coachmen and ball gown for Cinderella, and off they go. The Prince is immediately charmed by the beautiful stranger and dances with her the rest of the evening, until the clock strikes midnight. Cinderella runs off, losing her slipper on the way. The Prince searches the kingdom for the owner of the shoe. Meantime, Cinderella discusses with her stepsisters what she "imagines" the ball must have been like. Ultimately, her Godmother leads the searchers to Cinderella and she marries the Prince. Cinderella's relatives participate in the ceremony and now treat her very nicely.

CBS claimed that this program drew more than 107 million viewers, the most ever for an entertainment program up to that time. But the only record of this live color special is a black-and-white kinescope. Oscar Hammerstein II based the book on the Charles Perrault version of the fairy tale, but made the stepmother and stepsisters more comic than cruel, and the fairy godmother attractive, young and down-to-earth. Julie Andrews, fresh from *My Fair Lady,* made a delightful Cinderella. This was Rodgers and Hammerstein's only television musical, and they worked as long and hard as they had on Broadway shows, unusual for television productions. The show had Emmy nominations for Julie Andrews, camera work and music, but no wins.

This show, with variations, has been performed on stage as an English Christmas pantomime and across the U.S. in summer stock and by opera companies. In 1993 the New York City Opera Company gave the first New York stage production. A 1965 television production (filmed and therefore available on video tape) is listed separately.

Reviews: *Variety* (May 1, 1957): "Artistry of the first order ... The lyrics were clever, yet remained romantic and sweet; the pomp and circumstance was lushly regal ... executed with finesse and exacting skill...."

Time (April 15, 1957): "Julie

Andrews fitted the heroine's role as if it were a glass slipper," wrote the reviewer, who went on to praise Richard Rodgers' score for "warmth and plenty of whirl," but faulted Hammerstein's script for "shifting between the sentimental and the sophisticated ... lovers' dialogue stilted."

Newsweek (April 8, 1957): "Grueling schedule of tryouts, rehearsals, run-throughs ... all the work paid off handsomely for viewers. The songs were first-rate R&H ... Julie in title role once more demonstrated that sweet and sugary aren't necessarily synonyms."

38. *Cinderella*   90 minutes. Musical. Broadcast February 22, 1965 (Monday, 8:30–10:00 P.M.) CBS

Executive Producer Richard Rodgers; *Associate Producer* James S. Stanley; *Producer/Director* Charles S. Dubin; *Associate Director* James Clark; *Writer* Joseph Schrank; *Lyricist* Oscar Hammerstein II; *Composer* Richard Rodgers; *Musical Director* John Green; *Choreographer* Eugene Loring; *Art Director* Edward Stephenson; *Costumes* George Whittaker; *Set Decorator* Antony Mondello; *Lighting* Ed S. Hill; *Makeup* Bud Sweeney; *Record* LP Columbia OS 2730; *Video* Playhouse Video; *Sheet Music* Williamson Music (9).

Cast: Lesley Ann Warren, Stuart Damon, Ginger Rogers, Barbara Ruick, Jo Van Fleet, Walter Pidgeon, Celeste Holm, Pat Carroll, Don Heitgerd, Joe E. Marks, Butch Sherwood, Bill Lee, Betty Noyes, Trudi Ames, Myra Stephens, Linda Howe, Francesca Bellini, Alicia Adams, Rosemarie Rand, Judy Chapman, Debbie Megowan, Jackie Ward, Robin Eccles, Alice Mock, Jack Tygett, Robert Courtleigh

Songs: "Loneliness of Evening," "Ten Minutes Ago," "In My Own Little Corner," "Stepsisters' Lament," "The Prince Is Giving a Ball," "Do I Love You Because You're Beautiful?," "Impossible/It's Possible," "When You're Driving Through the Moonlight," "A Lovely Night."

Orchestra: "Overture," "March," ("Where Is Cinderella?"), "Gavotte," "Waltz for a Ball."

Story: The Prince, returning from his travels, stops by Cinderella's house to ask for a drink of water, which she gladly furnishes from the well, though she is forbidden to talk to strangers. Cinderella's stepmother and stepsisters come home and discuss the Prince, wondering who he will marry. The King and queen decide to throw a ball for the Prince, in hopes that he will find a girl. When Cinderella wishes very hard that she can go to the ball, her fairy Godmother comes to her aid, outfitting her with dress and coach but telling her she must be home by midnight.

Cinderella enters the ball and the Prince is smitten, dancing the night away with her. When the clock strikes midnight Cinderella flees, losing her slipper. The Prince searches the kingdom for the owner of the shoe, and is leaving Cinderella's home when she offers him a drink. He finally recognizes her, finds the slipper fits, and triumphantly takes her home to the palace.

This elaborate filmed version began with an "Overture," like a Broadway show before the curtain opens; the overture was played while only the title appeared on the screen. The song "Loneliness of Evening," dropped from *South Pacific*, was added to this production. Oscar Hammerstein II died before the revival was made, and the script was revised by Joseph Schrank.

This show is among the top 50 most-watched TV specials (as of 1990).

Nielsen ratings only started in 1960, so this cannot be compared with the original production.

Reviews: *New York Times* (Jack Gould): "Richly costumed, sumptuously mounted."

New York Journal-American (Jack O'Brien): "Music and lyrics remain wonderful [but] stolid, static studio-imprisoned production."

Variety (Feb. 24, 1965): "The magic of the Cinderella story hovered over this [production] ... but only upon occasion was it truly captured. ... Staging was occasionally breathtaking but ... the pace was ponderous."

39. *Cinderella '53* 60 minutes. Musical. *Studio One.* Broadcast December 21, 1953 (Monday, 10:00–11:00 P.M.) CBS

Writer Arnold Schulman; *Songs* Cole Porter.

Cast: Ann Crowley, Conrad Janis, Nydia Westman, David Atkinson

Story: A beautiful woman of Tenth Avenue, New York City, is in love with an international socialite she has never met.

The Porter biographies do not indicate that he wrote songs for this show, so it appears that existing songs were used.

40. *Cindy* 2 hours. Musical. Broadcast March 24, 1978 (Friday, 9:00–11:00 P.M.) ABC

Producers/Writers James L. Brooks, Stan Daniels, David Davis, Ed Weinberger; *Director* William A. Graham; *Songs* Stan Daniels; *Other Music* Howard Roberts; *Choreographer* Donald Mc-Kayle; *Costumes* Sandra Stewart; *Art Director* Jim Vance.

Cast: Charlaine Woodard, Scoey Mitchell, Mae Mercer, Nell-Ruth Carter, Alaina Reed, Cleavant Derricks, Clifton Davis, W. Benson Terry, Richard Stahl, Noble Willingham, Burke Byrnes, John Hancock, Helen Martin, Graham Brown, Bill P. Murry, Don Dandridge, Spo-de-ooee, Boyd Bodwell, Joseph George

Songs: "Sugar Hill Ball," "Men's Room Attendant," "When It Happens," "Love Is the Magic."

Traditional vocal: "Jesus, Lover of My Soul."

Instrumentals: "Tuxedo Junction," "Mood Indigo," "Stompin' at the Savoy," "It's Easy to Remember," "I Got It Bad and That Ain't Good," "I'm Getting Sentimental Over You," "Take the 'A' Train."

Story: It is 1943 in Harlem, and Cindy has just come up from the South to live with her loving father, nagging stepmother and nasty stepsisters. Her father is a men's room attendant at the Plaza Hotel, and though well-intentioned he is weak. Cindy is made the household drudge but keeps her bubbly disposition. Cindy gets her big night out at the Sugar Hill Ball, where she dances with a handsome Marine named Joe Prince. When midnight arrives she dashes off, leaving a sneaker behind. Prince hires a scruffy detective to find the owner of the sneaker, but Cindy falls in love with a neighborhood boy, and they live happily ever after.

Reviews: *Variety* (March 29, 1978): The critic noted that this Cinderella story was slow to establish mood but improved a great deal in the last hour, with unexpected plot turns livening up the story. "The ball music was of the right period, but entirely too square sounding for a Harlem society crowd.

... In the title role, Charlaine Woodard was a delight."

New York Times (John J. O'Conner, March 24, 1978): "An original musical product of considerable merit ... inventive and charming."

41. *Cindy's Fella*   60 minutes. Musical. *Lincoln-Mercury Startime.* Broadcast December 15, 1959 (Tuesday, 9:30–10:30 P.M.) NBC

Producer William Frye; *Director* Gower Champion; *Writer* Jameson Brewer; *Lyricist/Composer* Conrad Salinger

Cast: Lois Smith, George Gobel, James Stewart, James Best, Kathie Brown

Songs: "Cindy's Fella."

Story: Yankee peddler Azel Dorsey is involved in a saloon brawl in a western town. Drifter, a guitar-strumming, impish wandering minstrel, comes to his rescue. Drifter then lures Azel to the farm of Widow Parke and her two daughters and stepdaughter Cindy, a mystical sprite. The sisters go off to a square dance; Azel and Drifter help Cindy to get outfitted and carried to the dance. She meets the rich, handsome son of a rancher, but in the end turns him down for her true love, Azel.

An updated Western version of the Cinderella story, where Drifter turns out to be the Godmother, and Azel's wagon serves as Cindy's coach to the ball.

Review: *Variety:* "Opening barroom brawl one of the funniest ever staged. ... Conrad Salinger music [is] a definite plus. ... Champion directs film ... with charm and restraint, giving it a leisurely pace."

42. *Come to Me*   60 minutes. Musical. *Kraft Television Theatre.* Broadcast

December 4, 1957 (Wednesday, 9:00–10:00 P.M.) NBC

Director William Graham; *Writers* Robert Crean, Peter Lind Hayes; *Lyricist* Peter Lind Hayes; *Composer* Robert Allen; *Record* 45 Vik 4X 0312; *Sheet Music* Korwin Music.

Cast: Farley Granger, Julie Wilson, Margaret O'Brien, J. Pat O'Malley, Steve Dunne, Robert Dane, Gordon Connell, Norman Shelley, James Harkins, Stan Schneider

Songs: "Lilac Chiffon," "Come to Me."

Story: The hero is obsessed with a gorgeous singer and chases her, but to no avail. He settles for her plain sister, but cannot forget his earlier love. He finally strangles his wife with a lilac chiffon scarf.

Star Julie Wilson recorded the two songs. A Johnny Mathis recording of "Come to Me" reached #22 on the charts.

Reviews: *Time* (Dec. 16, 1957): "Farley Granger agonizing over Julie Wilson for a full, tortured, bewildering hour."

Variety (Dec. 11, 1957): "Ran aground … in a murky melodrama … a trio of unsympathetic characters in a murder story that lacked both suspense and credibility."

43. Cop Rock 60 minutes. Musical/Drama Series. Broadcast September 26, 1990, to December 26, 1990 (Wednesday, 10:00–11:00 P.M.) ABC

Producer Steven Bochco; *Directors* Various; *Music Director* Mike Post; *Theme* "Under the Gun" by Randy Newman.

Cast: Barbara Bosson, Ronny Cox, Larry Joshua, Peter Onorati, David Gianopoulos, Anne Bobby, Ron McLarty, James McDaniel, Mick Murray, Paul McCrane, Vondie Curtis-Hall, William Thomas, Jr., Teri Austin, Dennis Lipscomb, Jeffrey Allan Chandler

Story: A crime show where everyone sang. Taking place in Los Angeles, each weekly episode had a story about police precinct activities, with courtroom follow-ups.

This innovative show had four or five original songs in each week's episode. These included rock, rap and gospel songs, and they were sung by criminals, politicians, judges, juries and cops. While the theme and songs for the show's premiere were written by Randy Newman, others composed songs for subsequent episodes. The interruption of action by songs was not generally well-received.

This was the second try at a musical series with continuing characters. *That's Life* in 1968–9 lasted a whole season, but it was a comedy which would probably have survived without the music. There were other series with musical numbers; the two series based on the film *Seven Brides for Seven Brothers* had lots of singing and dancing (one with original music by Jimmy Webb), and there were any number of family sitcoms with music in which one or more family members were performers, but most of these were never intended to be book musicals. *Cop Rock* was a real pioneer, and it's too bad it didn't last long enough for more people to see it. A salute to creators Steven Bochco and William M. Finkelstein!

Review: *Washington Post* (Sept. 26, 1990): Critic Tom Shales noted that with or without songs, *Cop Rock* was "an arrestingly good cop show." Admitting that some viewers might find the songs intrusive, Shales nevertheless praised the show's creators for "a daring departure, one that sometimes works spectacularly and sometimes goes clunk into the nearest brick wall. … The show, he

The jury offers a musical opinion in *Cop Rock* (1996). Photofest.

said, was "a true original," with "moments of brilliance that are almost blinding."

44. *Copacabana* 2 hours. Musical. Broadcast December 3, 1985 (Tuesday, 9:00–11:00 P.M.) CBS

Executive Producer Dick Clark; *Producer* R. W. Goodwin; *Director* Waris Hussein; *Writer* James Lipton; *Lyricists* Bruce Sussman, Jack Feldman; *Composer* Barry Manilow; *Production Designer* Tracy Bousman; *Choreographer* Grover Dale; *Record* LP RCA SML 1-7178; *Sheet Music* Kamakazi Music, Appoggiatura Music, Camp Songs Music.

Cast: Barry Manilow, Annette O'Toole, Estelle Getty, James Callahan, Andra Akers, Silvana Gallardo, Joseph Bologna, Ernie Sabella, Cliff Osmond, Dwier Brown, Stanley Brock, Clarence Felder, Hamilton Camp, Hartley Silver, Ralph M. Clift, John Petlock, Rafael Mauro, Lonnie Burr, James Martinez, Whitney Rydbeck, Robert Broyles, Brad Logan, Dickson Hughes, Hugo Stanger, Lew Horn, Richard Kuller, Carole Meyers, Artie Butler, James Gillian, Copacabana Girls, dancers

Songs: "Copacabana," "Man Wanted," "Let's Go Steppin'," "Aye Caramba," "Changing My Tune," "Call Me Mr. Lucky," "Blue," "Big City Blues," "Who Needs to Dream," "Sweet Heaven," "Lola," "El Bravo."

Story: Songwriter-pianist Tony Starr wins a radio talent contest, beating singer Lola Lamar. His prize is a job at the Copa—tending bar. He moves up to lounge pianist. In love with Lola, he gets her a job in the Copa chorus. Sinister Rico Castelli, club owner from Havana, spots Lola and woos her to his club. Years later, Lola sits alone in the Copa, mourning her lost youth and Tony.

This was based on Barry Manilow's song hit "Copacabana," which won him a Grammy for Best Pop Vocal (Male). (Manilow also co-wrote the song, but was not nominated as songwriter.) A Latin-disco song, it told the story of Lola and Tony in less than three minutes. The story was greatly expanded with dance numbers and songs for the TV show. The program won an Emmy for best direction and was nominated for choreography.

Reviews: *Variety* (Dec. 11, 1985): "Adds yet another fillip by gently spoofing Hollywood 30s–40s tuners. Silly complications don't interrupt songs and dance. ... A fond sendup with a smile or two of recognition."

New York Times (John J. O'Conner, Dec. 3, 1985): "Impeccably directed.... Score for *Copacabana* less inspired than serviceable. ... Mr. Manilow is to be congratulated for reminding us that, given imagination and talent, the [original musical] form can still work on television."

45. ***The Cricket on the Hearth*** 60 minutes. Animated Musical. *The Danny Thomas Hour.* Broadcast December 18, 1967 (Monday, 9:00–10:00 P.M.) NBC

Executive Producer Danny Thomas; *Producers* Arthur Rankin, Jr., Jules Bass; *Writer* Romeo Muller; *Lyricist* Jules Bass; *Composer* Maury Laws; *Record* LP RCA LSC 1140; *Video* MGM/UA.

Cast (voices): Roddy McDowall, Danny Thomas, Marlo Thomas, Ed Ames, Hans Conried, Abbe Lane, Paul Frees

Songs: "Cricket on the Hearth," "Smiles Go with Tears," "Through My Eyes," "That Was Yesterday," "The First Christmas," "Fish 'n' Chips," "Don't Give Your Love Away," "Parade of the Toys."

Story: Cricket Crockett arrives in London Christmas morning and takes up residence with Caleb Plummer, a poor toymaker, and his daughter Bertha. Caleb works for skinflint Tackleton. Tragedy hits the family when Bertha's fiancé is lost at sea, Caleb goes

bankrupt and Bertha becomes blind. Cricket rescues Caleb and Edward returns to Bertha.

A much simplified version of Charles Dickens' 1845 story nevertheless retains the spirit of the original. Marlo Thomas sings for and is the voice of Bertha. *The Danny Thomas Hour* was a weekly series offering assorted entertainment forms: musical-variety specials, dramatic plays and light comedies.

46. ***The Dangerous Christmas of Red Riding Hood (or, Oh Wolf, Poor Wolf)*** 60 minutes. Musical. Broadcast November 28, 1965 (Sunday, 7:00–8:00 P.M.) ABC

Producer Richard Lewine; *Associate Producers* James Stanley, Dorothy Dicker; *Director* Sid Smith; *Writer* Robert Emmett; *Lyricist* Bob Merrill; *Composer* Jule Styne; *Conductor/Arranger* Walter Scharf; *Choral Director/Vocal Arranger* Buster Davis; *Choreographer* Lee Theodore; *Scenery and Costumes* Raoul Pène Du Bois; *Makeup* Bob O'Bradovich; *Record* LP ABC-Paramount 536; *Sheet Music* Chappell-Styne (4).

Cast: Liza Minnelli, Cyril Ritchard, Vic Damone, Bette Henritze, Mort Marshall, Marlene Dell, The Animals

Songs: "My Red Riding Hood," "I'm Naive," "Snubbed," "We're Gonna Howl Tonight," "Woodman's Serenade," "Ding-a-Ling, Ding-a-Ling," "Granny's Gulch," "Granny," "Along the Way," "We Wish the World a Happy Yule."

Story: The Wolf, in his cage at the zoo, says he is a gentleman who only tried to make friends with Red Riding Hood, and that the fairy tale is a lie. He then tells his version of the story. Red is getting ready to go to her grandmother's with her Christmas gifts. The

Liza Minnelli on her way to Granny's *The Dangerous Christmas of Red Riding Hood*
(1965). © 1996 Capital Cities/ABC.

family is poor, and Red wishes she had a better coat, as she tells her feelings to a mute dancing field mouse. Her mother decides to give her her Christmas present before she leaves, a new coat. Red is disappointed that the coat is blue, but finds it is lined in red, so wears it inside out, and leaves for Granny's house. As Red starts through the forest she meets —and dances with—a variety of ani-

Cyril Ritchard is the misunderstood wolf in *The Dangerous Christmas of Red Riding Hood* **(1965). © 1996 Capital Cities/ABC.**

mals. The Wolf tells the Wolf Pack that he will make friends with Red (real name Lillian), and he introduces himself as Mr. Lone T. Wolf. Red then meets a singing woodsman who says he's really an enchanted Prince. She gives him the knee warmers she made for her grandmother, and he gives her a present of a song. Mr. Wolf, watching this scene, tells the Wolf Pack that he will get rid of the woodsman, or eat both Red and the woodsman. Mr. Wolf then pretends to be a woodcutter himself, but Red recognizes that he is the wolf and goes on her way. The wolf arrives first, puts Granny in the wood box, and disguises himself as Granny. When Red arrives they talk about the party they're going to have. He plays the organ and Red sings. The wolf says (aside) he was going to give Red another chance, but she has said too many unkind things about wolves, and he plans to have her for dinner. As he tries to put her into the kettle, the field mouse runs to get the woodcutter, who rescues Red while the wolf is led off. Back at the zoo, the wolf says he has no friends and doesn't understand why. Finally a skunk invites him to their family party, which he concedes is better than nothing.

The Animals, a British rock group of the 1960s, played the Wolf Pack. The song "I'm Naive" was later used in the 1992 British version of Styne's musical *Some Like It Hot*. Composer Styne and lyricist Merrill had collaborated on the Broadway musical *Funny Girl*, still running at the time of this show. This show was repeated December 25, 1966.

Review: *Variety* (Dec. 1, 1965): "A thoroughly engaging performance of Cyril Ritchard ... [who] personally carried this slim and pointless musical retelling of Red Riding Hood. ... Songs were neither catchy enough for youngsters nor mature enough for grown folks."

47. *The Danny Kaye Show* 60 minutes. Musical. Broadcast March 8, 1967 (Wednesday, 10:00–11:00 P.M.) CBS

Producer Robert Scheerer; *Director* Bill Foster; *Songs* Billy Barnes; *Musical Director* Paul Weston; *Choreographer* Tony Charmoli.

Cast: Danny Kaye, Amzie Strickland,

Harvey Korman, Harold Gould, Joyce Van Patten, Tony Charmoli dancers, Earl Brown singers

Songs: "What She Mean By That?," "I'm a No Jealous," "Too Old to Be Young."

Story: Italian immigrant Giovanni finds his true love, but is too shy to pursue her. The romantic adventures of this bashful young man form the story.

For this show only, the variety format was replaced by a musical, with book music, and lyrics by Danny Kaye's regular eight-writer team. The show was repeated on June 7, 1967, the last episode of the series.

Review: *Variety* (March 15, 1967): "Libretto was a throwback heart comedy with a pinch of farce. ... Kaye's own vid-savvy repertory company was yeoman in the breach. ... Ingratiating enough for the home screen."

48. *David Copperfield* see *Charles Dickens' Copperfield*

49. *The Death Goddess* 60 minutes. Opera. *NET Opera Theater*. Broadcast January 22, 1973 (Monday, 8:00–9:00 P.M.) PBS

Executive Producer Peter Herman Adler; *Producer* Kametaro Aramaki; *Director* Norikazu Sugi; *Writer* Shohei Imamura; *Composer* Shinichiro Ikebe; *Conductor* Hiroshi Wakasugi.

Cast: Masako Saito, Yoshiharu Nakamura, Echiko Narita, Tokyo Broadcasting Chorus

Story: An undertaker is unhappy with his life. The Death Goddess falls in love with him and gives him the power to save lives, provided he makes love to her each time he uses his power. He develops into a faith healer, becomes rich and is pleased with what he is able to do until he discovers that his resurrected patients are doing evil deeds, causing more deaths. He realizes the Death Goddess is using him, so he deliberately lets a gangster die, but is knifed by the dying man and dies himself.

This Japanese opera, written for television, uses Japanese theater techniques, a modern setting and electronic music.

Reviews: *Opera News* (Speight Jenkins, March 3, 1973): "Honor, humor and a largely atonal musical palette came together to make extraordinary entertainment. ... The music was solid and original ... mates opera with TV to make an honest hybrid...."

(Shirley Fleming, April 1973): "Sci-fi and soap, based on the Brothers Grimm, made in Japan. ... The music was chop-chop percussion and a good deal of brass."

50. *The Decorator* 30 minutes. Opera. *The Catholic Hour.* Broadcast May 24, 1959 (Sunday afternoon) NBC

Executive Producer (series) Martin H. Work; *Producer (series)* Richard J. Walsh; *Librettist* Frank Getlein; *Composer* Russell Woollen.

Cast: Catholic University students

Story: A family of four buys a suburban home and hires a decorator. The decorator overwhelms the husband and wife with a monologue on the various styles available, and what they can do to be competitive with their neighbors. He pushes the family into a collective identity crisis, but all is happily resolved.

One of four operas commissioned by the National Council of Catholic Men for use on *The Catholic Hour.*

Review: *Musical America* (Charles Crowder, May 5, 1959): "Brittle, sophisticated and comic commentary on ambitious wifery.... Intoxicating rhythmic drive. The music and text are inseparably wedded and throughout the total is witty, charming, and frolicsome."

51. *Deseret* 2 hours. Opera. Broadcast January 1, 1961 (Sunday, 3:00–5:00 P.M.) NBC

Producer Samuel Chotzinoff; *Director* Kirk Browning; *Librettist* Anne Howard Bailey; *Composer* Leonard Kastle; *Conductor* Peter Herman Adler; *Set Designer* Jan Scott.

Cast: Kenneth Smith, Judith Raskin, John Alexander, Mac Morgan, Marjorie McClung, Rosemary Kuhlmann

Story: At a Utah Mormon colony called Deseret, a sweet young girl is brought to Mormon leader Brigham Young by her parents to be his 25th bride. The girl is reluctant, but finally agrees to the marriage because of Young's kindness, and she dreams of herself as first lady of Deseret. When a handsome young Army officer arrives from Washington, the youngsters are attracted to each other, but unwilling to hurt Young. When the officer breaks in on the ceremony, Young realizes he has a rival, and allows the young couple to be together.

Deseret was subsequently performed on the stage by the Memphis Opera Theater in 1967. Versatile composer Kastle has also fashioned musical works from Walt Whitman's poems, and written and directed a film, *The Honeymoon Killers.* He wrote the opera "The Swing," performed on the *Home* show in 1956.

Reviews: *Musical America* (John Clark, Feb. 1961): "Mr. Kastle's treatment of this romantic episode is so abundantly melodic and vocal he must be considered as a born writer of operas."

Saturday Review (Irving Kolodin, Jan. 14, 1961): "Kastle has put the drama in motion with music of atmosphere and purpose, achieved its climax successfully, and resolved the cyclical scheme with no suggestion of artificiality or contrivance."

Nicholas Slonimsky, *Music Since 1900:* "Set to music in a liltingly melodious and meltingly harmonious manner, with pleasing arias, vocal duets, trios, quartets, quintets and sextets."

Time (Jan. 6, 1961): "Composer Kastle provided a surgingly lyrical score admirably suited to the moods of the text."

Variety (Jan. 11, 1961): "Pleasant if somewhat pallid ... conventional format musically and dramatically."

52. *A Diamond for Carla*   60 minutes. Musical. *Westinghouse Desilu Playhouse.* Broadcast September 14, 1959 (Monday, 10:00–11:00 P.M.) CBS

Producer John Green; *Director* Claudio Guzman; *Writer* Will Foren; *Lyricist* Paul Francis Webster; *Composer* Sammy Fain; *Conductor* Frank DeVol

Cast: Anna Maria Alberghetti, Johnny Desmond, Robert Strauss, Frank Puglia, Laurie Carroll, Armand Alzamora

Songs: "Fountain of Dreams," "Amigos," "For the Love of You," "Gossip," "A Diamond for Carla."

Story: An orphaned girl living on a remote Caribbean island is deeply in love with shy Miguel. The girl makes friends with a visiting American fisherman and he leaves behind a diamond ring as a trousseau for the couple. This generates unwarranted village gossip and feeds Miguel's jealousy.

Desilu Playhouse's first musical.

Review: *Variety* (Sept. 16, 1959): "Held forth considerably more promise than was achieved.... Simplicity translated to a stilted and awkward pretentiousness that lacked feeling or seldom rang true."

53. *Dr. Jekyll and Mr. Hyde*   90 minutes. Musical. Broadcast March 7, 1973 (Wednesday, 9:30–11:00 P.M.) NBC

Producer Burt Rosen; *Director* David Winters; *Writer* Sherman Yellen; *Lyricists/Composers* Lionel Bart, Mel Mandel, Norman Sachs; *Musical Director* Irwin Kostal; *Choreographer* Eleanor Fazan; *Makeup* Neville Smallwood; *Costumes* Emma Porteous; *Art Director* Jack Shampan; *Video* Image Entertainment.

Cast: Kirk Douglas, Susan George, Michael Redgrave, Susan Hampshire, Stanley Holloway, Donald Pleasence, Judy Bowker, Geoffrey Chater, John C. Moore, Geoffrey Wright

Songs: "Our Time Together," "The Way the World Was Meant to Be," "Something Very, Very Good," "Experiment (Whatever It Is)," "Two Fine Ladies," "Rules," "Poor Annie," "Who's a Naughty Boy," "Right Before My Eyes," "I Bought a Bicycle," "If Smudge Can't Do It—It Can't Be Done."

Story: Dr. Henry Jekyll, a respected and well-loved London physician, develops a drug mixture which transforms his personality, freeing him from civilized constraints and allowing his most evil characteristics to take over as Mr. Hyde. His girlfriend Isabel drives him to his appointment at the local insane asylum, where he asks to try his solution on patients, but is refused. On his way home he meets Smudge and tells him he needs a lunatic for a patient. As Hyde, Dr. Jekyll tours Soho with Smudge, carouses all night and finds himself in jail. Having transformed back to Dr. Jekyll, he is released. With a bit of Hyde's personality remaining, Jekyll visits Isabel with a bicycle, which her father says is inappropriate. Back to Hyde, he finds singer Annie Lyons, who won't join him for a drink; he gets her fired, then offers to be her patron. Once in their rented room, he tells her she is to stay there forever. Hyde brings a young match girl to the room to wait on Annie; the girls conspire to escape, but as Smudge guards the room, only the match girl gets away. Hyde takes Annie out to the cemetery where he injects her with a chemical. Back in his laboratory, Dr. Jekyll says his experiment is over, but Hyde appears to taunt him until he threatens to kill himself. Smudge brings Annie, now hopelessly insane, to Jekyll as a patient, and Jekyll takes her to the asylum. Too late, Jekyll realizes the error of his ways. He goes to Isabel, who says she will support him; but he changes to Hyde and attacks her father. Jekyll's butler will not let him in as Hyde, but he breaks into his laboratory and drinks the potion, changing back to Jekyll. The police arrive to tell him Isabel's father is dead. Jekyll denies having anything to do with the death, but Smudge now recognizes him as Hyde. He changes once again, fights the police and is killed trying to escape.

This show, based on the Robert Louis Stevenson novel of 1886, was filmed in London. The show was nominated for Emmys for musical direction, costume design and makeup. British composer Lionel Bart wrote book, lyrics and music for the London and New York hit *Oliver*, as well as other stage musicals and pop songs. Writer Sherman Yellen wrote the book for the Broadway musical *The Rothschilds*.

The fascination with musicalizing the Jekyll and Hyde story continues, with several attempts being made in recent times.

Reviews: *TV Guide* (March 7, 1973): "A hearty musical adaptation. ... Kirk Douglas is a treat. ... Brightly scored by Tony winner Lionel Bart."
Variety (March 14, 1973): "Ditties were undistinguished.... Douglas played Jekyll as a superannuated schoolboy, Hyde as a bumptious braying loudmouth. ... Straight, unrelieved boredom...."

54. *Dr. Seuss' How the Grinch Stole Christmas* 30 minutes. Animated Musical. Broadcast December 18, 1966 (Sunday, 7:00–7:30 P.M.) CBS

Producers Chuck Jones, Ted Geisel; *Director* Chuck Jones; *Writer/Lyricist* Theodore Seuss Geisel; *Composers* Albert Hague, Eugene Poddany; *Music Director* Eugene Poddany; *Record* LP MGM LEO LES 901; *Video* MGM UA 500176; *Sheet Music* Robbins (3).

Cast (voices): Boris Karloff (narrator), Thurl Ravenscroft, June Foray

Songs: "You're a Mean One, Mr. Grinch!" "Welcome Christmas," "Trim Up the Tree."

Story: The Grinch, who hates the holiday, dresses up as Santa, with a dog as his reindeer, and rides around stealing gifts from residents of Whoville. But the Whos remain cheerful, and the Grinch realizes that Christmas doesn't have to do with gifts, but with feelings. He gives back the gifts and enjoys Christmas dinner with the Whos.

The first of Dr. Seuss' books adapted for television, this show has been repeated annually since its premiere. The story is in rhyme, and Karloff's narration is delightful. The

Boris Karloff

recording won a Grammy for best children's album. Chuck Jones is a world-class animator and director who not only originated Wile E. Coyote and the Road Runner (and contributed significantly to development of other Warner Bros. cartoon characters) but has brought many storybook characters to animated life.

Reviews: *Women's Wear Daily* (Rex Reed, Dec. 27, 1966): "Happy delight. ... Songs were tuneful and smart, Karloff's make-believe villainy a perfect wedding of misery, meanness and mellifluous cheer."

Variety (Dec. 21, 1966): "A literate half-hour cartoon. The animation excellently captured the spirit of Seuss' fictional characters and had enough farcical sight gags."

55. *Dolcedo* 30 minutes. Opera. *The Catholic Hour.* Broadcast May 17, 1959 (Sunday afternoon) NBC

Executive Producer (series) Martin H. Work; *Producer (series)* Richard J. Walsh; *Librettist* Dominic Rover, O.P.; *Composer* Emerson Meyers.

Cast: Catholic University students

Story: Dolcedo, an aging agnostic, is dying and struggling toward faith. He is both a spiritual realist and an optimist. He goes to live in a convent of perpetual prayer in Rome. Sister Leo, noted for her impatience, tends Dolcedo in his illness. Sister Ursula gives Dolcedo confidence and tenderness. Father Richard is a man of total faith and personal hesitancy. The story concerns the interplay of the four characters.

Commissioned by the National Council of Catholic Men for *The Catholic Hour.*

Review: *Musical America* (Charles Crowder, May 1959): "In a score ingeniously constructed on four melodic fragments Mr. Meyers ... create[s] a musical flow of highly emotional and intellectual impact. ... A dry distant libretto ... finds warmth under Mr. Meyers' pen as each character comes alive with descriptive musical moods."

56. *A Doonesbury Special* 30 minutes. Animated Musical. Broadcast November 27, 1977 (Sunday, 9:30–10:00 P.M.) NBC

Producers/Directors John Hubley, Faith Hubley, Garry Trudeau; *Writer* Garry Trudeau; *Composer* Jimmy Thudpucker; *Harmonica Solo* John B. Sebastian; *Record* Windsong BLXI 2589; *Video* Pacific Arts.

Cast (voices): Richard Cox, Barbara Harris, David Grant, Charles Levin, Richard Bruno, Rebecca Nelson, Rev. William Sloane Coffin, Jr., Jack Gilford, Mark Baker, Eric Elice, Ben Halley, Jr., Will Jordan, Linda Baer, Eric Jaffe, Michelle Browne, Thomas Baxton, Lenny Jackson, Patrice Leftwich, Jimmy Thudpucker

Songs: "Stop in the Middle," "I Do Believe."

Story: The story opens with Zonker Harris in a pond at the Walden commune where he lives with friends Mike, B.D., Mark, Boopsie and Joanie. Zonker goes inside, dripping wet, and turns on the television where Jimmy Thudpucker is singing "Stop in the Middle." This causes Zonker to think about their earlier years and he proposes at dinnertime that the group "disband, intermarry and move into condominiums." The others reminisce about their years of protest, and we see a rock concert and a football game. They realize the '60s are over, and Joanie Caucus, who now runs Walden Day Care Center, observes that perhaps changes can be made through the next generation. We see scenes from the day care center, where new attitudes about women are being taught. We then see a Christmas pageant with the day-care children participating. The group realizes that times have changed and they must move on. Many issues of the era are brought out, but the story contains humorous scenes typical of the *Doonesbury* characters.

Producer John Hubley died before the show was completed. This sole *Doonesbury* TV special was adapted by Garry Trudeau from his comic strips. The script and animation scenes from this show are captured in *A Doonesbury Special: A Director's Notebook* by Trudeau. This show won an award at the Cannes

Film Festival. Trudeau had earlier won a Pulitzer Prize for his strip.

Reviews: *Variety* (Nov. 30, 1977): The reviewer was impressed enough to note that a series of *Doonesbury* specials could conceivably rival the popular *Peanuts* offerings. "The half hour generally recaptured the strip's high points. ... Voices good. ... Casting Rev. William Sloan Coffin, Jr., was inspired. ... Jimmy Thudpucker had a couple of very strong songs."

Video Hound: "*Doonesbury* ... is a humorous view of our changing patterns and lifestyles, showing that change and transition are natural and inevitable parts of the human condition."

57. *A Drum Is a Woman*   60 minutes. Musical. *U.S. Steel Hour.* Broadcast May 8, 1957 (Wednesday, 10:00–11:00 P.M.) CBS

Composed and narrated by Duke Ellington; *Dialogue* Will Lorin; *Arrangers* Duke Ellington, Billy Strayhorn; *Record* LP Columbia CL 951.

Cast: Joya Sherrill, Margaret Tynes, Ozzie Bailey, Carmen de Lavallade, chorus.

Instruments: reeds, drums, trumpets, trombones, piano, bass, harp.

Songs: "A Drum Is a Woman," "You Better Know It," "Rhythm Pum Te Dum," "Madam Zajj," "What Else Can You Do with a Drum?" "Ballet of Flying Saucers," "Zajj's Dream," "New Orleans," "Rhumbop," "Hey, Buddy Bolden," "Pomegranate," "Caribee Joe," "Finale," "Congo Square."

Story: A jazz fantasy, this composition endeavors to trace the history of jazz from its African origins, through the Caribbean to New Orleans, then to New York, ultimately to the moon. This allegorical tale features jazz in the person of Madam Zajj. After presenting jazz rhythms, Ellington introduces Carribee Joe in the West Indies, where a drum becomes Madam Zajj. Zajj leaves for Barbados and meets another Joe, then on to New Orleans and Buddy Bolden. Moving on to the cities of the world, Madam Zajj becomes more popular and less primitive but still thinks of Carribee Joe. She dreams Joe visits her in New York City, but it is only a dream. Many Joes later Madam Zajj is still gathering fame and fortune while Joe remains in the jungle with his drums.

This was a most unusual production. Except for some Big Band concerts, there had been very little jazz on television, and the presentation of an experimental work was even more surprising. Ellington considered this work one of his most satisfying and particularly liked the "radiant presence" and superb dancing of Carmen de Lavallade, as he always loved to see people dancing to his music.

Orson Welles had talked to Ellington in 1941 about doing a film history of jazz. Ellington developed an outline and perhaps some music, but all of Welles' projects were scrapped after a dispute with his studio. Over the years, on his travels, Ellington composed bits and pieces to fit his concept, and finally put the work together for its television premiere. It appears the recording was made around the time of the television production. Jazz is hard to define, and even more difficult to evaluate. Ellington was always experimenting with new and different music, and much of his work has been only truly appreciated in recent years. Music from *A Drum Is a Woman* was used in a bicentennial dance performance by the Alvin Ailey dance company, and later in a musical (*Queenie Pie)* aspiring to Broadway.

Reviews: *Time* (May 20, 1957): "Duke Ellington's most ambitious project in years, and also one of the fleshiest seen on the home screen ... a pretentious mishmash of primitive rhythms, pop tunes and sensuality ... interesting but meaningless collage."

Variety (May 15, 1957): "The show didn't quite come off ... things didn't fit."

Derek Jewell, author of *Duke: A Portrait of Duke Ellington*, found the script, written by Ellington, "naive," and thought the humor "labored" and "the whole concept ... rather self-indulgent." Ellington biographer James Collier (*Duke Ellington*) said the music was "pedestrian," the text "embarrassing."

58. *Drummer Man* 60 minutes. Drama with Music. *Kraft Television Theatre.* Broadcast May 1, 1957 (Wednesday, 9:00–10:00 P.M.) NBC

Director William A. Graham; *Writer* Mel Goldberg; *Title Song* Joe Allison; *Song* "Start Movin'" by David Hill, Robert Stevenson; *Sheet Music* Unart Music

Cast: Sal Mineo, Ruda Michelle, Robert Emhardt, Mike Kellin, Dave Farrell, Paul Mazursky, Stefan Gierasch, Henry Lascoe, Joe Silver, Jean Sheppard, Leo Bayard, Sorrell Booke, John Squeri, David Leland, John Abildsan; Jazz by Phil Woods & Quartet

Song: "Start Movin'."

Story: The second-rate orchestra in the seedy dance hall is only a job to drummer Tony Russo, who has big dreams; he hopes the combo he has formed will make it, and then he can marry Gina, a dance hall hostess. An offer for the combo to play at Carnegie Hall looks like the big break to Tony, but another combo member has found the group a job on a cruise ship, which pays well and offers job security. Tony begs the boys to stay with him and play at Carnegie Hall.

Not really a musical, this show is included here because of the success of the song. (See also *The Singin' Idol.*) Kraft's ad in *TV Guide* read, "Intimate moving story of a jazz player's life." The song "Start Movin'," pre-recorded by Mineo for the show, became a million seller, reaching #9 on the charts, and Kraft claimed once again to be a "hit maker." Mineo was already known from his films, though not as a singer.

Review: *Variety* (May 8, 1957): "Mel Goldberg fashioned a mood-vignette for Sal Mineo in *Drummer Man* and the teenage thesp did the best he could within the limitations of the script." The reviewer felt that Mineo was more convincing as a drummer than as a lover, being "out of his league" in romantic scenes.

59. *The Easter Bunny Is Comin' to Town* 60 minutes. Animated Musical. Broadcast April 6, 1977 (Wednesday, 8:00–9:00 P.M.) ABC

Producers/Directors Arthur Rankin, Jr., Jules Bass; *Writer* Romeo Muller; *Lyricist* Jules Bass; *Composer* Maury Laws; *Conductor/Arranger* Bernard Hoffer; *Designer* Paul Coker, Jr.; *Video* Vestron.

Cast (voices): Fred Astaire (narrator), Skip Hinnant, Robert McFadden, Ron Marshall, James Spies, Meg Sargent, Allen Swift, Jill Choder, Karen Dahle, Michael McGovern, Laura Dean, George Brennan, Gia Anderson, Stacey Carey

Songs: "The Easter Bunny Is Comin' to Town," "What Came First, the Chicken or the Egg?" "Someone's Gotta Take a Taste," "You Think Nobody

Loves You (But They Do)," "Big Rock Candy Mountain," "Trainyard Blues," "Think Can Do."

Story: A live "newsreel" shows everyone getting ready for Easter. The mailman comes with letters asking how Easter customs got started. This time the mailman (who looks like Fred Astaire) is driving a train named "Chugs" (The Little Engine Who Could). The mailman tells the story of the baby bunny who is found by the children of Kidville. The children name the bunny "Sunny," and raise him there. When he is grown, Sunny attempts to visit the nearby Town which allows only grownups, except for seven-year-old King Bruce. Carrying a basket of eggs for gifts to the people of Town, Sunny is stopped by Gadzooks, a bear who lives on Big Rock Mountain. Undaunted, Sunny tries again—with colored eggs to fool the bear. Young King Bruce is tired of eating beans and likes the eggs, but Bruce's Aunt Lily Longtooth instructs Bruce to pass a law banning eggs. In subsequent years Sunny and his friends invent chocolate bunnies, jelly beans, and other Easter treats. Other customs such as hiding eggs, rolling eggs, the Easter Parade and Easter toys are also explained. Finally the kids and Sunny build a railroad to carry the Easter goodies to Town. Aunt Lily and the soldiers try to stop the train, but it gets through, and Aunt Lily's heart melts when she is shown the flower named for her.

Review: *Variety* (April 13, 1977): "*The Easter Bunny Is Comin' to Town* resembled *Santa Claus Is Comin' to Town.* ... Story logical (if fictional) ... music pleasant ... script worked *Little Engine That Could* in."

60. ***The Emperor's New Clothes***
60 minutes. Musical. Broadcast Sep-

tember 4, 1967 (Monday, 7:30–8:30 P.M.) CBS

Executive Producer Richard R. Rector; *Producer* Ethel Burns; *Directors* Jim Eiler, Nick Havinga; *Writer* Jim Eilers; *Songs* Jim Eiler, Jeanne Bargy; *Arranger* Richard Hayman; *Conductor* Alfredo Antonini

Cast: Jim Eiler, Jeanne Bargy, Fred Graves, Vicki Morales, Marcie Stringer, Will B. Able

Songs: "If I Could Be a Princess," "You've Got to Blow Your Own Trumpet."

Story: A vain Emperor spends his time looking for beautiful clothes. Swindlers, posing as weavers, tell the Emperor that they can make him the finest suit, but that those unfit for office or stupid will not be able to see the cloth. No one wants to admit to not seeing the fabric or the suit, so all pretend they can see it. The Emperor parades in his invisible suit until a child speaks the truth, that he has no clothes on.

A production of the Prince Street Players, Ltd.

Review: *New York Times* (Jack Gould, Sept. 5, 1967): "A slapstick version ... with indifferent results ... labored and predictable. ... Jeanne Bargy's score had more promise than was perhaps being realized ... [It] warranted fuller staging."

61. ***The Emperor's New Clothes***
60 minutes. Live/Animated Musical. *Enchanted World of Danny Kaye.* Broadcast February 21, 1972 (Monday, 8:00–9:00 P.M.) ABC

Producers/Directors Arthur Rankin, Jr., Jules Bass; *Associate Producer* Herbert Bonis; *Lyricist* Jules Bass; *Composer* Maury Laws; *Video* Viacom.

Cast (voices): Danny Kaye (narrator), Cyril Ritchard, Imogene Coca, Allen Swift, Robert McFadden

Songs: "Come Along with Me," "Clothes Make the Man," "Creation," "I See What I Want to See," "The Tailor's Song."

Story: Marmaduke, a con man turned tailor, fools Emperor Klockenlocher into ordering a suit of invisible cloth. Completely hoodwinked, the Emperor leads a parade in the altogether; his subjects believe in the invisible suit until a small boy reveals the truth.

Based on a Hans Christian Andersen fairy tale, this show's live-action portions were filmed in Denmark. Danny Kaye had earlier played Hans Christian Andersen in a 1952 movie.

Review: *Variety* (Dec. 17, 1975): "Handled with verve and imagination, aided no end by apt vocal interpretations by Cyril Ritchard and Imogene Coca. Songs ... helped sustain the necessary mood of the tale."

62. *The Entertainer* 2 hours. Drama with Music. Broadcast March 10, 1976 (Wednesday, 9:00–11:00 P.M.) NBC

Producers Beryl Vertue, Marvin Hamlisch; *Director* Donald Wrye; *Writer* Elliott Baker; *Lyricist* Robert Joseph; *Additional Lyrics* Tim Rice; *Composer* Marvin Hamlisch; *Choreographer* Ron Field; *Art Director* Robert MacKechan; *Set Decorator* Sam Jones.

Cast: Jack Lemmon, Ray Bolger, Sada Thompson, Tyne Daly, Michael Cristofer, Annette O'Toole, Mitch Ryan, Allyn Ann McLerie, Dick O'Neill, Leanna Johnson Heath, Rita O'Conner, Alan De Witt

Songs: Not found

Story: Archie Rice, a conceited third-rate vaudevillian, plays in a seedy California burlesque house during the 1940s. His main concern is survival; he lies, cheats, exploits others and is insensitive to the harm he causes. A total heel, he destroys his wife, his children and finally his father.

The Entertainer was based on the John Osborne play, previously made into a movie with Sir Laurence Olivier. This version, set in California, was Jack Lemmon's first dramatic TV work in many years. Composer Hamlisch wrote music to songs for the Broadway hit *A Chorus Line* and arranged Scott Joplin music for the film *The Sting*, for which he won an Oscar.

Review: *Variety* (March 17, 1976): "Televersion did not try for or succeed at the high level of aspiration of the original play or film [but] Baker's rewrite was just right for Lemmon. Cast was excellent."

New York Times (John J. O'Conner, March 10, 1976): "Vaudeville, not the empire in decline. ... Admirably persistent, occasionally quite moving portrait of defeat in a world of shabby fantasies."

63. *Evening Primrose* 60 minutes. Musical. *ABC Stage 67*. Broadcast November 16, 1966 (Wednesday, 10:00–11:00 P.M.) ABC

Executive Producer John Houseman; *Producer* Willard Levitas; *Director* Paul Bogart; *Writer* James Goldman; *Lyricist/Composer* Stephen Sondheim; *Other Music* David Shire; *Orchestrator* Norman Paris; *Record* see below; *Sheet Music* Burthen Music.

Cast: Anthony Perkins, Charmian Carr, Dorothy Stickney, Larry Gates, Margaretta Warwick, Margaret Baker, Dorothy Sands

Anthony Perkins and Charmian Carr in *Evening Primrose* (1966). © 1996 Capital Cities/ABC.

Songs: "I Remember," "Take Me to the World," "I'm Here," "When."

Story: An unhappy poet, fleeing from the pressures of the outside world, seeks refuge inside a department store, thinking he is at last alone. Exploring the store at night, he has only to avoid the single night watchman. But then he finds he is not alone, meeting a strange assortment of wraith-like creatures who inhabit the store. He learns of their ways and joins in their nightly activities. These creatures have been living in the store for many years and guard their privacy. He meets Ella, who was left in the store at age six and kept by the group as a maid. Unlike the others, she is young and luminous, and the poet finds himself falling in love. When the others are out for an evening, he arranges a pretend picnic and confesses his love. Ella tells him of her feelings for the watchman, and of her yearning to see birds and trees and to join the outside world. She also tells the poet of the Dark Men who are called upon to dispose of those who threaten the secrecy of the group. The heartbroken poet tells another group member of his love for Ella and of her hope to escape. He then sees Ella being carried off, and knows he will meet the same fate.

Evening Primrose was based on a short story of the same name by John Collier. Network ads read, "*ABC Stage 67* will captivate you tonight ... an eerie yet charming story." The show was shot on location in Stern Bros. department store, at 42nd Street and Sixth Avenue in Manhattan. Although not recorded at the time, songs from *Evening Primrose* have been performed in Sondheim retrospectives, especially the poignant "I Remember." On the 1990 album "Dress Casual," Mandy Patinkin and Bernadette Peters perform all four songs.

Reviews: *New York Daily News* (Ben Gross): "The book was literate enough. The music and lyrics, although passable, were in no way as good [as Sondheim's other works]. ... An appealing basic idea ... withered before it could bloom."

Variety (Nov. 23, 1966): "It might have made a passable hour of fantasy drama but for the intrusion of song. Some fiction ought not to be musicalized. ... The songs were the best original music written for the series ... the

most creative and experimental elements of the show."

New York Times (Jack Gould, Nov. 17, 1966): "[The show] tripped over its own inordinate complexity. ... The score as a whole proved richer in promise than in realization. The songs were simply too much alike."

64. *Feathertop* 60 minutes. Musical. Broadcast October 19, 1961 (Thursday, 8:30–9:30 P.M.) ABC

Producer Tony Charmoli; *Director* Dean Whitmore; *Writer* John Marsh; *Lyricist* Martin Charnin; *Composer* Mary Rodgers; *Music Director* Richard Probor-sky; *Arranger* Harry Zimmerman; *Choreographer* Tony Charmoli; *Costume Designer* Robert Carleton; *Art Director* Robert Kelly; *Record* LP Mars Candy LB 2931; *Sheet Music* Williamson Music (2).

Cast: Jane Powell, Hugh O'Brian, Hans Conried, Cathleen Nesbitt, Jackie Joseph, Shirley Mills, Pat Lloyd, Anthony Teague

Songs: "The Day I Say I Do," "Family Tree," "Incantation Ballet" (orchestra), "Easy Come, Easy Go," "Gentleman of Breeding," "Intimate Friends," "I'm a Man," "Perfect Strangers."

Story: In ante-bellum Louisiana, Madame Eau Charme, a socially ambitious witch, is miffed when she is evicted from the Governor's ball. She constructs a scarecrow and brings him to life, naming him "Feathertop." She teaches him to talk and gives him advice about the ways of polite society, then sends him off to gain the love of Julie Balfour, the Governor's beloved daughter. He is then to break her heart so as to bring about Madame's revenge on the Governor. Feathertop falls in love with Julie, but Madame causes everyone to see in the mirrors that Feathertop is only a scarecrow. Feathertop denounces Madame and destroys her; having found a heart, he becomes a true mortal.

Feathertop was based loosely on a Nathaniel Hawthorne story, with a change of scene and period. Composer Mary Rodgers wrote music for the Broadway show *Once Upon a Mattress*; lyricist Martin Charnin wrote lyrics for revues and night club acts, and would much later write lyrics for *Annie*. Cathleen Nesbitt was an actress of long standing on British and American stages.

Reviews: *Variety* (Oct. 25, 1961): "Earthbound vehicle snagged in recurrent thickets of puns and clichés. ... Flawed by fundamental and flagrant confusion of styles in both its scripting and its music." Despite these problems, the reviewer praised the "excellent cast," especially Cathleen Nesbitt in the sorceress role.

New York Times (Jack Gould): "A lovely touch of theatre ... a musical fantasy of beguiling and tuneful gentleness."

New York Herald Tribune (Richard K. Doan): "Television audiences seldom are treated to such little musical delights."

65. *Fenwick* 30 minutes. Animated/Live Musical. Broadcast December 8, 1968 (Sunday, time unknown) NBC

Executive Producer Edwin H. Mahoney; *Producer* James Loren; *Director* Charles S. Dubin; *Writer* Joseph Schrank; *Lyricist* Patti Jacob; *Composer* Jack A. Boring; *Musical Director* Ralph Burns; *Choreographer* Tony Charmoli; *Record* LP Motorola FLP 621; *Video* Homestead Video.

Cast: Walter Slezak (narrator/Santa), Michael Link, Johnnie Whitaker, Della Sharman, Devin Anderson, Paul Lizotte, David McFarland, Kyle Nelson, Peter Villabenor

Songs: "Santa Land," "In the Toy Shop," "Fenwick," "Keep Thy Faith, Children."

Story: An orphan elf named Fenwick has a dream of going to the North Pole to help Santa make toys. After much wandering he comes to the toy factory. He is young and inexperienced, and the other elves say there is no place for him, but Santa says to give him a chance. Fenwick doesn't work out in toy production, but decides he can help with delivering gifts, and stows away on Santa's sleigh. The reindeer cut up but Fenwick calms them, showing he has a special knack with them. When deliveries are finished, Santa puts Fenwick in charge of the reindeer. All the elves celebrate the new addition to the family; the show's message is "Peace in the world starts with love and faith."

Based on an original concept by J. Frederick Hughes. Anita Bryant sings "Keep Thy Faith, Children," with musical supervision by Don Elliott.

Review: *Variety* (Dec. 11, 1968): "Well enough launched ... although not without some shortcomings, especially in the handling of Michael Link and some difficult words handed him. ... Four song score, three of which are catchy tunes and the fourth more in the carol category."

66. *The Final Ingredient* 60 minutes. Opera. *Directions '65*. Broadcast April 11, 1965 (Sunday, 1:00–2:00 P.M.) ABC

Librettist Arnold Weinstein; *Composer* David Amram; *Music* C. F. Peters.

Cast: William Covington, Joseph Sopher, Malcolm Smith, Richard Frisch, Ezio Flagello, John Fiorito

Story: Prisoners in a Nazi concentration camp try to gather the ingredients for their Passover seder, especially the final ingredient, an egg.

The *Directions* series was ABC's Sunday morning non-denominational religious program, identified with the year. This opera, commissioned by ABC, was based on a Reginald Rose TV play, and was composer Amram's first opera. Amram has also been a conductor and has composed music for motion pictures, television and jazz combos, as well as writing orchestral, choral and chamber works.

Review: *Musical Journal* (Owen Anderson, May 1965): "More impressive in individual scenes than as a unified whole. ... There were numerous moments of beauty and dramatic tension." Anderson noted that composer Amram, working within the traditional structure of opera rather than reaching for the avant garde, "displayed a fine technical grasp of the medium and the ability to write music of considerable poignancy."

67. *Freedom Is* 30 minutes. Animated Musical. Broadcast Summer 1976 (Syndicated)

Executive Producer Martin J. Neeb, Jr.; *Production Executive* Rev. Ardon D. Albrecht; *Writer* Don Hall; *Lyricist* Don Hinchey; *Composer* Jimmy Haskell.

Cast (voices): David Kelly, Jonathan Winters, Richard Roundtree, Joseph Cotten, Ed Asner, Dan Dailey, Philip Morris

Songs: "Freedom Is," "The Search," "Freedom Is, March."

Story: In his dreams, young Benji and his dog are transported back to Revolutionary War times. He meets messenger Jeremiah Goodheart, who has lost a letter to the Continental Congress, and a slave boy, Jason. Benji and Jason find the letter and deliver it to Jeremiah. Benji asks Thomas Jefferson whether the slave boy and his father will be free; Jefferson explains that the Congress is not yet ready for this step.

This program was made for the 1976 Bicentennial and sponsored by the Lutheran Church. Benji had been featured in previous "specials" produced by the church; the others were about religious holidays.

68. *Frosty Returns* 30 minutes. Animated Musical. Broadcast December 1, 1995 (Friday, 8:30–9:00 P.M.) CBS

Producers Eryk Casemire, Bill Melendez; *Directors* Bill Melendez, Evert Brown; *Writer* Oliver Goldstick; *Music* Mark Mothersbaugh; *Video* Broadway Video.

Cast (voices): Jonathan Winters (narrator), John Goodman, Jan Hooks, Andrea Martin, Brian Doyle-Murray, Elizabeth Moss, Michael Patrick Carter, Steve Stolisi, Philip Glasser, Gail Lynch, Mindy Martin

Songs: "We Love the Snow," "There's No More Snow," "I Could Live Without Snow," "Let There Be Snow."

Story: In the town of Beansboro, the children rejoice when a snowstorm closes the school and they can play in the snow, while the grownups grumble about the icy conditions. Charles and Holly are practicing a magic act for the Winter Carnival when Holly's magic topper blows away and lands on Frosty, bringing the snowman to life. But industrialist Mr. Twitchell has produced a product called "Summer Breeze" that when sprayed makes the snow disappear, and he is spraying the town. Alarmed, Holly puts Frosty in her refrigerator and goes off to school. The schoolkids, with the help of their teacher, Miss Carbuncle, realize that snow is needed to complete nature's cycles. At the Carnival, Holly convinces Mr. Twitchell that he is doing the wrong thing. It snows again, and Frosty is crowned King of the Carnival before he moves on.

Based on a story by Jim Lewis. The original *Frosty* aired in 1969.

Review: *Los Angeles Times* (Lynne Heffley, Dec. 1, 1995): "Most notable for its preachiness and forgettable music, frequently sung off-key."

69. *Frosty the Snowman* 30 minutes. Animated Musical. Broadcast December 7, 1969 (Sunday, 7:30–8:00 P.M.) CBS

Producers/Directors Arthur Rankin, Jr., Jules Bass; *Writer* Romeo Muller; *Music & Lyrics, Title Song* Jack Rollins, Steve Nelson; *Additional Lyrics* Jules Bass; *Additional Music* Maury Laws; *Record* LP MGM SE 4733; *Video* Viacom; *Sheet Music* Hill & Range (Title Song).

Cast (voices): Jimmy Durante (narrator), Jackie Vernon, Billy De Wolfe, June Foray, Paul Frees

Song: "Frosty the Snowman," with many additional verses

Story: A snowman comes to life by means of a magic hat. As the temperature rises, Frosty and his little human friend Karen search for a colder place, but are pursued by the villainous magician Professor Hinkle, who wants his hat back. Frosty and Karen take a train to the North Pole, with many adventures along the way, and finally meet Santa Claus. Santa promises the magician a new hat if he reforms.

The title song was originally written in 1950.

Review: *Variety* (Dec. 10, 1969): "Script barren of originality of wit ... borrowed sentimentality, cuteness ... strictly gimcrack."

70. *Galileo Galilei* 90 minutes. Opera. Broadcast May 14, 1967 (Sunday, 10:00–11:30 A.M.) CBS

Executive Producer Pamela Ilott; *Director* Bruce Minnix; *Librettist* Joe Darion; *Composer* Ezra Laderman; *Conductor* Alfredo Antonini; *Music* Oxford U. Press.

Cast: Ara Berberian, David Clatworthy, Ray de Voll, Joanna Simon, Camerata Singers

Story: Galileo, 17th-century Italian physicist and astronomer, concludes that ocean tides confirm the theory of Copernicus that Earth revolves around the sun, while contemporary doctrinal orthodoxy of the philosophers holds that the planets circle a fixed Earth. For this and other published scientific findings, Galileo is accused of heresy and is summoned to Rome by the Inquisition to stand trial. During the trial Galileo tries to decide whether to recant. He does so at first but then changes his mind.

Commissioned by CBS, this work was listed as an oratorio when first presented on television, but has also been called an opera and a drama with music. The composer later presented a revised version on stage as *The Trials of Galileo* (1979). This production was taped at Riverside Church in New York City.

Composer Laderman wrote many operas and won an Oscar for his soundtrack for *The Eleanor Roosevelt Story*.

Lyricist Darion wrote lyrics for *Man of La Mancha*, still running on Broadway at the time of this production.

Review: *New York Times* (May 15, 1967): Reviewer Theodore Strongin noted that the material was enhanced, rather than diluted, by dramatic simplification of Galileo's story. In visuals, language, and action, he wrote, "the oratorio was underplayed, but not musically.... Mr. Laderman's score was grand, feverish, ominous and entirely appropriate to Galileo's inner dilemma. ... Everything fit. ... A production of unusual distinction."

71. *Gallantry* 30 minutes. Opera. *Arias and Arabesques.* Broadcast August 30, 1962 (Thursday, 10:00–11:00 P.M.) CBS

Producer Pamela Ilott; *Librettist* Arnold Sundgaard; *Composer* Douglas Moore; *Music* G. Shirmer (Vocal Selections).

Cast: Ronald Holgate, Laurel Hurley, Charles Anthony, Martha Wright

Story: Surgeon Dr. Gregg is making passes at Nurse Lola. She tells him she is engaged. The doctor appeals to her sympathy by telling her she reminds him of his mother and recalling childhood sadness. When a patient is wheeled in, Nurse Lola is horrified to discover he is her fiancé, Donald. Together for a moment, they swear their love. When the doctor arrives, Donald asks him about his wife. Lola is appalled to learn that the doctor is married. As surgery begins, Lola becomes nervous about the scalpel-wielding doctor; she stops him and threatens to expose his unfaithfulness. She rushes out and Dr. Gregg follows. Donald, left alone, sings once more of his love. Lola returns to tell him she has sent for another surgeon. The opera is complete with commercials, also sung.

"Gallantry" was not written for television, but it is *about* television, specifically a soap opera. Performed on the stage in 1958, it was shown on television as half of a "special" called *Arias and Arabesques*, the other part being a dance called "Parallels." Authors comment, in their introduction to the score, that this show is a tribute to soap opera, a "peculiarly American art," which juxtaposes traditional virtues and fundamental vices to present essential truths. Composer Moore wrote the opera "The Ballad of Baby Doe." The first two reviews below are of the stage production.

Reviews: *Musical America* (April 1958): "Clever score ... is jazzy, piquant, and at the same time tender.... The workmanship and timing of composer and librettist raised the opera to the level of a work of art....Cast well chosen, staging exemplary."

Time (March 31, 1958): "A tuneful romp through the world of the daytime TV serial ... score alternately jazzy and sugary."

Variety (Sept. 5, 1962): "The opera, however, was less a takeoff on the soap opera than on opera itself and the satirical commercials were not nearly as comical as the real thing on television. Moore failed to bite very hard into the subject."

72. *Gift of the Magi* 60 minutes. Musical. Broadcast December 9, 1958 (Tuesday, 9:00–10:00 P.M.) CBS

Producers Albert Selden, George Schaefer; *Director* George Schaefer; *Writer* Wilson Lehr; *Lyricist/Composer* Richard Adler; *Music Director* Hal Hastings; *Orchestrator* Don Walker; *Record* LP United Artists UA 4013.

Cast: Eli Wallach (narrator), Gordon MacRae, Sally Ann Howes, Sally Gracie,

Sally Ann Howes and Gordon MacRae in *Gift of the Magi* (1958). Photofest.

Allen Case, Bibi Osterwald, Howard St. John, Tammy Grimes, Mildred Trases, Home Town Quartet

Songs: "The Name's the Same," "A Better Word Than Love," "He's a Company Man," "What to Do?" "Christmas in Your Heart," "It's Much Too Nice to Cut," "My Sugar Is the Salt of the Earth."

Story: Jim and Della Young are a young married couple very much in love, but neither has the money to buy a Christmas present for the other. Della finally decides to sell her beautiful long hair so that she can buy a watch chain for Jim's prized possession, his grandfather's gold watch. At home again, she anxiously awaits Jim's reaction to the loss of her crowning glory. He seems stunned as he hands her a gift: tortoise shell combs for her hair! She gives him her gift, the watch chain, only to find that he has sold the watch to get the money to buy her the combs.

This is a musical version of the O. Henry short story, padded out with period scenes of gaslight-era activities. Composer Richard Adler, with his partner Jerry Ross, had Broadway hits with *Pajama Game* and *Damn Yankees*, but Ross died shortly after the latter opened. Absent a partner, Adler wrote both music and lyrics for TV shows *Gift of the Magi* and *Little Women*. Sally Ann Howes had taken over the role of Eliza in *My Fair Lady* and married Adler earlier in the year. Gordon MacRae sang in many movies and television shows and had his own TV series.

Review: *Variety* (Dec. 17, 1958): "Enjoyable Yuletide fare. … Among the thin threads of the book was a tapestry of some seven tunes, written and composed by Richard Adler, and delightfully sung by MacRae and Howes."

73. *Gift of the Magi* 90 minutes. Musical. Broadcast December 21, 1978 (Thursday, 8:30–10:00 P.M.) NBC

Director Marc Daniels; *Writer* Sidney Michaels; *Lyricist* Stanley Lebowsky; *Composer* Fred Tobias.

Cast: Debby Boone, John Rubinstein, Jo Anne Worley, Peter Graves, Jim Backus, Alan Young, Judith Chapman, Biff McGuire, Joe Bennett

Songs: "My Christmas Wish for You," "We Owe It to the Irish to Succeed," "Open Your Arms, America," "The Promise of What I Could Be," "Love to Last a Lifetime," "On This Happy Occasion," "Is It Gone?" "A Little Less Worry, a Little More Faith."

Story: Della, a blue-eyed, blonde Italian girl meets Jim, a charming young Irishman, and they fall in love, despite their close-knit immigrant families' different ways. All join to salute the newlyweds, and they are very happy but poor. When Christmas comes, they are at a loss for presents for each other. Della decides to sell her fine long hair to buy a watch chain for Jim, only to find that he has sold the watch to buy her combs for the fine hair she no longer has.

This musical version of the O. Henry short story features songs and ethnic dances covering the immigration experience and life in New York. Two weeks earlier, a non-musical version with Marie Osmond, *Gift of Love*, had aired.

Review: *New York Times* (John J. O'Conner, Dec. 21, 1978): "Songs can best be described as serviceable."

74. *Gnomes* 60 minutes. Animated Musical. Broadcast November 11, 1980 (Tuesday, 8:00–9:00 P.M.) CBS

Executive Producers Thomas W. Moore, Anne E. Upson; *Producer/Director* Jack Zander; *Writers* Sam Moore, Maurice Raff; *Lyricist* Phyllis Levinson; *Composer* Neil Warner; *Video* Magic Window.

Cast (voices): Lee Richardson (narrator), Arthur Anderson, Rex Everhart, Anne Francine, Hetty Galen, Gordon Halliday, Bob McFadden, Corinne Orr, Joe Silver

Songs: "Sing-a-Long Wedding Day," "With Your Hand in Mine."

Story: Gnomes are friendly, peace-loving creatures. One Gnome family looks forward to the marriage of their eldest son, but the son and his bride-to-be are kidnapped by the vicious Trolls. In the battle that follows, the Gnomes are helped by the woodland animals to defeat the Trolls, after which the wedding takes place.

Based loosely on the book by Wil Huygen and illustrator Rien Poortvliet.

Review: *TV Guide* (Nov. 11, 1980): "A whimsical, colorful new cartoon. Unusual good guys confront unusual bad guys."

75. Golden Child 90 minutes. Opera. *Hallmark Hall of Fame.* Broadcast December 16, 1960 (Friday, 8:30–10:00 P.M.) NBC

Producer George Schaefer; *Director* Robert Hartung; *Librettist* Paul Engle; *Composer* Philip Bezanson; *Musical Director* Peter Herman Adler; *Conductor* Herbert Grossman; *Choreographer* Matt Mattox; *Set Designer* Warren Clymer; *Costume Designer* Noel Taylor; *Music* Hallmark (Score).

Cast: Patricia Neway, Brenda Lewis, Jerome Hines, Stephen Douglass, Judy Sanford, Enrico Di Giuseppe, David Lloyd, Chester Ludgin, Patricia Brooks, John Wheeler

Story: California in 1849 is the site of the Gold Rush. At Sutter's Fort, drunken, gold-greedy prospectors are celebrating Christmas Eve by square dancing, drinking, brawling and carousing. Captain Sutter cannot quiet them down. Meanwhile, a family consisting of Martin, his pregnant wife Martha and their daughter Rachel, crossing the Sierras in a covered wagon, are near death from cold and starvation. The family stumble into Sutter's Fort; they are met with hostility from the miners who suspect them of claim jumping. Captain Sutter protects the family, Martha gives birth to a baby boy, and the spirit of love is renewed.

Called an "original Christmas folk opera," this drama told a Nativity story in the old West. Patricia Neway had performed in many television operas; Stephen Douglass starred in *Damn Yankees* on Broadway.

Reviews: *Musical Courier* (Jan. 1961): "This ambitious production had a thorough musical preparation. Settings were atmospheric and a capable singing cast was assembled. ... The music, while written and scored capably, is highly conventional."

Time (Dec. 26, 1960): "Sounded like Menotti gone western and gone weak. Music kept attempting to soar melodically but kept being dashed to the ground again by its own heaviness. Still, score had its stirring, lyrical moments...."

Variety (Dec. 21, 1960): "Sponsor Hallmark should be given credit for trying. ... Bogged down by petty sentimentality, didn't have one rousing or memorable tune. ... Cast of professional caliber except little girl who had a small voice."

New York Times (Harold C. Schoenberg, Dec. 17, 1960): "Musically ... rather nondescript. Score is too unmelodic to attract most listeners and it does not have enough compositional drive to compensate for its lack of melody. Buckets of sentimental slosh."

76. Goldilocks 30 minutes. Live/Animated Musical. Broadcast March 31, 1970 (Tuesday, 8:30–9:00 P.M.) NBC

Producers David H. De Patie, Friz Freleng; *Director* Marc Breaux; *Associate*

Producer Walter N. Bien; *Co-Producers* Richard M. & Robert B. Sherman; *Animation Supervisor* Lee Mishkin; *Writer* A. J. Carothers; *Lyricists/Composers* Richard M. & Robert B. Sherman; *Music Arranger* Doug Goodwin; *Record* LP Disneyland DL 3511; *Video* Yes; *Sheet Music* Sherbro Music (2).

Cast (voices): Paul Winchell (narrator), Mary Frances Crosby, Bing Crosby, Kathryn Crosby, Nathaniel Crosby, Avery Schreiber

Songs: "Take a Longer Look," "The Human Race," "Don't Settle for Less."

Story: A father takes his family into the mountains on a fishing trip. His daughter (who looks a little like Goldilocks) runs after a butterfly and is led into a strange (animated) world. She finds the three bears' house, eats their porridge and falls asleep. The bears find her, but other animals see her and are afraid humans will spoil their forest. Led by a militant bobcat, the animals tell the girl to get out of the forest. The girl runs, falls and stuns herself. But she is all right, and the relieved animals show her the way out of the forest. They realize there is room in the forest for everyone.

This was a Crosby family venture. The Sherman brothers wrote songs for many Disney films, including *Mary Poppins*. Narrator Paul Winchell was best known as a ventriloquist and voice of the Smurfs.

Review: *Variety* (April 8, 1970): "Its half-hour length and lack of new directions were not worth the effort. ... A couple of pleasant original tunes. ... The mixture of animation and live action was well handled and acting was passable."

77. La Grande Bretèche 60 minutes. Opera. *NBC Opera Theater.* Broadcast February 10, 1957 (Sunday, 3:00–4:00 P.M.) NBC

Producer Samuel Chotzinoff; *Director* John Schwartz; *Librettists* Stanley Hollingsworth, Harry Duncan; *Composer* Stanley Hollingsworth; *Music/Artistic Director* Peter Herman Adler; *Sets* Gerald Ritholz; *Costumes* John Boxer.

Cast: Gloria Lane, Hugh Thompson, Adelaide Bishop, Davis Cunningham, Jimi Beni

Story: In a mansion (La Grande Bretèche) on the banks of the Loire live a Count and Countess with their servants. In his daily routine, the husband goes to his business and to his club in the evenings. When he arrives home he inquires if his wife is asleep (as she has been ill for several months) and then retires to his separate bedroom. One night he comes home later than usual and decides to visit his wife, whose health seems to have improved. When he enters her room, he hears the closet door close, and assumes the maid is in there until the maid enters the room. When the maid leaves, he accuses his wife of having someone in the closet. She swears on her crucifix that there is no one there. The husband summons a mason and has the closet door plastered over. The next morning, after the husband leaves, the wife tries to pry open the closet, but the husband returns and remains in his wife's room for 20 days.

Commissioned by NBC for its opera series, this opera was based on the short story by Balzac.

Reviews: *New York Times* (Howard Taubman, Feb. 11, 1957): "Does not make a satisfactory drama. There is no real character development. ... Mr. Hollingsworth has not yet developed a personal style. ... Some striking moments ... An impressive production."

Variety (Feb. 13, 1957): "The music was modern, reminiscent of Menotti, but missing the lyrical touch ... poor balance between orchestra and singers. ... Well sung and acted, but music didn't support emotion."

78. The Great Man's Whiskers 2 hours. Musical. Broadcast February 13, 1973 (Tuesday, 8:00–10:00 P.M.) NBC

Producer Adrian Scott; *Director* Philip Leacock; *Writer* John Paxon; *Lyricist* E. Y. Harburg; *Composer* Earl Robinson.

Cast: Dean Jones, Ann Sothern, John McGiver, Harve Presnell, Beth Brickell, Dennis Weaver, Isabel Sanford, Cindy Eilbacher, Richard Erdman, Nicole Meggerson, John Hillerman, Maudie Prickett, Woodrow Chambliss, Alvin Hammer, Charles Lane

Songs: "The Wilderness Man," "Things That Go Bump in the Night."

Story: A young girl writes a letter to President Lincoln, suggesting he grow a beard to hide his sad face. The President has his train rerouted to meet the letter writer. The girl's father, a music teacher, becomes the town hero, thanks to the President's visit.

A show for Lincoln's birthday, this comedy-drama-musical was based on a one-act play by Adrian Scott. The title was also listed as *The Grate* (or *Great*) *Man's Whiskus.*

Reviews: *TV Guide* (Feb. 13, 1973): "A treat for the kids."

Steven H. Scheuer, *Movies on TV & Video*: "An old-fashioned drama. ... The best part—an ingratiating meeting between Lincoln and the youngster—comes in the last act."

79. Griffelkin 90 minutes. Opera.

NBC Opera Theater. Broadcast November 6, 1955 (Sunday 4:00–5:30 P.M.) NBC

Producer Samuel Chotzinoff; *Director* Kirk Browning; *Librettist* Alastair Reid; *Composer* Lukas Foss; *Music Director* Peter Herman Adler; *Decorator* Rouben Ter-Artunian; *Choreographer* Robert Joffrey.

Cast: Adelaide Bishop, Rose Geringer, Mary Kreste, Alice Richmond, Andrew McKinley, Paul Ukena, Lee Cass, Robert Holland, Oliver Andes, Chester Watson

Story: On his tenth birthday Griffelkin, a young devil, is given a magic fluid to turn live people to stone and bring stone people to life, and is sent to Earth for a day to create mischief. Full of deviltry, he pulls his share of pranks and gets himself into many scrapes. But he meets a young girl, experiences the beauty of the earth and learns about love. Griffelkin uses the last of his magic fluid to save the life of the girl's mother. For this violation of the rules, the devils banish him from Hell and he is forced to live on Earth like other boys. He is adopted by the mother he helped.

Based on a German folk tale. Composer Lukas Foss has also been a pianist, conductor and musical director with major symphony orchestras, and has composed many orchestral and instrumental works. Griffelkin was one of his earliest works.

Reviews: *New York Times* (Howard Taubman, Nov. 7, 1955): "A delightful production. Using all the flexibility that television makes possible, the expert staff assembled by Samuel Chotzinoff, producer, brought freshness and imagination to the work."

Saturday Review (Irving Kolodin, Nov. 19, 1955): "Affirms that Lukas Foss is a composer of talent in a special area of music, writing music for words. ... Too long. Reid nicely rhymed verse. [Foss'] ... harmonious feeling if savorous and distinctive."

Musical America (Robert Sabin, Nov. 15, 1955): "Wit, imagination, tenderness, fantasy and bubbling rhythmic mischief abound. The performance must have brought genuine pleasure to countless thousands of music lovers of all ages in the TV audience."

80. Hans Brinker or the Silver Skates   90 minutes. Musical. *Hallmark Hall of Fame.* Broadcast February 9, 1958 (Sunday, 6:30–8:00 P.M.) NBC

Producers: Mildred Freed Alberg, Paul Feigay; *Director* Sidney Lumet; *Writer* Sally Benson; *Lyricist/Composer* Hugh Martin; *Musical Director* Franz Allers; *Conductors/Arrangers* Irwin Kostal, Fred Katz; *Record* LP Dot DLP 9001; *Sheet Music* Cromwell Music (8).

Cast: Tab Hunter, Peggy King, Sheila Smith, Jarmila Novotna, Basil Rathbone, Dick Button, Carmen Matthews, Ralph Roberts, Ellie Sommers, Paul Robertson, Vinny Corrod

Songs: "Ice," "Trinka Brinker," "I'm a Very Lucky Boy/Girl," "Clop, Clop, Clop," "I Happen to Love You," "The More the Merrier," "A Job for Me," "Hello, Springtime," "Hans Brinker."

Story: Hans Brinker, his sister Trinka and their friends and neighbors enjoy skating in the Dutch wintertime, but Hans and his sisters are poor and have only wooden skates. Their father is ill and cannot work. Hans and Trinka go to Amsterdam to seek out Dr. Broek and ask for his help. Hans and Rikki (Rychie) become romantically involved.

Though not selected for their skat-

ing ability, Tab Hunter had won several California regional ice-skating championships, and Peggy King was also an experienced skater. Dick Button, who was chosen for his skating skill, had won two Olympic figure-skating championships. The show originated from NBC's color studio in Brooklyn, and used 50,000 pounds of ice. This "special" gave *Hallmark* its biggest audience up to that time. The show, based on the Mary Mapes Dodge children's story published in 1865, was nominated for an Emmy for art direction.

Review: *Variety* (Feb. 12, 1958): "Uneven production that ran from mediocre and frequently tedious fare to some spirited and zestful entertainment." (The skating production numbers were cited as being the best part of the show.)

81. Hans Brinker or the Silver Skates   2 hours. Musical. Broadcast December 14, 1969 (Sunday 7:00–9:00 P.M.) NBC

Executive Producer Allan A. Buckhantz; *Producer* Ted Kneeland; *Director* Robert Scheerer; *Writer* Bill Manhoff; *Lyricist/Composer* Moose Charlap; *Music Director* Harper MacKay; *Ice Choreographer* Ted Shuffle; *Art Director* Mathias Matthies; *Costumes* Irma Paull; *Set Decorator* Ellen Schmidt; *Makeup* Erick & Gisela Schmeckel; *Video* Warner Home Video; *Sheet Music* Charlico Music (1).

Cast: Robin Askwith, Sheila Whitmill, Eleanor Parker, Richard Basehart, Roberta Torey, John Gregson, Cyril Ritchard, Liam Redmond, Jane Anthony, Julian Barnes, Michael Wennick, David Auker, Colin Pilditich, Ivan Butler, Lo van Hensbergen, Ina van Faasen, Lex Goudschmid, Jason

Lindsey, Freddy Aalbeck, Hein Boele, Gerhard Hartig, The Kurt Lindenau Singers' Boys Choir

Songs: "Too Much Water," "Golden Tomorrows," "There Is a Way," "Proper Manners," "To Be Free," "How I Love You," "Amsterdam," "His Love Is Born Anew."

Story: Hans Brinker and his sister Gretel are the best skaters in town and hope to win the silver skates offered as prizes in a local competition, but they have no money for metal skates and have to make-do with home-made wooden ones. Their father, disabled from a fall, his mind and memory gone, is unable to work. He had buried his savings and the family doesn't know where. The mother works at whatever she can find, and Hans tries to find work to help out, but the family is struggling. When Hans learns that Dr. Boekman is in Amsterdam, he resolves to seek the doctor's help for his father. Hans earns enough to buy metal skates, and skates to Amsterdam with friends. The doctor finally agrees to visit the family. Hans returns home in time for the contest, and Gretel is given skates. The doctor operates on the father, who regains his memory and his strength, and the proud parents are able to watch the children in the races. Gretel wins the silver skates, but Hans gives his skate strap to a friend and does not participate. It turns out the father holds an undelivered message to the doctor from his long-lost son; they are reunited and offer to take Hans in as an apprentice doctor. Side stories involve a romance between Hans and Annie, and the hilarious time had by the boys in Amsterdam.

This production, filmed in Holland, was done as a flashback for no apparent reason. Songwriter Charlap had done songs for several earlier TV specials, and wrote music for some of the songs in *Peter Pan.*

Reviews: *Variety* (Dec. 17, 1969): "First hour ... seemed inordinately drawn out and puerile. ... Second hour tightened up, thanks to Richard Basehart. Music never did impress except *Golden Tomorrows.* Songs slowed down the pace. No one sang especially well."

New York Times (Jack Gould, Dec. 15, 1969): "Disappointingly uneven production ... [taken up with] excessive telling of the Brinker family psychodrama. ... A strong adult flavor to the proceedings.... Numbers were wanting in a trace of melodic distinction."

Despite the lukewarm reviews for the overall production, the actors won applause; *Variety* praised Eleanor Parker and Richard Basehart, and the *New York Times* was grateful for Cyril Ritchard's "element of style."

82. *Hansel and Gretel* 60 minutes. Musical. Broadcast April 27, 1958 (Sunday, 6:30–7:30 P.M.) NBC

Executive Producer David Susskind; *Producer* Herbert Moss; *Director* Paul Bogart; *Writer* Yasha Frank; *Lyricist* William Engvick; *Composer* Alec Wilder; *Music Director* Glenn Osser; *Choreographer* Onna White; *Art Director* Sam Leve; *Costumes* Sal Anthony; *Record* LP MGM E 3690; *Sheet Music* Edward B. Marks.

Cast: Red Buttons, Barbara Cook, Risë Stevens, Rudy Vallee, Stubby Kaye, Paula Laurence, Hans Conried, Shai K. Ophir, Sondra Lee, Will B. Able, May Questel, Diki Lerner, Harrison Muller, Jessie Elliott, Paul Hartman

Songs: "Much Too Happy Dancing," "Morning Song," "Market Today," "Eenie Meenie Mynie Moe," "Men

Rule the World," "What Are Little Boys/Girls Made Of?" "Evening Song," "Finale," "Evening Prayer."

Story: The Town Crier narrates the story. As he opens the market, the poor woodworker and his wife display their wares but they do not sell. The Gingerbread Witch and her apprentices Eenie, Meenie, Mynie and Moe come to town looking for children to use to make gingerbread cookies, but don't see any. When the woodworker mentions his Hansel and Gretel, the Witch buys all of his goods and gets directions to the house. At the house, the Witch tells Hansel and Gretel of a wonderful berry patch, then by magic lures them ever deeper into the woods. The lost children spend the night sleeping, while their parents and the townspeople search for them. The next day, the children find the Witch's candy house and, in eating it, forget their home and family. While the Witch is away, the children teach the apprentices games and tell them the advantages of being good. When the Witch tries to put Hansel into the oven, there is a scuffle, the witch is shoved in, the spell is broken, and all return to a town celebration.

This different version of the fairy tale was done as a verse play with music and much dancing. Risë Stevens sang the Humperdinck "Evening Prayer" from the opera *Hansel and Gretel.* Stubby Kaye was then appearing in *Li'l Abner* on Broadway.

Review: *Variety* (April 30, 1958): The reviewer praised the cast—Red Buttons for his boyish enthusiasm, Risë Stevens for her excellent singing, Stubby Kaye for singing and acting, and Hans Conried for his delightful—"though perhaps too cute"—portrayal of the witch. The review continued: "Wilder's tunes were pleasant. ... Diffusion of interest by details added to the plot ... with so many facets to the story, the interest was divided. The musical moments were many and good."

83. *The Happiest Day*   60 minutes. Musical. *Chevy Show.* Broadcast April 23, 1961 (Sunday, 9:00–10:00 P.M.) NBC

Producer Bob Finkel; *Directors* Bob Finkel, Dean Whitmore; *Writer/Lyricist/Composer* Irvin Graham; *Conductor* Axel Stordahl.

Cast: Wally Cox, Jack Carson, Charlie Ruggles, Bea Benaderet, Janis Paige, Craig Stevens

Songs: "Too Old," "Dancing in a Dream."

Story: Earth is in a miserable state, and a heavenly messenger is sent down to deliver commercials. The angel shows a day in the life of Kathy Hewitt, assisted by himself as guardian angel, where he arranges for Kathy to have a date with her boss, her "happiest day."

Wally Cox, best known for his *Mr. Peepers* and *Hiram Holiday* TV series, had a uniquely lovable way of playing the shy, retiring guy.

Review: *Variety* (April 26, 1961): "A frothy tale hardly worthy of great effort but certainly not deserving of the poor handling given by the co-directors. ... Cox [is] delightful. ... Shrillness in other actors. ... Lyrics deft, music served its purpose."

84. *Happily Ever After*   60 minutes. Animated Musical. *Wonderworks.* Broadcast October 21, 1985 (Monday, 8:00–9:00 P.M.) PBS

Executive Producers Henry Winkler, Roger Birnbaum; *Producers (Original Story)* Linda Balahoutis, Marilyn Katzenberg; *Producer/Director (London)*

Steven Melendez; *Associate Producer (London)* Graeme Spurway; *Director* Bill Melendez; *Writer* Bill Scott; *Lyricists* Randy Edelman, Bill Scott; *Composer* Randy Edelman.

Cast (voices): Carol Burnett (narrator), Cassandra Coblentz, Carrie Fisher, Henry Winkler, Danny Colby, Danny De Vito, Rhea Perlman, Jeremy Schoenberg, Dana Ferguson, Gini Holtzman, Karrie Ullman, Carl Stevens, Keri Houlihan, Brett Johnson

Songs: "Give Life All You've Got," "Skywalker's Rule."

Story: Molly Conway is upset and blames herself when her parents divorce. She and her friends, the "Skywalkers," hatch a scheme to bring Molly's parents back together, but their plan backfires. Molly and Tommy (whose parents are not getting along) run away, but they are quickly found. When Molly plays the Fairy Godmother in the school play *Cinderella*, she says, "Happily ever after is dumb." But after her father moves out, and with the help of her teacher and friends, Molly learns that it is still possible to be happy.

85. *Heidi*   90 minutes. Musical. Max Liebman Presents. Broadcast October 1, 1955 (Saturday, 9:00–10:30 p.m.) NBC

Producer/Director Max Liebman; *Writers* William Friedberg, Neil Simon; *Lyricist* Carolyn Leigh; *Songs* Clay Warnick, Mel Pahl, Irwin Kostal; *Music Director* Charles Sanford; *Choreographer* James Starbuck; *Choral Director* Clay Warnick; *Scenery* Fred Fox; *Costumes* Paul du Pont; *Sheet Music* Morley Music (6); *Libretto* Samuel French.

Cast: Jeannie Carson, Wally Cox, Elsa Lanchester, Natalie Wood, Jo Van Fleet, Richard Eastham, Robert Clary, Bill Gibberson, Lee Goodman, Phil Faversham, Eleanor Williams, Claire Chatwin, The Schmeed Trio, Bil and Cora Baird's Marionettes

Songs: "Heidi," "I Got My Way," "Greener Pastures," "I Love to Rumble," "Right or Wrong," "The Etiquette Song."

Story: Heidi lives with her grandfather in the Swiss Alps; she is sent to Frankfurt to be a companion to an invalid girl, Clara. Heidi visits a public square with an organ grinder to see a marionette show. Back in the mountains, Heidi spends time with her goatherd friend and is visited by Clara, who regains her strength.

Based on the Johanna Spyri novel of 1880, in which Heidi is five years old when the story begins. The songs are based on the music of Robert Schumann.

Reviews: *New York Times* (Oct. 3, 1955): "The casting of Carson was unfortunate. ... Several of the musical interpolations were most ill-advised, destructive of illusion and mood."

Variety (Oct. 5, 1955) commended the scenery, costumes and yodeling by the Schmeed Trio, but thought Jeannie Carson unbelievable as the young girl of the story. The reviewer thought only Elsa Lanchester as Fraulein Rottenmeier and Natalie Wood as Clara were true to the spirit of *Heidi*.

86. *Here Comes Peter Cottontail*   60 minutes. Animated Musical. Broadcast April 4, 1971 (Sunday, 7:00–8:00 P.M.) ABC

Producers/Directors Arthur Rankin, Jr., Jules Bass; *Director* Kizo Nagashima; *Writer* Romeo Muller; *Title Song* Steve

Nelson, Jack Rollins; *Other Lyrics* Jules Bass; *Other Music* Maury Laws; *Video* Viacom; *Sheet Music* Hill & Range (Title Song).

Cast (voices): Danny Kaye (narrator), Casey Kasem, Vincent Price, Iris Rainer, Joan Gardner, Paul Frees, Greg Thomas, Jeffrey A. Thomas

Songs: "Here Comes Peter Cottontail," "The Puzzle of Life," "Improvise," "Be Mine Today."

Story: Peter Cottontail campaigns to become chief Easter Bunny, but his rival, Irontail, demands a contest to see who can give away the most eggs on Easter. Peter oversleeps and loses the contest. Seymour S. Sassafras tries to send Peter back to the day before, but the machine sends him back through the year's holidays. He finally lands on St. Patrick's Day and is able to give away green eggs to win the contest.

This story was based in part on the song written in 1950, and also on a book, *The Easter Bunny Overslept,* by Priscilla and Otto Friedrich.

Review: *Variety* (April 7, 1971): "The puppet animation characters were appealing. Danny Kaye did yeoman duty … music was good but the overall story line strayed from simplicity. … Songs [have] a pleasing lyrical content."

87. The Hero   60 minutes. Program with Opera. *Lincoln Center.* Broadcast September 24, 1965 (Friday, 8:00–9:00 P.M.) PBS

Producer Jac Venza; *Librettist* David Rogers; *Composer* Mark Bucci.

Cast: Arthur Rubin, Anita Darien, Kirsten Falke, Elaine Bonazzi, Chester Watson

Story: Michael St. John becomes a hero for shooting a murderer on Far Rockaway beach. He doesn't remember

what happened. As a hero, he is promoted and receives favorable attention from others, but he begins having nightmares. As his memory returns, he recalls that the murderer, lying helpless on the beach, had handed Michael his gun. He didn't have to kill him, so he believes himself to be a murderer. He goes to the police, his priest and the man's wife, but no one blames him. He cannot live with the guilt so drowns himself at Far Rockaway.

This unusual program was put together for the third anniversary of New York's Lincoln Center. To illustrate the diversity of artists "who can produce something quite individual from the same theme," producer Venza commissioned a drama, a ballet and an opera, all based on Frank Gilroy's short story "Far Rockaway." All three works were part of this 60-minute program; the opera lasted 12 minutes. Composer Bucci was co-winner of the Prix Italia, an international television award, for his opera.

88. He's for Me   60 minutes. Musical. *Alcoa Hour.* Broadcast July 21, 1957 (Sunday, 9:00–10:00 P.M.) NBC

Director Herb Hirechman; *Writer* Michael Dreyfuss; *Lyricist/Composer* Michael Brown.

Cast: Roddy McDowall, Jane Kean, Larry Blyden, Joan Hovis

Songs: "She's for Me," "A Dollar and a Quarter and a Dime," "They Don't Know What Love Is."

Story: The comedic adventures of two boys who fall in love with the two girls in the apartment across the hall.

Jane Kean filled in at the last minute for Elaine Stritch.

Review: *Variety* (July 24, 1957): "Book was dull padding of a thin theme. Music was fine, musical not so hot, the cast pleasant and grave."

89. *High Pitch*   60 minutes. Musical. *Shower of Stars*. Broadcast May 12, 1955 (Thursday, 8:30–9:30 P.M.) CBS

Producer Nat Perrin; *Director* Seymour Burns; *Associate Producer/Musical Staging* James Starbuck; *Writer* Milton Lazarus; *Additional Dialogue* Karen de Wolfe; *Original Songs* David Rose, Milton Pascal; *Conductor/Arranger* David Rose; *Vocal Director/Arranger* Norman Luboff; *Art Director* Robert Tyler Lee; *Set Decoration* Buck Henshaw; *Miss Piazza's Gowns* Florence Lustig; *Video* Classic Television.

Cast: Marguerite Piazza, Tony Martin, Vivian Vance, William Frawley, Mel Allen (guest), Bill Lundigan (host)

Songs: "I Feel a Song Comin' On," "Take Me Out to the Ball Game," "Life of a Ballplayer's Wife," "Let's Fall in Love," "Dance with Me Henry," "How Deep Is the Ocean."
    Several operatic arias were sung by Piazza.

Story: The Hooligans are a losing baseball team. Opera star Dorothy Meadows, who grew up rooting for them, decides to buy the team and make them into winners. She explains the game to her opera partners in a syndicate and they agree to the purchase. She entices star baseball player Ted Warren to join the team and fall in love with her. The Hooligans start winning and the syndicate members are out there rooting for "their" team. But Dorothy's jealous manager tells Ted that she was just toying with him, and sends Dorothy on tour. Ted starts having fights with the manager and the team starts losing. Gabby Mullins, the team manager, has not been happy with Dorothy's interference and influence, so

he is glad to see the couple break up. The tour is canceled, and Dorothy tries to see Ted, but he won't talk to her. She finally gets into his room by pretending to be the maid, and tries to reason with him, but they fight again. Ted says he has been a chump and will start playing well. The Hooligans win games and finally the pennant, but Dorothy and Ted are both unhappy. Dorothy threatens to leave the opera; her manager calls Gabby and asks him to convince Dorothy that Ted is no good. But instead, Gabby tells the truth, and Ted and Dorothy reconcile.
    Despite this show being advertised as "an original baseball mini-musical," most of the songs are standard tunes, used to show off the singing skills of its stars. Piazza was an opera singer who did some pop tunes; Martin then a top pop singer. The plot showed some originality, though.

Review: *Variety* (May 18, 1956): "A thin, hackneyed book mated too generously to cold-blooded song and production cues.... Good opportunity was muffed for slanted original songs out of the Dave Rose bag.... Strictly out of the lowercase boy-meets-girl heap."

90. *High Tor*   90 minutes. Musical. *Ford Star Jubilee*. Broadcast March 10, 1956 (Saturday, 9:30–11:00 P.M.) CBS

Producer Arthur Schwartz; *Director* James Neilson; *Writer/Lyricist* Maxwell Anderson; *Composer* Arthur Schwartz; *Conductor* Joseph J. Lilley; *Arrangers* Joseph J. Lilley, Skip Martin; *Record* LP Decca DL 8272; *Sheet Music* Chappell (6).

Cast: Bing Crosby, Everett Sloane, Julie Andrews, Nancy Olson, Hans Conried, Lloyd Corrigan, John Pickard

Songs: "Living One Day at a Time,"

The ghosts of Dutch sailors march to the mountaintop to await a rescue ship in *High Tor.* **Photofest.**

"When You're in Love," "Sad Is the Life of a Sailor's Wife," "A Little Love, a Little While," "John Barleycorn," "Once Upon a Long Ago."

Story: Van Van Dorn owns High Tor, a mountain along the Hudson River. He works only occasionally, hunts and fishes when he pleases, and lives from day to day. While Van and his girlfriend Judith are picnicking on the mountain two real estate men, Biggs and Skim-

merhorn, offer to buy it for its rock, but Van refuses to sell. Judith is dismayed that Van seems unwilling to think of their future, and she leaves in a huff. Alone on the mountain, Van sees the ghosts of shipwrecked Dutch sailors; the ghosts have climbed High Tor to wait for a rescue ship. Van hears Lise, the captain's wife, talk and sing of her longing for home and for the old days. She and De Witt, the ship's bosun, decide to fall in love with humans to remove the spell they think holds them in their ghostly state. Meanwhile, Biggs and Skimmerhorn can't find their way off the mountain and return. Bank robbers also come on the scene, but mistake De Witt for a state trooper and run, dropping their bag of money. De Witt opens the bag, but takes only coins, leaving the paper money between the sleeping Biggs and Skimmerhorn. When they waken, they pocket the money. The ghosts return and tell Biggs and Skimmerhorn that they can get them off the mountain with a steam-shovel parked nearby; they convince the men to climb in the bucket, but leave them hanging there while they go off bowling. The robbers come back to get their money, and shoot De Witt, but he scares them off with his blunderbuss. The shots waken Biggs and Skimmerhorn. Van and Lise spend the night talking and falling in love. Judith comes back and meets De Witt, but refuses his overtures. Lise tells Judith she realizes that she and Van cannot be lovers, and she gives him back. The ghostly crew spots a ship, and the captain comes for Lise, who must return with her companions. Ultimately the bank offers Van a substantial amount of money for the mountain and he agrees to sell. He asks Judith to stay with him.

This was a 1937 verse play by Maxwell Anderson, performed on Broadway at that time. Julie Andrews made her television debut in *High Tor*.

Review: *Variety* (March 14, 1956): "Songs were good ... a stunning performance by Julie Andrews. But basically ... a flimsy boy-meets-girl story. Through it all Crosby was ... strictly Crosby and not Van Dorn, a man in love with his mountain."

91. *Hi-Hat* Mini-Musical. *The Carol Burnett Show*. Broadcast January 8, 1978 (Sunday, 10:00–11:00 P.M.) CBS *Songs* Stan Freeman, Arthur Malvin

Cast: Roddy McDowall, Ken Berry

Story: A song-and-dance salute to the romantic musicals of the 1930s.

This mini-musical was only a portion of *The Carol Burnett Show*, which offered a variety of features, but the segment was recognized by an Emmy to the songwriters for "outstanding achievement in special musical material (music & lyrics)."

92. *The Hobbit* 90 minutes. Animated Musical. Broadcast November 27, 1977 (Sunday, 8:00–9:30 P.M.) NBC

Producers/Directors Arthur Rankin, Jr., Jules Bass; *Animation Director* Toru Hara; *Lyricist* Jules Bass; *Composers* Maury Laws, Lois Winter; *Conductor/ Arranger* Maury Laws; *Record* LP Buena Vista 103; Disneyland 3819; *Video* ABC Video.

Cast (voices): Glenn Yarbrough (balladeer), Orson Bean, John Huston, Hans Conried, Richard Boone, Theodore, Otto Preminger, Cyril Ritchard, Jack De Leon, Paul Frees, Don Messick, John Stephenson

Songs: "The Greatest Adventure," "In the Valley," "Roads," "The Mountain King's Return," "The Dwarfs of Yore," "Down, Down to Goblin Town," "The Misty Mountains," "Funny Little Things," "Rollin' Down the Hole," "In the Valley, Ha! Ha!," "That's What Bilbo Baggins Hates," "Gollums Riddle."

Story: Bilbo Baggins is a Hobbit, a gnome-like creature only four feet tall, roly-poly, friendly, a resident of Middle Earth. He is commandeered by the wizard to help the 13 dwarfs retrieve their gold from Lonely Mountain. Bilbo and his colleagues encounter all sorts of creatures, good and evil, including some horrible goblins and a fearful dragon. With the help of a magical ring, Bilbo regains the treasure and returns home to his quiet life.

Based on the Tolkien book. NBC, Arthur Rankin, Jr., and Jules Bass won a Peabody award for the show, "a vividly original and enchanting version of J. R. R. Tolkien's classic."

Reviews: *Variety* (Nov. 30, 1977): "Never quite came to life. The creatures in the book are given chapters to develop and become familiar, but TV hurries them along. ... Good animation and fidelity to the book ... expertly cast voices."

Mark Satern, *Video's Best:* "Perhaps it is too much to expect that this fantasy masterpiece should translate well to the screen. Nevertheless, there is value for those familiar with the book, but please read the book."

Mick Martin and Marsha Porter, *Video Movie Guide:* "Disappointing. ... Unfortunately, all the strange creatures have a cutesy look."

Steven H. Scheuer, *Movies on TV & Video:* "Enchanting animated dramatization of J. R. R. Tolkien's popular novel."

93. *Holiday* 90 minutes. Musical. *Max Liebman Presents.* Broadcast June 9, 1956 (Saturday, 9:00–10:30 P.M.) NBC

Producer/Director Max Liebman; *Producer* Bill Hobin; *Director* Charles S. Dubin; *Writer* None listed; *Lyricist* Edward Eager; *Music* Clay Warnick, Mel Pahl; *Music Director* Charles Sanford; *Choreographer* Rod Alexander.

Cast: Doretta Morrow, Keith Andes, Kitty Carlisle, Bambi Lynn, Rod Alexander, Tammy Grimes, George Irving, Anthony Eisley, Jacques D'Amboise, Charles Weidman

Songs: "Escape It All," "According to the Baedeker," "I Want So Much," "Qu'est-ce Que C'est?" "Pantomime Ballet," "It Mustn't Happen Now," "Chit Chat," "Tra-la-la," "Once There Was a Man," "When a Woman Is a Wife."

Story: A New England schoolteacher en route to Europe falls in love with a married banker. She discovers he is an embezzler, sacrifices her inheritance to cover his embezzlement, but returns him to his wife. The story moves from Paris to Venice to Rome.

Based on the 1951 Elmer Rice play *The Grand Tour*, this show adapted the music of Johann Strauss.

Review: *Variety* (June 13, 1956): "Started off brightly but failed to maintain the pace. ... A maudlin yarn ... with further development would have been a better story. Topnotch production, camera work, settings. ... Neat hoofing...."

94. *The Honeymooners* *The Jackie Gleason Show.* Broadcast 1966–1970 (Saturday, 7:30–8:30 P.M.) CBS

Executive Producer Jack Philbin; *Producer* Ronald Wayne; *Director* Frank Bunetta; *Writer* Marvin Mars; *Songs* Lyn Duddy, Jerry Bresler; *Conductor* Sammy Spear.

Cast: Jackie Gleason, Art Carney, Sheila MacRae, Jane Kean, June Taylor Dancers

Songs: "Daddy, Won't You Baby Me," "It Looks Like We're Goin' to the Big Convention," "The Day a Woman Can't Outsmart a Man," "Raccoon Anthem."

Story: Ralph Kramden wants to go to the Raccoon convention, but has no money. He finds a hypnotist, "Fatchoo-mara," and persuades him to try to hyp-notize his wife Alice so she will give him the money.

Songs and story above are from the episode of September 28, 1968, with guest Richard Deacon. This story was recycled from an earlier non-musical episode.

The Honeymooners is a show not to be overlooked, but almost impossible to write about. The 39 "classic" half-hour episodes are not musicals. The "lost episodes" pieced together from skits on early Gleason shows did have sung-through skits, though not as a regular feature. When *The Honeymooners* returned in January 1966, it was with a full-hour musical show. In the fall of that same year *The Honeymooners* reap-peared but with Sheila MacRae and Jane Kean replacing Audrey Meadows and Joyce Randolph. Of the shows from 1966 to 1970, over half devoted the full hour to the honeymooners, but some were full book musicals and some were without music. The above episode is one of those done with music, and the credits listed apply only to the 1966–1970 shows, though it appears these songwriters also did musical shows in the 1956–57 season, some with the same plots.

In 1976 through 1978 there were four *Honeymooners Reunion Specials* for which Audrey Meadows returned. Music was composed and conducted by Jackie Gleason, but these specials do not appear to be musicals.

There are a number of books on *The Honeymooners* for those wanting to explore the history of this show in more detail.

95. *How the Grinch Stole Christ-mas* see *Dr. Seuss' How the Grinch Stole Christmas*

96. *I'm Getting Married* 60 min-utes. Musical. *ABC Stage 67.* Broadcast March 16, 1967 (Thursday, 10:00–11:00 P.M.) ABC

Writers/Lyricists Betty Comden, Adolph Green; *Composer* Jule Styne.

Cast: Anne Bancroft, Dick Shawn

Songs: "I'm Getting Married," "Roots," "Venezia," "Forbidden Fruit," "Love Is Our Umbrella."

Story: Paul Benderhof and his girl Virginia are about to get married. Paul is a young executive on the way up. Vir-ginia is concerned that Paul will turn into a faithless, inconsiderate husband and a horror like other husbands she has heard about.

Comden and Green intended this show to be a satire on marriage, express-ing the views of well-known but widely divergent authors on love and marriage. The two principals were accompanied by two pianos.

Review: *New York Times* (March 17, 1967): Reviewer George Gent com-plained that the production violated a basic principle of comedic fantasy, namely that those involved were required to play the story as though they believed it. Instead, wrote Gent, this musical was "played as two young lovers caught in a credibility gap with a wickedly perceptible wink at the audi-ence." The result was "a witless pas-tiche.... Mr. Styne's music did nothing to lighten the hour."

97. *In Fashion* 90 minutes. Musi-cal. *Theater in America.* Broadcast March 13, 1974 (Wednesday, 9:30–11:00 P.M.) PBS

Producer Matthew N. Herman; *Direc-tor/Writer* Jon Jory; *Lyricist* Lonnie Burstein; *Composer* Jerry Blatt; *Choreo-grapher* Donald Saddler.

Cast: Susan Kaslow, Pamela Hall, Charlotte Rae, Max Wright, Ken Jenkins, Daniel Davis, Patricia Tovatt, Donna Curtis

Songs: "In Fashion," "After Just Six Months of Marriage," "When a Pretty Woman Walks By," "My Children! Mama!," "A Woman's Glove," "But Not to You," "They'll Never Understand Us," "Married Women," "This Is the First Time for Me," "A Lovers' Hideaway," "The New Woman," "We Can't Ever Let Him Know," "Poor Sick Thing," "I'd Know You Anywhere," "I Married an Imbecile," "The Queen of Greenland," "Don't Ever Go Away," "I Only Found Her Yesterday," "A Man Is a Man for All That," "It Isn't She."

Story: Dr. Moulineaux, though married only six months, has spent the night on a park bench after a failed tryst with a female patient and hoped-to-be mistress, Suzanne. To his suspicious wife, Yvonne, he claims to have been taking care of a very ill patient, Bassinet, but just then Bassinet arrives to announce that he has an apartment for rent. Yvonne tells her mother that she doubts her husband's story, but the doctor tells his mother-in-law that Bassinet is contagious, while Bassinet is trying to rent his apartment to the mother-in-law. Dr. Moulineaux rents the apartment, and arranges to meet there with Suzanne. The apartment formerly belonged to a dressmaker, and is filled with equipment and tools of that trade. Suzanne's husband arrives while the doctor is kneeling and embracing Suzanne, and assuming the doctor is the dressmaker, refers his mistress Rosa to him. Suzanne accuses Rosa of being the doctor's mistress, but Rosa says her husband is with her, and introduces her lover—Suzanne's husband. Suzanne runs off, her husband chases her, and Rosa swoons into the doctor's arms.

Yvonne arrives to see this scene and runs off; the doctor hands Rosa to Bassinet and runs after Yvonne. Bassinet discovers that Rosa is his long-lost wife who had earlier run off with a soldier. There are many more scenes of mistaken identity and complications, but all are reconciled at the end.

Georges Feydeau was a master of French farce. *In Fashion* is based on his 1886 play *Tailleur pour dames* ("A Gown for His Mistress"), his first full-length play and his first major triumph. Since his plays revolve around deception, mistaken identities and coincidences, his scripts contain detailed instructions for the action. The humor relies on rapid action and exact timing, which cannot be described in a summary. Feydeau's best-known works are *A Flea in Her Ear* and *Hotel Paradiso*, both of which have been made into films, but the films lack the delicate touch of the stage productions. This musical version was first staged by the Actors Theatre of Louisville, so is not really a written-for-TV musical, but it is impossible to resist a Feydeau farce with so many songs, a rare musical event for television.

Review: *Variety* (March 20, 1974): "Entirely admirable production.... The Feydeau play was charming and excellently done; the new music and lyrics are spirited. But they seldom come together and are sometimes at odds." The reviewer called Burstein's lyrics "clever" but found them an uncomfortable fit with the spoken dialogue. The reviewer praised the "excellent" cast and director Jan Jory's "surehanded" management of "the carefully controlled and orchestrated chaos."

98. ***The Incredible, Indelible, Magical, Physical Mystery Trip***   60 minutes. Animated/Live Musical. *ABC*

Afterschool Special. Broadcast February 7, 1973 (Wednesday, 4:30–5:30 P.M.) ABC

Executive Producer Stanley E. Paperny; *Producers* David H. De Patie, Friz Freleng; *Director Animation* Herbert Klynn; *Director Live Action* Jim Gates; *Writer* Larry Spiegel; *Lyricist/Composer* Edward Newmark.

Cast: Hal Smith, Michael Link, Kim Richards

Voices: Len Maxwell, Peter Broderick, Kathy Buch

Songs: "Follow Me," "The Food Song," "Sailing Down the River," "Look on the Bright Side," "Have a Heart," "The Brain Song," "Missy's Song."

Story: Two children, Joey and Missy, miniaturized by a magician, tour the unhealthy body of their Uncle Carl; they learn how organs work, and of the damage that smoking, overeating, abuse and neglect can do.

Review: *Variety* (Feb. 14, 1973): "A pretty good idea was accorded a somewhat erratic production ... animation consistently good. Songs were okay but the message became a little preachy. Weakness of the hour was the live-action sequences of Uncle Carl."

99. *It's a Brand New World*   60 minutes. Animated Musical. *NBC Special Treat.* Broadcast March 8, 1977 (Tuesday, 4:00–5:00 P.M.) NBC

Executive Producer Eddie Elias; *Producer* Al Elias; *Directors* Ronald Fritz, Dan Hunn; *Writers* Romeo Muller, Max Wilk; *Musical Director* Sammy Lowe; *Record* LP Redbird RB 1001.

Cast (voices): Joe Silver, Malcolm Dodd, Dennis Cooley, Boni Enten, George Hirsch, Charmaine Harma.

Vocals: Sylvester Fields, Hilda Harris, Maeretha Stewart

Songs: "It's a Brand New World," "Samson's Gonna Be Born," "Four Would-Be Angels," "Down Along the Vineyards," "They Laughed for 120 Years," "The Riddle," "Shem, Ham and Japeth," "300 Foxes," "It Rained 30 and 10," "Jaw Bone of a Donkey," "Noah's Ark," "Young Samson."

Story: Four fun-loving children learn the stories of Noah and Samson through a remedial Bible class for aspiring angels.

100. *It's Sunny Again*   30 minutes. Musical. *General Electric Summer Originals.* Broadcast July 3, 1956 (Tuesday, 9:00–9:30 P.M.) ABC

Producers: Norman & Irving Pincus; *Director* Don Wels; *Writer* William Bowers.

Cast: Vivian Blaine, Jules Munshin, Casey Adams, Shirley Mitchell

Songs: "New York, New York," "Singin' in the Rain."

Story: A theatrical agent is unable to find work for his talented client, but his trickery gets him fired. The singer's sweet sister and a leering Lothario are involved in her life.

This tidbit is included because it is listed as a musical comedy; it was the premiere show of the series *General Electric Summer Originals.* The summer series was described as "30-minute dramatic films never before seen on television." It appears standard songs were used in this show.

Review: *Variety* (July 11, 1956): "Miss Blaine is misused by a weak script and some badly employed canned laughter."

101. *Jack: A Flash Fantasy* 60 minutes. Opera. *NET Opera Theater.* Broadcast July 26, 1977 (Tuesday, 9:00–10:00 P.M.) PBS

Executive Producer Neil Sutherland; *Coordinating Producers* David Griffiths, Sam Paul; *Producers/Writers* Rob Iscove, Peter Mann; *Director* Rob Iscove; *Songs* Peter Mann; *Music Director* Rick Wilkins; *Choreographer* Rob Iscove; *Costume Designer* Csilla Marki; *Scenic Designer* Arthur Herriot.

Cast: Jeff Hysop, Laurie Hood, Victor Garber, Gilda Radner, William Daniel Grey, Vera Biloshisky, Alan Thicke, Patricia Gaul, Jerry Sroka, Valri Bromfield

Songs: "Written in the Cards," "Baby Legs."

Story: Playing cards come to life and assume distinct personalities.

A rock opera musical variety program, commissioned for TV by the Canadian Broadcasting Corporation.

102. *Jack and the Beanstalk* 90 minutes. Musical. *Producer's Showcase.* Broadcast November 12, 1956 (Monday, 8:00–9:30 P.M.) NBC

Producer Alvin Cooperman; *Director* Clark Jones; *Writer/Lyricist* Helen Deutsch; *Composer* Jerry Livingston; *Record* LP RKO Unique 111; *Sheet Music* Remington Music (7).

Cast: Joel Grey, Celeste Holm, Cyril Ritchard, Peggy King, Arnold Stang, Leora Dana, Billy Gilbert, Dennis King (Narrator), Ray Charles Chorus

Songs: "The Ballad of Jack and the Beanstalk," "Looka Me," "I'll Go Along with You," "He Never Looks My Way," "Song of the Harp," "People Should Listen to Me," "Twelve Feet Tall," "Sweet World," "This Is the One," "Where Are the White Birds Flying?" "The March of the Ill-Assorted Guards."

Story: A poor farm boy named Jack trades the family cow for some magic beans. The beans grow into a giant beanstalk. Jack climbs the stalk and runs into all sorts of characters in a dream sequence where the characters resemble the townspeople, and a teenager's fantasies are acted out.

Jack and the Beanstalk was nominated for an Emmy for best live camera work. The *Time* review noted that the show pulled in the largest audience of any 90-minute production ever aired up till that time.

Reviews: *Time:* Its charm ... was sporadic. Top-heavy with talent and electronic gimmickry.... The music just wasn't very good. ... Newcomer Joel Grey showed promise."

Variety (Nov. 14, 1956): "Instead of fantasy there was psychoanalysis, set to music. It didn't quite come off.... Too much shell, too little substance."

103. *Jack and the Beanstalk* 60 minutes. Musical. Broadcast December 19, 1966 (Monday, 7:30–8:30 P.M.) CBS

Executive Producer Richard R. Rector; *Producer* Ethel Burns; *Directors* Jim Eiler, Nick Havinga; *Writer* Jim Eiler; *Songs* Jim Eiler, Jeanne Bargy; *Arranger* Richard Hayman; *Conductor* Alfredo Antonini.

Cast: Joan Roberts, Hal Holden, Fred Grades, Bob Lussier, Robert Dagny, Will B. Able, Dorothy Greener, David Lile, John Joy, Marcie Stringer

Songs: "It's a Magical, Musical Day," "Fee, Fi, Fo, Fum," "Beans, Beans!" "Take a Giant Step," "Goodby, Little Cow," "Plinka, Plunka," "I'm Gonna

Gene Kelly

Climb Up," "Oh, Them Golden Eggs," "Go Way," "We Must Get Out of Here."

Story: Jack goes to town to sell the family cow and comes home with some beans from which a giant beanstalk grows. Jack climbs the beanstalk and finds Giant Land, where he makes friends with the giant, meets the golden harp and the golden goose, and has many adventures.

A production of the Prince Street Players, Ltd.

104. *Jack and the Beanstalk* 60 minutes. Live/Animated Musical. Broadcast February 26, 1967 (Sunday, 7:30–8:30 P.M.) NBC

Producer/Director Gene Kelly; *Writers* Michael Norris, Larry Markes; *Producers/Directors* William Hanna, Joseph Barbera; *Lyricist* Sammy Cahn; *Composer* James Van Heusen; *Music Director* Lennie Hayton; *Record* LP HBR 8511; *Video* Worldvision.

Cast (voices): Gene Kelly, Bobby Riha, Ted Cassidy, Marian McKnight, Marni Nixon, Cliff Norton, Leo Delyon, Chris Allen, Dick Beals

Songs: "Half Past April and a Quarter to May," "It's Been Nice," "The Woggle Bird Song," "A Tiny Bit of Faith," "Stiffen Up," "One Starry Moment," "I Sure Hate Love."

Story: Jack trades his cow for some beans, and the beans grow into a giant beanstalk. Jack and the peddler climb the beanstalk, and they share adventures with some mice, the giant, an enchanted harp-girl named Serena and a goose. They rescue Serena, escape from the giant with the help of the mice and the goose, slay the giant as he follows them down the beanstalk, and collect his gold. Jack's mother is coincidentally named Serena, and she and the peddler get acquainted.

Gene Kelly was already noted for his dance with cartoon mouse Jerry in the film *Anchors Aweigh*, and in this show he once again interacted with animated figures. This program won an Emmy for outstanding children's program. Sammy Cahn and James Van Heusen wrote many songs for movie musicals.

Review: *Variety* (March 1, 1967): "Kelly is excellent as a dancer, fetching as a singer, but did not register as a Yankee peddler. Riha was the perfect Jack."

105. *Jack Frost* 60 minutes. Animated Musical. Broadcast December 13, 1979 (Thursday, 8:00–9:00 P.M.) NBC

Producers/Directors Arthur Rankin, Jr., Jules Bass; *Writer* Romeo Muller; *Lyricist* Jules Bass; *Composer* Maury Laws; *Video* Lightning Video.

Cast (voices): Buddy Hackett (narrator), Robert Morse, Debra Clinger, Paul Frees, Dave Garroway, Larry Storch, Dee Stratton, Don Messick, Diana Lynn

Songs: "Me and My Shadow," "There's the Rub," "The Christmas Song," "She Is Beautiful," "Jack Frost," "Just What I Always Wanted," "Lonely Being...," "The Groundhog's Song."

Story: Jack Frost's story is told by ground hog Pardon-Me-Pete. Jack moves from the South Pole to January Junction, and there falls in love with snowwoman Elisa. In order to be seen, the invisible Jack kills Kubla Kraus, an evil giant, and in return is granted a season of human life. But he finds Elisa (now human) is marrying someone else, so Jack leaves, giving the newlyweds the gift of springtime.

This tale is based on a 1902 story by L. Frank Baum, creator of *Oz*.

Review: *Variety* (Dec. 19, 1979): "One of the better holiday programs to have surfaced this season ... a visual treat."

106. *The Juggler* 30 minutes. Opera. *The Catholic Hour*. Broadcast May 3, 1959 (Sunday afternoon) NBC

Executive Producer (series) Martin H. Work; *Producer (series)* Richard J. Walsh; *Librettist* Jean Lustberg; *Composer* William Graves.

Cast: Rudy Caringi, William Lowry, Mary Kennedy, Mary Ann Stabile, Jan Nugent, Daniel Tomaselli, Robert Hubbard, Ann Ricardo

Story: On the festival-feast day of the Virgin Mary, a deaf-mute juggler offers as his gift a small bouquet of wild flowers which he presents with adoration. The Padre, who preaches materialism, humiliates the juggler for his gift, but the juggler is lifted to immortality when the statue of the Virgin Mary comes to life.

Commissioned by the National Council of Catholic Men for *The Catholic Hour*, this story is based on the legend of the juggler of Notre Dame.

Reviews: *Musical America* (Charles Crowder, May 1959): "With miracles at work, William Graves construed his music to suit the sentiment of the story. Most effective is his use of madrigal texture in several chorus scenes: closely knit harmony and narrow melodic line."

Washington Post (Paul Hume, April 5, 1959): "This simple story has a sympathetic setting in music which is not unlike the most familiar of Menotti. It gains its high emotional powers from the beautiful miming of Rudolph Caringi in the title role."

America (May 23, 1959): "Once again *The Catholic Hour* has been demonstrating its capacity for presenting original ideas in an attractive way on the TV screen."

107. *Junior Miss* 90 minutes. Musical. *Du Pont Show of the Month.* Broadcast December 20, 1957 (Friday, 7:30–9:00 P.M.) CBS

Producer Richard Lewine; *Director* Ralph Nelson; *Writers* Joseph Stein, Will Glickman; *Lyricist* Dorothy Fields; *Composer* Burton Lane; *Record* LP Blue Pear 1019; *Sheet Music* Chappell (5).

Cast: Don Ameche, Joan Bennett, Carol Lynley, Diana Lynn, Jill St. John, Suzanne Sidney, David Wayne, Paul Ford.

Songs: "Junior Miss," "A Man Is an Animal," "Happy Heart," "Have Feet—Will Dance," "I'll Buy It," "Let's Make It Christmas All Year Round."

Story: Teenagers Judy Graves and Fuffy Adams are convinced that Judy's father is having an affair with the daughter of his boss. The girls try to arrange another affair for the femme fatale, leading to all kinds of misunderstandings and complications.

Based on the book *Junior Miss* (1941) by Sally Benson, which was made into a Broadway play and a movie prior to this show. Carol Lynley had been a child model and shortly before this production had won recognition for work on the Broadway stage. Composer Burton Lane wrote the score for Broadway's *Finian's Rainbow*, and lyricist Dorothy Fields wrote words to an amazing number of songs for stage and film, and wrote the books for many musicals also.

Review: *Variety* (Dec. 25, 1957): "Engaging…. The lusciously uncomplicated adolescence of Miss Lynley's portrayal warmed the old-fashioned script. … Music unimportant and uninspired, but incidental to the comedy."

108. *Keep in Step* 60 minutes. Musical. Broadcast January 23, 1959 (Friday, 9:00–10:00 P.M.) CBS

Producer Edward J. Montagne; *Directors* Aaron Ruben, Al De Caprio; *Writers* Billy Friedberg, Arnie Rosen, Coleman Jacoby, Terry Ryan; *Lyricist/Composer* Ronny Graham; *Conductor* Hal Hastings; *Choreographer* Jack Cole.

Cast: Phil Silvers, Diana Dors, Sydney Chaplin, Jerry Carter, Paul Ford, Joe E. Ross, Beatrice Pons, Harvey Lembeck, Allan Melvin, Maurice Gosfield, Hope Sansberry, Nick Saunders, John Alexander, Jimmy Little, Billy Sands,

Don Ameche and Carol Lynley, stars of *Junior Miss* **(1957). Photofest.**

Herbie Faye, Bernie Fein, Mickey Freeman, Jack Healy, Maurice Brenner

Songs: "I've Got the World on a String," "Plea to Col. Hall," "Famous Beauties," "Emma," "Freeze!"

Story: Sgt. Bilko is frustrated in trying to put on a musical at Camp Fremont. He hears that Sydney Chaplin is being recalled to active duty for a recruiting drive, and pulls strings to get Chaplin assigned to Camp Fremont and to his motor pool. He convinces Chaplin to write a musical about Bilko's life for the men, but is upset when Chaplin wants to star actor Phil Silvers as Sgt. Bilko.

Phil Silvers was a master of comedy, and his TV series, in which he starred as Sgt. Ernie Bilko, a charming, unscrupulous, manipulative con man who hustled the military bureaucracy and everyone around him, was a big hit. He was surrounded by a motley but engaging assortment of characters. This "special," expanded to an hour, was presented during the last season of the series, with most of the regular cast participating. Phil Silvers had earlier starred in the Broadway musical *Top Banana* (1951), which was about a TV star.

Review: *Variety* (Jan. 28, 1959): "Great fun ... [in Bilko's typical fashion] intriguing, refreshing, sidekicks [as usual] funny. ... Musical numbers and score adequate."

109. *The King and Mrs. Candle*
90 minutes. Musical. *Producer's Showcase.* Broadcast August 22, 1955 (Monday, 8:00–9:30 P.M.) NBC

Producer Fred Coe; *Director* Arthur Penn; *Writer* Sumner Locke Eliott; *Lyricist* Chuck Sweeney; *Composer* Moose Charlap; *Music Director* Harry Sosnik; *Choreographer* Tony Charmoli; *Sets* Paul Barnes; *Costumes* Gary Kent; *Sheet Music* Harms (2).

Cast: Cyril Ritchard, Irene Manning, Joan Greenwood, Richard Haydn, Donald Marye, Theodore Bikel, Agnes Doyle, Helen Raymond, Raymond Bramley, Philippa Bevans, Lulu Belle Clarke, Martha Greenhouse

Songs: "Young Ideas," "Absolutely Mad," "We Must Fly," "You're Lucky for Me," "What Is the Secret of Your Success?"

Story: King Rupert of Brandovia rules his country with an iron fist, while the residents are busy exporting bologna

and fighting off neighboring Carps and Gloats. A people's revolution deposes the king, and he has to learn to live in a democracy. He works at various odd jobs, and courts Lily Candle, a dance instructor.

Reviews: *New York Times* (J. P. Shanley, Aug. 23, 1955): "A highly improbable bit of Graustarkian fluff, with no message and no moral ... relaxing and enjoyable.... [The poor singing] did not detract—the songs, like the book, are not to be taken seriously."

Variety (Aug. 24, 1955): "Less than satisfying. ... Dull and ordinary stretches of an unbelievable love story taken too seriously. [Leads] are good at comedy, not so good at singing. Tunes are far above the ordinary."

110. *Kingdom Chums: Little David's Adventure* 60 minutes. Live/Animated Musical. Broadcast November 28, 1986 (Friday, 8:00–9:00 P.M.) ABC

Executive Producer, Animation Jean Chalapin, Andy Heyward; *Executive Producer, Live Action* Diana Kerew; *Director, Animation* Bernard De Viries; *Director, Live Action* Colin Chilvers; *Writers* Jeff Scott, Jeanne Betancourt; *Lyricist/Composer* Joe Raposo.

Cast: Jenna Van Oy, Christopher Fitzgerald, Andrew Cassese

Songs: "Greatest Stories of All," "Child of God," "Your Love Makes Me Strong."

Voices: Sandi Patti, Scott Menville, John Franklin, Billy Bowles, Jim Cummings, Town-send Coleman, Paul Winchell, Phil Proctor

Story: Some bullies are picking on a Jewish boy, Sauli, and he falls on Mary Ann's bird. At home, the "Love Light" pulls the children into the computer and they become cartoons. Christopher, the tiger, Magical Mose, a cat, and Little David, a raccoon, are Kingdom Chums who lead the children 3000 years into the past. The children relive David's adventures with him while he plays the harp, slays a bear and ultimately defeats the giant Goliath. The children learn that with faith one has the courage to overcome fear. Back home, Sauli stands up to the bullies, and Mary Ann finds her bird is alive.

This show was based on the book *Little David's Adventure* by Squire D. Rushnell, ABC's Vice President of Long Range Planning and Children's Programs. The story follows the book. A sequel, *Kingdom Chums: The Original Top Ten*, fully animated and made by a different crew, was shown as an *ABC Weekend Special* (daytime).

Review: *Variety* (Dec. 10, 1986): "Didn't seem like an appropriate network kids fare ... overtly religious message ... completely undisguised retelling of Biblical stories. ... Plodding story has too little action or humor or plot to keep many kids entertained."

111. Kingdom Chums: The Original Top Ten 60 minutes. Animated Musical. *ABC Weekend Special.* Broadcast April 10, 1993 (Saturday, Local Option) ABC

Producer/Director Rick Reinert; *Writer* Peter Sauder; *Lyricists/Composers* Al Kasha, Joel Hirschhorn; *Director of Animation* Dave Bennett; *Music Director* Roger Laroque; *Voice Director* Susan Blu.

Cast (voices): Debby Boone, Marilyn McCoo, Tony Orlando, Billy Preston, Frankie Valli, Mayim Blalik, Scott Menville, Marne Patterson

Songs: "Follow the Love Light," "Respect Your Mom and Dad," "Be Glad for What You've Got," "Thank You God," "Lies," "Honor His Name," "Stop Before You Steal," "Idols," "Be Loyal to the One You Love," "He's All You Need," "Learn to Love," "Love One Another."

Story: Peter, his sister Annie and a troublesome boy named Osborne meet in a restaurant. Osborne has stolen a top hit record from the library, and Peter talks to him about honesty. The children are drawn into the jukebox and once again meet the Kingdom Chums: Christopher, Lion of Love, and Marvelous Mose, Chum of Joy, who tell the children about the all-time top ten hits, the Ten Commandments, in song. Each Commandment is presented as a quiz, and one of the boys wins the record for understanding the message. When the children return to the restaurant, they fully understand the Commandments; Osborne returns the record and changes his ways.

This is a sequel to *Kingdom Chums: Little David's Adventure.*

112. Labyrinth 60 minutes. Opera. *NBC Opera Theater.* Broadcast March 3, 1963 (Sunday, 2:00–3:00 P.M.) NBC

Producer Samuel Chotzinoff; *Director* Kirk Browning; *Librettist/Composer* Gian Carlo Menotti; *Conductor* Herbert Grossman; *Settings* Warren Clymer; *Costumes* Noel Taylor.

Cast: Judith Raskin, John Reardon, Elaine Bonazzi, Robert White, Beverly Wolff, Frank Poretta, Leon Lishner, Nikiforos Naneria, John West, Eugene Green, Bob Rickner

Story: This is an allegory about man's journey through life and his search for life's meaning. The story is told through

**A flooded train compartment is part of the mysterious journey in *Labyrinth* (1963).
Photofest.**

a bridgegroom and his bride, lost in the corridors of a grand hotel, trying to find the key to their room. They try to stop the bellboy, but he slips a note under a door, then leaves. They meet a spy, then an old man, who asks the groom to play chess. The groom leaves his bride in the corridor but does not get answers from the old man, who falls asleep. The groom rejoins his bride. The spy drops a note with an arrow on it. The couple go to the executive director's office, but she is busy giving orders and is no help. The groom then enters a room that turns into a rocket ship, where an astronaut sings of the wonders of space but then cries "meteors" as the ship explodes, catapulting the groom back to the hall. The groom grabs the bellboy as he comes by, but the spy stabs the bellboy to death. The bride screams and runs through the corridors. The groom chases her and is seen running through forests, mountains and rivers. He finds himself in a flooded train compartment where people are swimming and fishing; on cue, the water runs out and people, now fully clothed, arrange themselves in seats as the conductor comes in. When he leaves, the car refills and people go back to their swimming and fishing. A storm approaches, and the groom finds himself being tossed in a raging sea. The bride tries to swim out to meet him and drowns. The groom floats into a ballroom and drags himself to the lobby, where the manager makes him lie down on a bench. The manager and his assistant build a coffin around the groom, but when they carry the coffin off, the man is left lying on the bench. He opens his hand to show the key.

According to the author, the bellboy represents religion, the spy any field that claims to have an explanation of life and the world. The old man represents the past, the female executive the present, the astronaut the future, and the manager death. The hotel is the world.

This one-act opera was commissioned by NBC, and was nominated for an Emmy for outstanding music. The opera had only the one performance; it has never been done in a theater, and the special effects would probably preclude doing so. Menotti himself calls this story "a puzzling concoction." The message is that death is the key that finally reveals to man the answer to his metaphysical questions.

Reviews: *Musical America* (John Ardoin, April 1963): "Sound theatrical possibilities but the punch it might have packed was diluted by its patchy libretto and score. ... Seems like a last-minute job ... a mere rejuggling of familiar mannered harmonic and melodic clichés."

Opera News (April 13, 1963): "The music runs the gamut from grand opera parody to da capo arias to pop euphoria of the Weill variety. ... Displays a chastened lyricism, as if Menotti had found new roots." The critic noted that the show's "engaging whimsey" worked well for television but might prevent the work from succeeding in another medium.

TV Guide (March 3, 1963): "The composer's melodic style is there but his story is surrealistic or dreamlike, and it takes a medium like TV, for which it is written, to handle it."

113. *The Land of Green Ginger*   60 minutes. Musical. *Shirley Temple Storybook Special.* Broadcast April 18, 1958 (Friday, 7:30–8:30 P.M.) NBC

Producer Alvin Cooperman; *Director* Robert P. Singlair; *Writer* Noel Langley; *Lyricist* Mack David; *Composer* Jerry Livingston; *Set Designer* Sidney Clifford.

Cast: Kuldip Singh, Charles Halton, Billy Curtis, Angelo Rossitto, Eugene Jackson III, Roy Jenson, Joey Faye, Jack Albertson, Sue England, Antony Eustrel

Songs: "You're a Hero," "We're on Our Way."

Story: Ali, son of Aladdin, is unable to find a bride. The Genie tells him of Princess Silver Bird of Samarkand; Ali must win her love for himself alone, not because he is wealthy. Using the lamp, Genie and a magic carpet, Abu overcomes the opposition of a smoke-breathing dragon and two villainous Oriental princes, and wins the Princess' hand and heart.

Based on Noel Langley's book. Songwriters Livingston and David had written songs for Disney's *Cinderella*. Kuldip Singh, Kashmiri-born singer, had appeared on Groucho Marx's TV show.

There is some indication that all or most of the *Shirley Temple Storybook/Theatre* productions have at least some songs, but there is insufficient information to include them all.

Reviews: *Time* (April 28, 1958): "As delightful a piece of fluffy nonsense as storyteller Temple has presented this season ... satirically spoofy enough to entertain adults ... was tricked up with a passel of fantastic gimmicks to bewitch children."

Variety (April 23, 1958): "A mishmash, part fairy tale, part burlesque. ... Had a number of imaginative concepts, but was lacking the fairy-tale magic. ... Sets were incongruous, between reality and abstractions."

114. *The Legend of Robin Hood*   90 minutes. Musical. Broadcast February 18, 1968 (Sunday, 7:30–9:00 P.M.) NBC

Producers Bob Wynn, Alan Handley; *Director* Alan Handley; *Writer* Harry Kleiner; *Lyricist* Sammy Cahn; *Composer* James Van Heusen.

Cast: David Watson, Noël Harrison, Roddy McDowall, Steve Forrest, Walter Slezak, Douglas Fairbanks, Jr., Victor Buono, Lee Beery, Arte Johnson, Bruce Yarnell

Songs: "Out in the Open Air," "Ever So Gently," "Prithee Please," "Nottingham Fair," "A Happy Happenstance," "The Star Beyond the Star."

Story: A merry romp through Sherwood Forest where Robin Hood and his men rob the rich and help the poor, making life miserable for the sheriff. The Merrie Men sing, carouse and have a jolly time.

Songwriters Cahn and Van Heusen a few years earlier wrote songs for the Sinatra film *Robin and the Seven Hoods*, as well as award-winning songs for other movies and TV shows.

Review: *Variety* (Feb. 21, 1968): "Plush production ... winning cast. ... Cahn/Van Heusen tunes were OK but not incidental enough. Airs, refrains, minstrelsy, etc. smothered the plot and character development."

115. *Let Me Go, Lover*   60 minutes. Drama with Music. *Studio One.* Broadcast November 15, 1954 (Monday, 10:00–11:00 P.M.) CBS

Producer Herbert Brodkin; *Writer* Henry Misrock; *Title Song* Jenny Lou Carson, new words by Al Hill; *Record* Columbia 40366; *Sheet Music* Hill and Range.

Cast: Joe Maross, Anthony Ross, Cliff Norton, Connie Sawyer\Title song sung by Joan Weber

Song: "Let Me Go, Lover."

Story: A midnight TV disk jockey correctly suspects an ex-con and his girlfriend are using his apartment for a rendezvous. There is skullduggery in the recording industry and a murder to complicate the plot.

Not really a musical, this show is worthy of note because through the power of television the song became an instant hit. It was written by Jenny Lou Carson in 1953 with the title "Let Me Go, Devil." Mitch Miller at Columbia Records had Al Hill write new lyrics and had Joan Weber record the song. Bits of the song were played six times during the show. The song rose to #1 on *Billboard* charts on December 4, 1954, and remained there for four weeks, and in the top 40 for 16 weeks. The drama was based on a *Redbook* short story, "Who's Been Sitting in My Chair?"

The practice of introducing new songs via TV dramas was particularly prevalent in 1954 and 1955, once it was discovered that songs could be plugged in this medium, but successor shows are not included here. Songs and the shows included "Hard to Get" on *Justice*, "Play Me Hearts and Flowers" on *Philco Television Playhouse*, "Chance at Love" on *Studio One*, "My Love Song to You" on *The Jackie Gleason Show*, and "Any Questions" on *Dragnet*. These song plugs are to be distinguished from series themes (vocal or instrumental), many of which rose to fame.

Review: *Variety* (Nov. 17, 1954): "*Studio One* had one of its off nights, when a mystery meller failed to be either mysterious or melodramatic."

116. *The Life and Adventures of Santa Claus*   60 minutes. Animated Musical. Broadcast December 17, 1985 (Tuesday, 8:00–9:00 P.M.) CBS

Producers/Directors Arthur Rankin, Jr., Jules Bass; *Writer/Lyricist* Julian P.

Gardner; *Composer* Bernard Hoffer; *Video* Warner Home Video.

Cast (voices): Alfred Drake, Earl Hammond, J. D. Roth, Robert McFadden, Lesley Miller, Earl Hyman, Larry Kenney, Joey Grasso, Amy Anzelowitz, Josh Blake, Ari Gold, Jamie Lisa Murphy, Lynne Lipton, Peter Newman

Vocalists: Al Dana, Margaret Dorn, Arlene Martell, Marty Nelson, David Ragaini, Annette Sanders.

Songs: "Ora E Sempre," "Ho-Ha-Ho," "Babe in the Woods," "A Child," "Big Surprise."

Story: Found as an abandoned baby, Santa Claus is raised by the Immortals in the Forest of Bursee. As a mortal, he tries to help others. He moves to the Laughing Valley of Ho-Ha-Ho and begins his tradition of making gifts for a nearby orphanage. Some nasty creatures who hate children try to stop the giving but Claus gets help from the reindeer to carry his gifts, and from the Immortals to banish the evil-doers. Claus' good deeds finally earn him immortality, with the title of Santa (Saint).

117. *Li'l Abner* 60 minutes. Musical. Broadcast April 26, 1971 (Monday, 8:00–9:00 P.M.) ABC

Producers Allan Blye, Chris Bearde; *Director* Gordon Wiles; *Writers* Coslough Johnson, Ted Zeigler, Allan Blye, Chris Bearde; *Songs* Earl Brown, Jimmy Dale.

Cast: Ray Young, Nancee Parkinson, Billie Hayes, Billy Bletcher, Bobo Lewis, Dale Malone, Jennifer Narin-Smith, Inga Neilson, Jackie Kahane, H. B. Haggarty, Tom Solari

Songs: "Your World," "Infamous Revival Stomp," "Super Gettin' Method Power."

Story: Dogpatch-and the World-are about to be destroyed by some indescribable lumps called "Deadly Glops." Mammy Yokum and her cohorts set out to save the day.

Pilot for a proposed series. Several earlier attempts had been made to bring *Li'l Abner* to TV, but none made the grade.

Review: *Variety* (April 28, 1971): "Played at full shout by its principals, it resembled a high-school play during the first dress rehearsal with a rambling script." The reviewer called the music "serviceable," singling out the opening and closing numbers for praise, "but nothing could excuse this silly excuse for a network special."

118. *Li'l Abner in Dogpatch Today*
60 minutes. Musical. Broadcast November 9, 1978 (Thursday, 8:00–9:00 P.M.) NBC

Producer George Schlatter; *Director* Jack Regas; *Writers* Digby Wolfe, Billy Barnes; *Lyricist/Composer* Billy Barnes.

Cast: Stephen Burns, Debra Feuer, Polly Bergen, Kaye Ballard, Louis Nye, Rhonda Bates, Don Potter, Deborah Zon, Susan Tolsky, Cissy Cameron, Diki Lerner, Charlene Ryan, Ben Davidson, Candy McCoy, Prudence Holmes

Songs: Not found

Story: Feminism hits Dogpatch with a bang as Bella Asgood lectures the gals they should be looking for careers instead of husbands on Sadie Hawkins Day.

This attempt to bring *Li'l Abner* to television tried to modernize the story. Songwriter Billy Barnes wrote a number of West Coast revues, and did specialty numbers for pop singers.

Review: *Variety* (Nov. 15, 1978): "Did not make it on any count. The satiric quality ... was completely absent, replaced by mindless caricatures.... Performances were generally listless, except for Charlene Ryan (as Stupefyin' Jones)."

119. *Little David's Adventure* **see** *Kingdom Chums: Little David's Adventure*

120. *The Little Drummer Boy* 30 minutes. Animated Musical. Broadcast December 19, 1968 (Thursday, 7:30–8:00 P.M.) NBC

Producers/Directors Arthur Rankin, Jr., Jules Bass; *Director of Animation* Takeo Nakamura; *Writer* Romeo Muller; *Title Song* Katherine Davis, Henry Onorati, Harry Simeone; *Other Lyrics* Jules Bass; *Other Music* Maury Laws; *Musical Director* Colin Romoff; *Design* Charles Frazier; *Video* Viacom.

Cast (voices): Greer Garson (narrator), José Ferrer, Teddy Eccles, Paul Frees, June Foray, Vienna Boys Choir

Songs: "When the Goose Is Hanging High," "Why Can't the Animals Smile?," "One Star in the Night," "The Little Drummer Boy."

Story: Aaron is a farm lad, son of a shepherd. Earlier his parents gave him a drum and he played while his animals danced, but his parents were killed by desert bandits, and Aaron now roams the land with Samson, his donkey, Ben, Ba Ba, his lamb, and Joshua, his camel. Aaron hates and mistrusts people. He is kidnapped by Ben Haramed to play with the roving musicians, and they entertain crowds in Jerusalem but are chased out. The band of musicians then meets the three kings who are following the star. One of their camels is

ill, and Ben Haramed sells Aaron's camel to the kings, over Aaron's protests. Aaron leaves the troupe and with his lamb and donkey goes looking for the kings and his camel by following the star to Bethlehem. His lamb is injured by a soldier, and Aaron asks a king's help to heal the lamb. The king says he is only mortal and cannot help, but that the true King, the baby, can. Aaron says he has no gift for the child, but then plays his drum. The lamb is healed and Aaron realizes he should love, not hate, others.

The song "The Little Drummer Boy" was written in 1958. Recorded by the Harry Simeone Chorale, the single record was a perennial best seller for many years, and an album containing the song had even better sales. The song was also recorded by many pop singers over the years. NBC aired the original version of this show for eight consecutive years. A sequel to the animated special (also available on video) was made in 1976.

121. *Little Women* 60 minutes. Musical. Broadcast October 16, 1958 (Thursday, 8:30–9:30 P.M.) CBS

Executive Producer David Susskind; *Producer* Albert Selden; *Director* William Corrigan; *Writer* Wilson Lehr; *Lyricist/Composer* Richard Adler; *Musical Director* Hal Hastings; *Orchestrator* Don Walker; *Choreographer* John Butler; *Record* LP Kapp KL 1104.

Cast: Jeannie Carson, Risë Stevens, Florence Henderson, Bill Hayes, Roland Winters, Zina Bethune, Joel Grey, Margaret O'Brien

Songs: "How Do You Write a Book?," "I Don't Want to Be a Fly," "Love I Mean," "Dance, Why Not?," "Man of the Family," "Party Shoes," "The Letter," "The Four of Us."

Zina Bethune (left) and Florence Henderson in *Little Women*. Photofest.

Story: The March family of New England try to get by while their father is away serving as a chaplain in the Civil War. Songs introduce Jo, an aspiring writer who likes to devise plays and entertainment for her sisters; Meg, the oldest sister; Beth, the quiet one, and Amy, the baby of the family. Neighbors Laurie, his grandfather and his tutor John Brooke also appear in scenes of family fun and a few problems.

This story, from the Louisa May Alcott book of 1868, was a popular one for television; NBC did versions in 1939 and 1945, CBS in 1949 and 1950, and NBC again in 1956. This was, however, the only attempt at a musical version. Jeannie Carson was known through her TV show *Hey Jeannie*.

Review: *Variety* (Oct. 22, 1958): "Jeannie Carson was a delight to watch...."

The show sought to accomplish too much in a short time, and ... emerged ... as a fluffy petite-four for dainty palates with not much to sink the choppers into."

122. *The Littlest Angel* 90 minutes. Musical. *Hallmark Hall of Fame.* Broadcast December 6, 1969 (Saturday, 7:30–9:00 P.M.) NBC

Executive Producers Lan O'Kun, Lester Osterman; *Producer* Burr Smidt; *Director* Joe Layton; *Writers* Lan O'Kun, Patricia Gray; *Lyricist/Composer* Lan O'Kun; *Conductor* Warren Meyers; *Choreographer* Joe Layton; *Costumes* Fred Voelpel; *Choral Director* Will Bronson; *Record* LP Mercury 1-603; *Video* Karol Video.

Cast: Cab Calloway, Tony Randall, Connie Stevens, Fred Gwynne, Corinna Manetto, Johnnie Whitaker, E.G. Marshall, John McGiver, George Rose, James Coco, Evelyn Russell, Chris Alexander, George Blackwell, Mary Jo Catlett, Lee Leonard

Songs: "The Master of All I Survey," "Where Am I?," "You're Not Real," "The Heavenly Ever After," "What Do You Do?," "Where Is Blue?," "I Have Saved," "You Can Fly," "I Bring You Good Tidings," "Once Upon Another Time," "May It Bring Him Pleasure."

Story: A young shepherd boy named Michael falls off a cliff and floats to the heavenly gates, where he is welcomed by the angel Gabriel and a heavenly chorus. His boyish guardian angel, Patience, takes him under his wing, gets him a robe and halo, and takes him to flying class. But Michael, the Littlest Angel, doesn't feel that he fits in. He doesn't like the angel clothes, and he cannot fly. He applies for a job, but there is nothing for him, and he has lit-tle to do. He misses the blue skies, green grass, flowers, and mountains, and he prays to go home again. He finally asks Patience if he can go home to get his box of treasures, and Patience lets him go (for which he gets banished). When Michael returns, God is announcing the forthcoming birth of the baby Jesus. All the angels set about preparing gifts for the baby. The Littlest Angel does not yet have any skills or talents, and he doesn't know what he can give as a gift. He finally donates his box of childhood treasures, then is ashamed to have offered such a humble gift. But God is most pleased with this gift of the heart and sends the box into the sky to become the Star of Bethlehem.

Based on the Charles Tazewell story (1946), this show broke Hallmark's previous viewing record (for *Hans Brinker* in 1958).

Reviews: *Variety* (Dec. 10, 1969): "Whitaker good as a wide-eyed youngster ... Gwynne persuasive as guardian angel.... Musical score tuneful enough but tended to slow up action."

New York Times (Jack Gould, Dec. 8, 1969): "A story too often told [leaving] emphasis on setting and score.... More variety in music might not have been amiss.... An hour and a half conscientiously executed by the producer, and not without ingredients of pleasure."

123. *Liza Minelli in Sam Found Out: A Triple Play* 60 minutes. Drama/Musical. Broadcast May 31, 1988 (Tuesday, 10:00–11:00 P.M.) ABC

Producers Alexander H. Cohen, Fred Ebb; *Director* Piers Haggard; *Writers* John Kander, Fred Ebb; *Lyricist* Fred Ebb; *Composer* John Kander.

Cast: Liza Minnelli, John Rubinstein

Buster Keaton and Kay Starr are members of a traveling circus in *The Lord Don't Play Favorites* **(1956). Photofest.**

Songs: "Sam," "Norma Gentle," "Sam Was There," "You Win Some, You Lose Some," "Empty Room."

Story: Norma and Johnny are a couple whose forthcoming marriage is jeopardized by Norma's best friend Sam—a jealous dog.

This show consisted of three diverse one-act plays: a drama, a comedy and a musical. Each starred Liza Minnelli and a different co-star. The cast, credits and story above relate only to the musical segment.

Review: *Variety* (June 15, 1988): "Liza Minnelli and the dependable John Rubinstein sing out about their courtship and about the third party in their affair. Rubinstein is as charming as Minnelli is disarming...."

124. *The Lord Don't Play Favorites*

90 minutes. Musical. *Producer's Showcase.* Broadcast September 17, 1956 (Monday, 8:00–9:30 P.M.) NBC

Directors Clark Jones, Bretaigne Windust; *Writer* Jo Swerling; *Lyricist* Irving Taylor; *Composer* Hal Stanley; *Music Director* Hal Mooney; *Choreographer* Tony Charmoli; *Record* 45 EP RCA EP 960 (Kay Starr, four songs), 45 RCA 47-6630 (Louis Armstrong, two songs).

Cast: Louis Armstrong, Kay Starr, Buster Keaton, Robert Stack, Dick Haymes

Songs: "Come One, Come All," "Rain, Rain," "For Better or Worse," "Hoedown," "I Never Saw a Better Day," "The Things I Never Had," "Soft Shoe Dance," "This Land," "The Good Book," "Dry, Oh Dry."

Story: A small traveling circus is stranded in a Kansas hick town in 1905. The town is experiencing a drought. The bankrupt circus prays for dry track on which to run its trick horse, but the Lord lets it rain and the horse wins anyway.

Based on a short story by Patrick Malloy.

Reviews: *Time* (Oct. 1, 1956): "The whole romp was a washout. Kay Starr's anvil voice led a lusty counterpoint.... But Armstrong as bandleader and Buster Keaton as clown were wasted. The 'original' Jo Swerling-Hal Stanley music had a too-familiar ring."

Variety (Sept. 19, 1956): "Tunes were serviceable and of good quality ... gave the show its few satisfying moments ... its winning moments came between the dialog. Buster Keaton was wasted."

New York Times (Jack Gould, Sept. 18, 1956): "Show had one fine number— a counterpoint in song between townsfolk who wanted rain and circus people who didn't. ... Score was decidedly reminiscent."

125. *Madeline* 30 minutes. Ani-

mated Musical. Broadcast November 7, 1988 (Monday, 7:00–8:30 P.M.) HBO

Executive Producers Andy Heyward, Saul Cooper, Richard Rosen, Pancho Kohner; *Producer* Cassandra Schlafhausen; *Director* Stephan Martinere; *Writer* Judy Rothman; *Composer/Conductor* Joe Raposo; *Video* Hi-Tops Video.

Cast (voices): Christopher Plummer (narrator), Marsha Moreau, Judith Orban, John Stocker, Loretta Jafelice, Linda Kash, Wendy Lands, Daccia Bloomfield, Tara Charenoff

Songs: "I'm Madeline," "Fly Air Madeline," "Something Is Not Right," "Ma Chérie-o Madeline," "Voilà My Scar," "Madeline."

Story: Madeline is the smallest and bravest (and the most mischievous) of 12 little girls in a convent school in Paris. With their teacher Miss Clavel, the girls are sometimes happy, sometimes sad, as they explore the city and play. But Madeline gets sick and has to have her appendix removed; when the girls visit her she proudly shows off her scar, and the other girls all want to have scars too.

Ludwig Bemelman's series of rhyming picture books about Madeline were written from 1938 to 1968. A theatrical cartoon version of this book made by UPA in 1952 had earlier been shown on television.

While the 1988 version is listed at 90 minutes, the video is only 30 minutes long, so it appears several of the *Madeline* story books were used for the broadcast. Christopher Plummer won an Emmy for his narration of *Madeline* in the 1993–4 season, when the picture was shown on the Family Channel.

Review: Mick Martin and Marsha Porter, *Video Movie Guide*: "Delightful animated short ... charmingly narrated in verse by Christopher Plummer."

126. *The Magic Horn* 60 minutes. Musical. *Alcoa Hour.* Broadcast June 10, 1956 (Sunday, 9:00–10:00 P.M.) NBC

Record LP RCA 1332.

Cast: Sal Mineo, Ralph Meeker, Ruby Braff, Buzzy Drootin, Milton Henton, Vic Dickenson, Peanuts Huche, Jimmy McPartland

Songs: "The Magic Horn," "Squeeze Me," "Sugar," "Loveless Love," "A Monday Date," "Dippermouth Blues," "Struttin' with Some Barbecue," "Ain't Gonna Give Nobody None of My Jellyroll," "On the Sunny Side of the Street."

Story: A Dixieland jazz band plays in 1920s Chicago. A young bandboy who hangs around is befriended by the trumpet player. When the horn player dies suddenly, the inconsolable boy runs off to his room. The trumpet won't play for anyone else, so the piano player finally delivers it to the boy in his room, and he makes it soar.

Mostly standard jazz numbers here, but a music-filled hour served as a pleasant diversion.

Review: *Variety* (June 13, 1956): "Players work better on notes than words. ... Mineo demonstrated nothing more than an out-of-this-world look. Meeker ... stiff and humorless. Braff's trumpeting gave the hour its only sparks."

127. *The Magical Mystery Trip Through Little Red's Head* 60 minutes. Animated/Live Musical. *ABC Afterschool Special.* Broadcast May 15, 1974 (Wednesday, 3:30–4:30 P.M.) ABC

Producers David H. De Patie, Friz Freleng; *Director* Herbert Klynn; *Writer* Larry Spiegel; *Lyricist* Johnny Bradford; *Composer* Dean Elliott.

Cast (voices): Lennie Weinrib, Diane Murphy, Ike Eisenmann, Sarah Kennedy, Joan Gerber

Songs: "Timer's Song," "Nightmare Song," "All Aboard," "Squirter's Song," "You've Got to Learn to Relax" "Come with Me," "Butterflies and Bushes," "Go Take a Walk in the Sunshine."

Story: Two children, Carol and Larry, reduced to microscopic size, take a fantasy trip through the brain of their older sister, Little Red. Loosely following the tale of "Little Red Riding Hood," they learn about time, choice and emotions.

128. *Manhattan Tower* 90 minutes. Musical. *Saturday Spectacular.* Broadcast October 27, 1956 (Saturday, 9:00–10:30 P.M.) NBC

Executive Producer Elliott Lewis; *Producer* Gordon Jenkins; *Associate Producer* Furth Ullman; *Director* Boris Sagal; *Writer/Lyricist/Composer* Gordon Jenkins; *Record* See below; *Sheet Music* Leeds Music; *Suite* Pickwick (MCA).

Cast: Peter Marshall, Helen O'Connell, Phil Harris, Cesar Romero, Ethel Waters, Edward Everett Horton, Hans Conried, Tommy Farrell, Bob Stevens, Richard Kean, Cheerio Meredith, Eddie Parks, Dick Ryan, Frank Marlowe, Ralph Sanford, Cyril Delevanti, Renny McEvoy, Steve Carruthers, Glenn Turnbull, Sylvia Bernstein

Songs: "New York's My Home," "Once Upon a Dream," "Never Leave Me," "Repeat After Me," "The Party," "Happiness Cocktail," "Magic Fire," "Learnin' My Latin," "March Marches On," "Married I Can Always Get," "This Close to Dawn."

Story: Intended as a love song to the city of New York, the sights, the sounds and the people, the everyday and night activities of the residents are captured in the words and music. A young mid-westerner finds and loses a dream girl on a visit to New York; a bartender, a dance instructor, students visiting the Statue of Liberty, a Greenwich Village artist, various night club habitués and Noah, the waiter, all people the tale.

Composer Jenkins said he first fell in love with New York City in 1929, and was inspired on a return visit in 1945 to compose what was then called "a musical narrative." The suite was recorded in 1945 and the recording sold well. In 1950 the suite was performed on *The Ed Sullivan show*, where the mayor of New York presented the composer with a key to the city. The original suite was expanded for the television production, with many more songs, so can be considered a new work for television. Jenkins said the people portrayed were based on real people he knew in the city.

Jenkins was a conductor and arranger for radio and television shows, has been a recording conductor for many noted singers, and has written a number of popular songs. He once wrote weekly operas for four years for a radio show.

There are four recordings (LPs) of *Manhattan Tower*, two undated; none are of the TV cast.

Review: *Variety* (Oct. 31, 1956): "The composition was stretched beyond its limit into an hour and a half color spectacular. ... Peter Marshall was in good voice, but wooden. ... Helen O'Connell as a New York girl played with a bounce."

129. *A Man's Game* 60 minutes. Musical. *Kaiser Aluminum Hour.* Broadcast April 23, 1957 (Tuesday, 9:30–10:30 P.M.) NBC

Producer David Susskind, Alfred Levy; *Director* Paul Lammers; *Writer* David Shaw; *Lyricists/Composers* Jack &

Madeline Segal (Maddy Russell); *Musical Director* Don Walker; *Choreographer* Robert Joffrey.

Cast: Nanette Fabray, Gene Nelson, Paul Ford, Bibi Osterwald, Kenneth Bowers, Fred Gwynne, Stephen Shaw, Lew Parker

Songs: "You I Love," "A Cold, Cold Winter," "Wonderful Wedding Day," "No Spring This Year," "A Man's Game," "Lament for the Whole Baseball World."

Story: Lew Daniels, manager of the New York Titans baseball team, travels to Alabama to look over a hot catcher prospect, farm boy Chub Evans. But he is astonished to see that Chub's pretty sister Jo is an outstanding pitcher, and he offers her a contract on the spot. Jo is eager to accept, but her fiancé Tom doesn't want to become a "baseball wife," sitting in the bleachers with a scorecard. Jo marries Tom and they arrive at spring training together. The players don't like having a female teammate, and their wives invade the locker room. Tom finds being left with the wives very uncomfortable and, on the way to the first game, leaves the train in a huff. Jo and Tom miss each other very much, so Tom travels with Chub to the opening game. On game day, Jo doesn't feel well and thinks it is nerves, but finds she is pregnant and benches herself. The team is relieved and Tom is pleased to have his wife back.

This story was based on a Robert Allan Aurthur comedy previously shown on the *Philco Television* playhouse. A pre-show publicity photo had Leo Durocher with Fabray, but he was not listed for the broadcast.

Review: *Variety* (May 1, 1957): "Despite a lot of hard work in the song and emoting departments by Nanette Fabray, the show remained a trite comedy effort. ... The script never developed.... The score [gave] nothing memorable."

130. *Maria Golovin* 2 hours. Opera. *NBC Opera Theater.* Broadcast March 8, 1959 (Sunday, 5:00–7:00 P.M.) NBC

Producer Samuel Chotzinoff; *Director* Kirk Browning; *Librettist/Composer* Gian Carlo Menotti; *Conductor* Herbert Grossman; *Settings* Rouben Ter-Artunian; *Costumes* Helen Pons; *Lighting* Charles Elson; *Record* 3LP RCA LM 6142; *Music* G. Recordi (libretto, vocal selections); Belwyn Mills (score).

Cast: Franca Duval, Richard Cross, Patricia Neway, Ruth Kobart, Lorenzo Muti, William Chapman, John Kuhn, Herbert Handt, Chester Ludgin, Craig Seehler

Story: The story takes place in a European villa shortly after World War II. Maria Golovin rents the upstairs apartment for the summer and arrives with her small son, a tutor and servants. Donato, a young veteran blinded in the war, lives in the villa with his mother and a maid who is in love with him. He makes bird cages for a living. Maria visits with Donato and learns that he is lonely and feels imprisoned by his blindness. She offers to read to him and play the piano. As they get acquainted, he asks to touch her face. Maria and Donato soon become intimate. He tells her of his earlier ambition to become an architect; she tells him of her husband, a prisoner of war, and of a previous summer affair. The maid encourages Donato to become suspicious of Maria, and his own insecurities fan his jealousy. An escaped POW from a nearby camp comes to the house and demands to be hidden overnight. The prisoner tells Donato that he will have to find his own escape from his fancied prison.

When the prisoner departs, he leaves his gun behind. Some time later, Maria receives a telegram saying her husband has been released, and she knows she should leave Donato. Everything that has happened has made Donato's love for Maria more obsessive, and he wishes Maria dead so that no one else can have her. At the end, Donato retrieves the prisoner's gun and in the heat of passion fires where he thinks Maria is. His mother deflects the shot, but tells him he has killed Maria and can now live in peace.

A romantic tragedy in three acts, seven scenes, *Maria Golovin* was commissioned and produced by NBC as one of the American entries at the International Exposition in Brussels in the summer of 1958. While the two-week performance there was its world premiere, the opera was en route to television. In the fall of '58 it was performed on Broadway, but had only five performances. Producer David Merrick had seen the opera in Brussels, and offered to produce it on Broadway (which he did), but when offered another show, he closed *Maria Golovin.* Composer Menotti believed with a longer run it would have been successful. New York theater critics had given mixed reviews to the stage production. One critic was put out because it was sold as a new Broadway musical, rather than an opera; another thought it dull. But there were favorable reviews too. NBC presented the opera on television in the spring of 1959.

Reviews: *Variety* (March 11, 1959): Like other reviewers, the *Variety* critic found *Maria Golovin* more successful on television than on the stage, thanks largely to the intimacy of the small screen. "Its reduced size projection made much more acceptable the melodramatic story, and more understandable the neurotic development of the blind, love-torn youth."

New York Times (Howard Taubman, March 9, 1959): "On television ... the story took on a fierce intensity that was almost too large for the home screen to contain. Fortunately, Kirk Browning, the director, moved his camera so fluidly that the opera did not overwhelm the television medium." According to Taubman, the libretto and the music together demonstrated the ample scope of Menotti's talent.

Time (March 23, 1959): "In this video treatment it was far and away the most successful translation of this lesser Menotti work. ... Singers all good ... camera work exceptionally fine, setting opulent. ... Music had spasmodic flashes of lyricism."

Donald Gramm

131. *The Marriage* 60 minutes. Opera. *NBC Opera Theater.* Broadcast February 7, 1953 (Saturday, 5:00–6:00 P.M.) NBC

Director John Block; *Librettist* Bohuslav Martinů; *Composer* Bohuslav Martinů; *Sets* Otis Riggs; *Costumes* Liz Gillelan.

Cast: Donald Gramm, Sonia Stollin, Michael Pollock, Winifred Heidt, Andrew McKinley, Lloyd Harris, Robert Holland, Ruth Kobart, Leon Lishner, Ann Pitoniak

Story: Podkolyossin, a civil servant and bachelor, believing he should marry, contacts a matchmaker to find him a wife. When the matchmaker announces she has found a suitable candidate, Miss Agafya, the reluctant Podkolyossin uses every excuse he can think of to postpone meeting the girl. His married friend Kotchkarev wishes to see the bachelor married and drags him to Miss Agafya's house, where they find several other candidates for her hand.

The girl is overwhelmed and announces she doesn't want any of them. Kotchkarev, after much conversation, persuades the other bachelors to leave, and brings Podkolyossin face-to-face with Miss Agafya. After some polite chitchat, Podkolyossin starts to leave, but his friend drags him back, elicits a proposal and acceptance from the couple, and leaves to make wedding arrangements. Podkolyossin, left alone with his thoughts, at first thinks of the pleasures of being married, but then is appalled at the permanency of the commitment. He panics, leaps out of the window and goes home, still a bachelor.

Based on the 1842 Gogol play.

Reviews: *Musical America* (James Lyons, Feb. 1953): "Gogol's story is full of the verismo that seems to lend itself so well to this medium; video's mono-dimensional scope is quite sufficient unto the simple annals of Everyman."

New York Times (Olin Downes, Feb. 8, 1953): "A production of singing actors whose technique was specifically appropriate to the television screen which is non-small praise. ... The opera is perfectly proportioned."

Time (Feb. 16, 1953): "Martinů's score is lighthearted and craftsmanlike, though it contains no memorable music. The production itself comes across as first-rate entertainment."

132. *Martin's Lie* 60 minutes. Opera. Broadcast May 30, 1965 (Sunday, 4:00–5:00 P.M.) CBS

Producers Bath Festival Society/Labyrinth Corp of America/CBS; *Director* Kirk Browning; *Librettist/Composer* Gian Carlo Menotti; *Conductor* Lawrence Leonard; *Settings and Costumes* Anthony Powell.

Cast: Michael Wennick, William McAlpine, Noreen Berry, Keith Collins, Donald McIntyre, Otakar Kraus, Roger Nicholas

Story: In the kitchen of an old convent which has been converted into an orphanage, the housekeeper is telling a story to the boys. The boys then say their prayers except for Martin, whose turn it is to sleep in the kitchen to guard the food from rats. Martin answers a knock on the door and finds a stranger who says he is being pursued as a heretic and asks for shelter. After Martin admits to waiting for his father, the stranger says, "I could be your father." Martin, because he wants to believe, finally accepts and hides the stranger. Soon the sheriff comes, looking for the heretic, and says he knows the man is there. Father Cornelius questions Martin, but Martin stubbornly refuses to

admit the man's presence. He finally confides to Father Cornelius that the man is his long-lost father. The priest tries to persuade him this is not so, but is unsuccessful. The sheriff searches the building, then threatens Martin; Martin drops dead.

This opera was commissioned by CBS and was performed at the Bristol Cathedral, Bath, England. The American television premiere, scheduled for January 24, 1965, was cancelled by CBS-TV owing to the death of Winston Churchill, and the program was shown in May.

Review: *New York Times* (June 14, 1964): Critic Gene Baro praised Menotti's treatment of a serious theme, calling it "skillful and moving." He went on: "Mr. Menotti has made an admirably terse and simple musical exposition of his dramatic material. His score represents every nuance of appropriate feeling but without flamboyance."

133. *The Mercer Girls* 30 minutes. Musical. *Hallmark Hall of Fame*. Broadcast June 28, 1953 (Sunday afternoon) NBC

Producer/Director Albert McCleery; *Writer/Lyricist* Poor Pray; *Composer* Albert Hague; *Conductor* Roy Shields.

Cast: Sarah Churchill, Bibi Osterwald, Stephen Douglass, Robert Wright, Peter Birch, Lloyd Buckley, Walter Donahue, Evelyn Ward, Renée Orin, Rosamund Vance, Vin Kehoe, Alan North, Fred Waring Glee Club

Songs: Not found

Story: Sarah Churchill played one of a troupe of eastern girls arriving at the Seattle frontier in 1864 to find husbands. Settler Asa Mercer had sent for the girls. Two men compete for the love of Sarah's character.

This was an early work of Albert Hague, who later composed music for the Tony-winning Broadway show *Redhead*, and much later played Professor Shorofsky in *Fame* (both the movie and TV series). Renée Orin, in the cast of *The Mercer Girls*, was Mrs. Hague and understudy to Sarah Churchill.

Review: *Variety* (July 1, 1953): "[Despite its 30 minute length looked like one of the better tunesmith tries in the medium. The Poor Pray lyrics [were] meaningful and punchy, and the Albert Hague music [was] a bit reminiscent but lusty.... Book ... was par for the course."

134. *The Mighty Casey* 90 minutes. Opera. *Omnibus.* Broadcast March 6, 1955 (Sunday, 5:00–6:30 P.M.) CBS

Writer/Lyricist Jeremy Gury; *Composer* William Schuman; *Conductor* Samuel Krachmalnuck; *Music* G. Schirmer (Vocal Selections).

Cast: E. G. Marshall, Danny Scholl, Elise Rhodes, Rufus Smith, Nathaniel Frey

Songs: "Championship of the State," "If Only Casey," "Strategy," "A Prayer," "Peanuts, Popcorn, Soda, Crackerjack," "The Mighty Casey," "Surprise," "Autograph," "The Gladdened Multitude," "You Look So Sweet Today," "You're Doin' Fine Kid," "Kiss Me Not Goodbye," "Rhubarb," "Two Out," "Hist'ry Hangs on a Slender Thread," "Oh, Somewhere."

Story: Mudville is playing Centerville for the state baseball championship, with big league scouts watching the game. If Casey does well, his girl Merry knows he will be leaving, but she prays for his success. But Casey, alas, at the crucial moment, strikes out.

This opera, based on Ernest L.

Thayer's 1888 poem "Casey at the Bat," was a much-expanded version of the poem set to music, with additional verses written by Gury. Schuman and Gury were both baseball lovers, and were said to have approached this project with enthusiasm. The opera premiered in Hartford, Connecticut, on May 4, 1953, but had only the one performance before its television debut. Famous entertainer De Wolf Hopper was known for reciting the poem on the stage.

Reviews: *Variety:* "...went wide of the plate musically and lyrically. Schuman's score was heavy handed.... Principals and chorus were hampered by a score which seemed too tough to sing."

Martin Gardner in *The Annotated Casey at the Bat:* "[Authors] have expanded the Casey myth with such loving insight, such full appreciation of the nuances in Thayer's ballad, that no Casey fan need hesitate to add the opera to the Casey canon."

135. *Minstrel Man* 2 hours. Musical. Broadcast March 2, 1977 (Wednesday, 9:00–11:00 P.M.) CBS

Executive Producers Roger Gimbel, Edward L. Rissien, *Producers* Mitchell Brower, Robert Lovenheim; *Director* William A. Graham; *Writers* Richard A. & Esther Shapiro; *Songs* Fred & Meg Karlin; *Choreographer* Donald McKayle; *Art Director* Hilyard Brown; *Sheet Music* Primus Artists Music.

Cast: Glynn Turman, Ted Ross, Stanley Clay, Saundra Sharp, Art Evans, Gene Bell, George Earl Billings, Anthony Ames, Amechi Uzodinma, Arthur Rooks, Carol Sutton, Wilbur Swartz, Robert Earle, Don Lutenbacher, Bill Holliday, Robert Harper, The Whitney Family

Songs: "Early in the Morning," "Precious Lord," "Ragtime Special," "Good News," "Coon, Coon, Coon," "Over the Waves," "Two New Coons in Town," "The Band Played On," "Remus Takes the Cake," "High Time in Old Dixie," "The Laughing Song," "Turkey in the Straw," "Coon Hollow Capers," "Just a Closer Walk with Thee," "Wait 'Till the Sun Shines, Nellie," "Hot Time in the Old Town Tonight."

Story: Brothers Harry and Rennie Brown have been earning their way in Mississippi performing as blackface minstrels, but have big ideas. Harry dances, sings and hustles his way to success by forming his own minstrel troupe in a field dominated by blackfaced whites; shy Rennie composes and plays ragtime piano like no one before him, and wants out of the minstrel business. The story of their lives is played out with plenty of music. When Harry baits a redneck audience and is lynched in front of the company, the other players take off their blackface in silent tribute.

Filmed on location in Mississippi, this program was nominated for Emmys for musical composition (dramatic underscore), special musical material and choreography. Composer Fred Karlin, noted for his many television and movie scores, consulted on the period ragtime music for this show, as well as composing the score. The songs listed above include authentic ragtime and popular music of the period; "Early in the Morning," an original song by Fred and Meg Karlin, was sung twice in the show. "Ragtime Special" was also an original song. In addition to the background music (themes), Fred Karlin composed a number of original instrumental pieces played by the performers on- and off-screen.

Reviews: *Variety* (March 9, 1977): "The script was a gem. Characters were subtly and strongly etched. ... Performances were flawless and frequently brilliant."

Leonard Maltin, *Movie & Video Guide:* "Engrossing drama.... Rich performances by Turman as ambitious song-and-dance man, Clay as dedicated musician racked by racial consciousness, Ross as a rascally impresario."

Steven H. Scheuer, *Movies on TV & Video:* "This compelling teleplay focuses on the efforts of a group of post–Civil War black minstrel performers to form their own troupe and to present material that would be less degrading to blacks."

136. *Miss Chicken Little*   30 minutes. Opera. *Omnibus.* Broadcast December 27, 1953 (Sunday, 5:00 P.M.) CBS

Producer Robert Saudek; *Librettist* William Engvick; *Composer* Alec Wilder; *Conductor* George Bassman; *Choral Director* Ray Charles; *Choreographer* John Butler; *Music* TRO

Cast: Jo Sullivan, Charlotte Rae

Songs: "It's a Fine Day for Walkin' Country Style," "Don't Deny."

Story: The traditional tale relates that Chicken Little is walking through the woods when an acorn falls, hitting her on the head. She tells all her feathered friends that the sky is falling. The group head off to tell the king, and meet a fox who says he will show them the way. Instead, he leads them to his foxhole, where he and his cubs eat them up.

Originally written for two pianos and performed on stage, the work was completely orchestrated "at lightning speed" for the *Omnibus* production. It has been variously referred to as a light opera, an operetta and a cantata. It is not known how closely the opera follows the traditional tale. *Omnibus* was a 90-minute program, but the opera was only 27 minutes long.

Review: No reviews were found, but Wilder biographer Desmond Stone reports that "Some who saw the *Omnibus* show, with its comic, light opera treatment, have called it 'stunning.'"

137. *Mr. Magoo's Christmas Carol*
60 minutes. Animated Musical. Broadcast December 18, 1962 (Tuesday, 7:30–8:30 P.M.) NBC

Executive Producer Henry Saperstein; *Producer* Lee Orgel; *Director* Abe Levitow; *Writer* Barbara Chain; *Lyricist* Bob Merrill; *Composer* Jule Styne; *Conductor/Orchestrator* Walter Scharf; *Video* Paramount.

Cast (voices): Jim Backus, Jack Cassidy, Morey Amsterdam, Joan Gardner, Jane Kean, Royal Dano, Les Tremayne, Paul Frees, Marie Matthews, Laura Olsher, John Hart

Songs: "It's Great to Be Back on Broadway," "Ringle, Ringle," "All Alone in the World," "The Lord's Bright Blessings," "Winter Was Warm," "We're Despicable."

Story: The nearsighted, cantankerous Mr. Magoo stars in a Broadway presentation of *A Christmas Carol*. The play opens with Scrooge counting his money. He refuses to make a donation to charity, and begrudges more coal to his clerk, Bob Cratchit. On his return home, Scrooge sees Marley's face on the doorknocker and in the fire. He is then visited by Marley's ghost, which he dismisses as a "bit of sour gruel." He is visited by a cheerful Ghost of Christmas Present (who accuses him of being too cheap to buy eyeglasses) and is taken to the Cratchit family home. A very young Ghost of Christmas Past takes him to

see himself as a lonely lad at school, to Fezziwig's Christmas party, and to a scene where Belle tells him she will no longer see him. The ominous Ghost of Christmas Yet to Come takes him past businessmen discussing his demise, rag-pickers going through his belongings, to the Cratchits' sad house and to his grave. He wakes up in his own bed. A joyful Scrooge dances around the room, then asks a lad to fetch the prize turkey and deliver it to the Cratchits anonymously. Strolling down the street, Scrooge contributes to charity, then visits the Cratchits', where a tree is delivered and Scrooge tells Bob he will get a raise. In the end, while taking his solo bows, Magoo causes all the scenery to fall down.

This was the first made-for-television animated cartoon special, and the first animated TV musical. The production closely followed the Dickens story and was done with imaginative drawings.

Mr. Magoo was created in 1949 as a theatrical cartoon, and many Mr. Magoo appearances followed. Beginning in 1960 Magoo began his own TV series, and other series came later. Jim Backus was the voice of Magoo for 40 years.

Composer Jule Styne wrote music for a number of Broadway shows and films as well as for the earlier TV musical *Ruggles of Red Gap*. Lyricist Bob Merrill wrote both words and music for several Broadway shows and wrote many popular songs.

Reviews: *Variety* (Dec. 26, 1962): "Slickly produced and entertaining kiddie fare. ... Dickens' story itself was nicely capsulized to get the feeling.... Animation first rate ... nice tunes, pleasant lyrics ... swift and entertaining pace."
Stephen H. Scheuer, *Movies on TV*

& Video: "Delightful animated version of the Dickens family classic, with a lovely score...."

Mick Martin and Marsha Porter, *Video Movie Guide:* "First rate animated musical of Charles Dickens' holiday classic which remains the best animated adaptation to date. The songs are magnificent."

138. *Mr. Willowby's Christmas Tree*
30 minutes. Musical. *CBS Holiday Special/Nabisco Family Classics.* Broadcast December 6, 1995 (Wednesday, 8:30–9:00 P.M.) CBS

Director Jon Stone; *Writer* Michael Kriegman; *Lyricists/Composers* Michael & Patty Silversher.

Cast: Robert Downey, Jr., Leslie Nielsen, Stockard Channing; Muppet performers: Kevin Clash, David Kudman, Julianne Ruscher, Steve Whitmire. Host: Kermit the Frog

Songs: "The Perfect Tree," "Long Long Ago," "Honeypot Waltz."

Story: Father mouse and his children go out to look for the perfect Christmas tree, and find a fine tree. But while they are climbing among the branches, the tree is cut by lumberjacks and delivered to Mr. Willowby's mansion. Mr. Willowby, too, thinks this is a fine tree, but it is too tall, so he has Baxter, the butler, cut off the top and take the smaller piece to Miss Adelaide, the maid. She is most pleased, and has Baxter join her in a Swedish Christmas celebration. The tree is too tall for her room, so the top is cut off and discarded. Papa bear finds the tree and takes it to his family, where they all dance the Honeypot waltz around the tree. This tree is too big for the bears' home, so they cut off the top. An owl takes the piece to his nest, and trims to fit. The leftover piece,

still containing the mouse family, is just right for Father mouse and his children to take home. Meantime, at the mansion, everyone is having a very Merry Christmas.

Based on the 1963 verse tale by Robert Barry. The main song, "The Perfect Tree," is sung by all of the characters in turn, with many verses.

139. *Mother Goose* 60 minutes.
Musical. *Shirley Temple's Storybook Special.* Broadcast December 21, 1958 (Sunday, 8:00–9:00 P.M.) NBC

Director Mitchell Leisen; *Writers* Malvin Wald, Henry F. Greenberg; *Lyricist* Mack David; *Composer* Jerry Livingston; *Choreographer* John Gregory

Cast: Elsa Lanchester, Carleton Carpenter, Shirley Temple, Billy Gilbert, Rod McKuen, Lloyd Corrigan, Gene Nash, Lynn Alden, Louise Glenn, Charles Black, Jr.

Songs: "Mother Goose Has Come to the Fair," "Beggar's March," "Moon Is Shining," "Wouldst," "Cushion Dance," "Georgy Porgy Comes to the Fair," "Dreams Are Made for Children."

Story: In 1785 the mayor of Skeddlestone, England, threatens to close the annual fair if last year's rowdyism is repeated. Mother Goose characters seen at the fair are Polly and Able Baker, Tom, Simple Simon, Willie Winkie, Jack and Jill and Sukey and Andy.

Review: *Variety* (Dec. 24, 1958): "Unimaginative hodge-podge. The songs and lyrics with the exception of one tune lacked spark and individuality. The able cast ... was largely wasted."

140. *The Mouse on the Mayflower*
60 minutes. Animated Musical. Broadcast November 23, 1968 (Saturday, 7:30–8:30 P.M.) NBC

Producers/Directors Arthus Rankin, Jr., Jules Bass; *Writers* Romeo Muller, Arthur Rankin, Jr.; *Lyricist* Jules Bass; *Composer* Maury Laws.

Cast (voices): Tennessee Ernie Ford (narrator), Eddie Albert, John Gary, Joanie Sommers, Paul Frees, June Foray

Songs: "Mayflower," "This Land," "Elbow Room," "When She Looks at Me," "One Day," "Good Times," "Time, Stand Still," "November."

Story: A brave mouse named Willum tells his version of the Pilgrims' voyage across the Atlantic on the *Mayflower*, and their arrival at Plymouth Rock. He tells of sailing with Miles Standish, John Alden, Priscilla Mullins, William Bradford and the other Pilgrims seeking religious freedom. Stormy seas damage the ship, seamen Quizzer and Scurv try to sabotage the trip, but Willum solves the problems admirably. The Pilgrims build a settlement at Plymouth and make friends with the Indians, though Quizzer and others try to start a war; a severe winter and illness threaten the settlers, but again Willum helps to solve the problems. Willum witnesses the first Thanksgiving feast.

While there have been a number of Thanksgiving-time specials, this appears to be the only one to deal specifically with the Thanksgiving story.

Review: *Variety* (Nov. 27, 1968): "Tasteless ... demeaned the holiday ... no service toward the education of the young."

141. *Mrs. Santa Claus* 2 hours. Musical. Broadcast December 8, 1996 (Sunday, 8:00–10:00 P.M.) CBS

Executive Producer David Shaw; *Producer* J. Boyce Harman, Jr.; *Director* Terry Hughes; *Writer* Mark Saltzman; *Lyricist/Composer* Jerry Herman; *Orches-* *trator* Larry Black; *Music Director* Don Pippin; *Choreographer* Rob Marshall; *Costume Designer* Bob Mackie; *Production Designer* Hub Braden; *Set Decorator* Ellen Totleben; *Record* CD.

Cast: Angela Lansbury, Charles Durning, Michael Jeter, Terrence Mann, Lynsey Bartilson, Bryan Murray, David Noroña, Debra Wiseman, Rosalind Harris, Grace Keady, Linda Kerns, Chachi Pittman, Sabrina Bryan, Bret Easterling, Mitchah Williams, Kristi Lynes, James Torocellini, Jean Kaufman, Stacy Sullivan, Cere Rae, Mick Murray, Ken Kerman, John Wheeler, Toni Perotta

Songs: "Seven Days 'til Christmas," "We Don't Go Together at All," "Mrs. Santa Claus," "Whistle," "Avenue A," "He Needs Me," "Almost Young," "The Best Christmas of All."

Story: It is 1910. Anna Claus heads up toy-making operations at the North Pole, but she is feeling neglected because Santa barely has time to talk to her. She suggests a different route for his sleigh, but he is not listening. Anna decides to try the run herself and takes off in the sleigh with the reindeer. A storm forces her off course, and she lands in New York City's melting pot. One of the reindeer is injured, and Anna seeks help from stable boy Marcello. After taking in the reindeer, Marcello takes Anna (now known as Mrs. North) to meet Mrs. Lowenstein and her suffragette daughter Sadie. Anna gets a job as supervisor in a toy factory and tries to help the exploited children working for mean Augustus P. Tavish. She does a little matchmaking on the side. In her absence Santa realizes how much he misses her. When Anna makes a mad dash back to the North Pole on Christmas Eve, Santa says he will follow her route, and he takes her along on his trip.

Other songs in the show using the tunes of those listed above include "A Tavish Toy," "Suffragette March," and "Dear Mrs. Santa Claus." Music of Herman's "We Need a Little Christmas" (from *Mame*) is used as the elves try to cheer up Santa. Jerry Herman appears briefly in the show as a ragtime pianist. This show was advertised by CBS as its first original musical for television since the 1957 "Cinderella," an inaccurate claim, as the material in this book demonstrates.

Lyricist/Composer Herman has written many Broadway musicals including *Mame* and *Hello, Dolly!* Angela Lansbury has appeared on stage, in movies and on television in both dramatic and musical roles, and has won four Tony awards for her stage musical performances.

Review: *TV Guide* (Dec. 8, 1996): "charming.... Angela Lansbury is enchanting in the title role ... catchy songs."

142. *My Heart's in the Highlands*
90 minutes. Opera. *NET Opera Theater.* Broadcast March 18, 1970 (Wednesday, 7:30–9:00 P.M.) PBS

Director Kirk Browning; *Writer/Lyricist/Composer* Jack Beeson; *Conductor* Peter Herman Adler; *Set Designer* Eldon Elder.

Cast: Gerard Harrington, Lili Chookasian, Alan Crofoot, Spiro Malas, Kenneth Smith, Jack Beeson

Story: At a ramshackle house in California a boy named Johnny, plays in the yard while his father tries to write poetry and his grandmother putters around inside the house. Suddenly the boy hears beautiful music; he sees a very old man playing "My Heart's in the Highlands" on a bugle. The old man is Jasper MacGregor, an actor. He asks for a drink of water, but the boy pesters him with questions. The father comes out and tells Johnny to get the stranger some water, then MacGregor asks for food. His father sends Johnny to the store but the family has exhausted its credit at the store and Johnny has no money to pay. Nevertheless, the boy charms the grocer and succeeds in bringing home bread and cheese. MacGregor plays another tune and, when neighbors gather to hear the music, MacGregor asks that they bring more food, which they do. MacGregor stays with Johnny and his family until several weeks later when a young man comes to take him back to the Old People's home, telling him they need him to play King Lear. MacGregor returns to the family to die. The family is evicted from their home and heads into the sunset.

This story was adapted from William Saroyan's 1939 one-act play. Composer Beeson also acted in the opera. He has written many other operas, including *Lizzie Borden*. This was the first stereo broadcast of a taped program (simulcast).

Reviews: *Opera News* (April 4, 1970): "An attractive bit of Americana. ... Saroyan's euphoric extravagance is matched by Beeson's full-bodied musical manner.... If [Beeson's] rhythms and melodizing seemed insistent at times, there were also moments of playfulness."

New York Times (Raymond Ericson, March 18, 1970): "Flawed though it is, the opera has charm and humanity. ... Music, tonal and easily accessible, is carefully constructed."

143. *Myshkin*   60 minutes. Opera. *Net Opera Theater.* Broadcast April 23, 1973 (Monday, 8:00–9:00 P.M.) PBS

Executive Producer Peter Herman Adler; *Producer* Herbert Seltz; *Directors* Herbert Seltz, Ross Allen; *Librettist* Patrick Creagh; *Composer* John Eaton; *Musical Director* John Reeves White; *Costume Designer/Scenic Designer* Andreas Nomikos.

Cast: Staff, faculty and students of the Indiana University School of Music

Story: Prince Myshkin is a simple, sincere, lovable man. Worn down by his epilepsy, he wishes only to live in peace with his world. He is engaged to Aglaia but has an affair with Nastasia; he feels unworthy of his fiancée, so decides to marry Nastasia. But she runs off with Rogozin, who murders her in a fit of jealousy. Myshkin, unable to deal with murder, disloyalty, vituperation and vindictiveness, has a mental breakdown and becomes the "idiot" he has been called.

Based on Fyodor Dostoyevsky's novel *The Idiot* (1868). The author was known for his character studies and portrayal of life in 19th century Russia, and was himself an epileptic.

Review: *Musical America* (Shirley Fleming, July 1973): "Vocal writing simply not very interesting, being short on rhythmic vitality and conveying little sense of dramatic shaping."

144. *The New Adventures of Heidi*
2 hours. Musical. Broadcast December 13, 1978 (Wednesday, 8:00–10:00 P.M.) NBC

Executive Producer Pierre Cosette; *Producer* Charles B. FitzSimons; *Director* Ralph Senensky; *Writer* John McGreevy; *Music* Buz Kohan; *Conductor* Allyn Ferguson; *Production Design* Michael Baugh; *Video* Homeland.

Cast: Katy Kurtzman, Burl Ives, John Gavin, Marlyn Mason, Sean Marshall, Sherrie Wills, Alex Henteloff, Charles Aidman, Walter Brooke, Amzie Strickland, Molly Dodd, Adrienne Marden

Songs: "I See Trees," "That Man!/Woman!," "Let Me Stay/Let Her Stay," "I Miss Christmas," "Heidi," "Why?," "What Have I Got?"

Story: Heidi lives with her grandfather in the Swiss Alps. She plays with Peter and the goats, where they are sometimes observed by a wild man. Grandfather finds he is losing his eyesight, and calls the cousins to come get Heidi. Elizabeth Wiler, in town with a busload of students from her school, wanders off from the group and follows Heidi and Peter home, and Grandfather takes her in for the night. Elizabeth's father has his office in Zurich, but runs hotels all over the world, and is rarely around to pay attention to his motherless daughter. Grandfather and Heidi take Elizabeth to town to meet her father, but she doesn't want to leave; Elizabeth's father says he will bring her back to visit.

When Heidi and Peter again see the wild man, Peter chases after him and doesn't return. Heidi tells her grandfather, and Peter's father and the others go looking for him. They rescue Peter from the river, but when they return find they have lost Grandfather. The men go back out and search, but can only find his cane. Heidi packs to go with the cousins, but Mr. Wiler's secretary calls to say they will take Heidi as a companion for Elizabeth. When Elizabeth's father is off on yet another trip, the secretary gets the idea of sending the girls along, thinking he will spend time with them. But in New York he is, as usual, busy, and after the girls have gorged themselves on room service foods, they decide to get lost, hoping the father will have to find them. Elizabeth cries over a music box in a store, because her mother used to give a music box to her father every Christmas. The girls return, the father solves the hotel problems, they all exchange Christmas gifts and are reconciled. Back in Switzerland, Heidi and Elizabeth return to school, but in the summer they take a trip to Heidi's mountain. The wild man has saved the Grandfather and brings him to see Heidi. He is now totally blind, but Mr. Wiler says there are doctors in Zurich who can operate on his eyes, and his vision is restored.

A much-changed and -modernized version of Johanna Spyri's 1880 novel. The New York City hotel and department stores lack the quaintness of the Frankfurt city portrayed in the story. Outdoor shots were filmed in Colorado.

Reviews: *New York Times* (Tom Buckley, Dec. 13, 1978): "Emotional content ... all but drained in this updating. ... Cast adequate except when they are called upon to sing the wispy songs ... The mountain scenery is fine."

145. *The Night the Animals Talked* 30 minutes. Animated Musical. Broadcast December 9, 1970 (Wednesday, 7:30–8:00 P.M.) ABC

Producers/Directors Pablo Zavala, Sheldon Riss; *Lyricist* Sammy Cahn; *Composer* Jule Styne; *Video* Worldvision.

Cast (voices): Frank Poretta, Joe Silver, Pat Bright, Bob Kaliban

Songs: "Parable," "It's Great to Communicate," "Let's Not Behave Like People," "A Place Like This," "The Greatest Miracle of All."

Story: On a cold winter night in Bethlehem, the animals are resting in their mangers when a couple and their donkey appear at the stable. When the child is born, the animals receive the miraculous gift of speech. Confused by the gift, at first they argue and disagree, but the dog pleads with them to accept the visitors with faith.

The story is based on a folk-legend that tells of the first gift of speech to the animals on the night of the Nativity.

Review: *Variety* (Dec. 16, 1970): "A charming and delightful Christmas parable for children."

146. *The Night They Saved Christmas* 2 hours. Musical. Broadcast December 13, 1984 (Thursday, 8:00–10:00 P.M.) ABC

Executive Producers Robert Halmi, Jr., Jack Haley, Jr., David Niven, Jr.; *Producers* David Kappes, Robert Halmi, Sr.; *Director* Jackie Cooper; *Writers* James C. Moloney, David Niven, Jr.; *Songs* Paul Williams; *Music* Charles Gross; *Production Design* George Costello; *Video* Cabin Fever.

Cast: Jaclyn Smith, Art Carney, Paul Le Mat, Mason Adams, June Lockhart, Paul Williams, Scott Grimes, Laura Jacoby, R. J. Williams, James Staley, Albert Hall, Anne Haney, Buddy Douglas, Billy Curtis, Michael Keys Hall, Randy Crosby

Songs: "Jingle Bells," "Gotta Be Ready by Christmas Eve," "If You Believe."

Story: Michael Baldwin and his crew are drilling for oil near the North Pole for a petroleum company, while his wife Claudia and children C. B., David and Marianne are unhappy with life in the isolated camp. Santa's chief elf Ed comes to Michael's office and tells him he must stop dynamiting or he will destroy North Pole City and blow up Santa Claus, but Michael thinks this is a practical joke. Ed decides he will have to convince the Baldwin family; he takes Claudia and the children to see Santa's toy factory and meet Santa and Mrs. Claus. Claudia and the older children are skeptical, but Santa answers their questions and finally convinces them he is real. They return home to find the oil crews are stepping up their dynamiting, at the boss' orders. The older children go off in a snowmobile to warn Santa; their mother flies out to find them lost in an ice fog. Santa rescues them and gets ready for his Christmas deliveries. While Michael is searching for his family, oil is found on the first site, drilling is stopped, the holiday is saved and the family reunited.

A charming Christmas fantasy, but not really much of a musical. Based on a story by James Moloney, David Niven, Jr., and Rudy Dochterman, this show was filmed in part at the Arctic Circle. The program was nominated for an Emmy for outstanding children's program.

Review: Leonard Maltin, *Movie & Video Guide:* "Amiable Yuletide fantasy. ... Carney's delightful...Williams is fun."

147. *No Man Can Tame Me* 30 minutes. Musical. *General Electric Theater.* Broadcast February 1, 1959 (Sunday, 9:00–9:30 P.M.) CBS

Director Gower Champion; *Lyricist* Ray Evans; *Composer* Jay Livingston; *Record* LP Blue Pear 1019; Empire EBC 59-7487.

Cast: Gisele MacKenzie, John Raitt, Eddie Foy, Jr.

Songs: "One Hand Tied Behind My Back," "How Can I Be Alone Again?," "I Heard."

Story: Matilda Haley's father wants to marry off his rough and tumble daughter, and approaches all the young men in town. He finally settles on the town dandy, but Matilda prefers a handsome trapper.

Livingston and Evans were well known for their movie music. Gisele MacKenzie was a singer on *Your Hit Parade* and had her own musical variety show; John Raitt starred in *Carousel* and *Pajama Game* on Broadway, and played many other roles in musicals.

Review: *Variety* (Feb. 4, 1959): "Tuning up a trite tale ... tunes ably handled."

148. *Noah and the Flood* 60 minutes. Musical Drama. Broadcast June 14, 1962 (Thursday, 9:00–10:00 P.M.) CBS

Director Kirk Browning; *Writer (Prologue)* Jack Richardson; *Librettist* Robert Kraft; *Composer* Igor Stravinsky; *Choreographer* Balanchine; *Production Designer* Rouben Ter-Artunian; *Choral Director* Gregg Smith; *Conductors* Robert Kraft, Igor Stravinsky; *Record* LP Columbia ML 5757, MS 6357; *Video* (See below); *Music* Boosey & Hawkes, London (Score).

Cast: *Actors* Laurence Harvey, Sebastian Cabot, Elsa Lanchester, Paul Tripp; *Singers* John Reardon, Robert Oliver, Richard Robinson; *Dancers* Jacques D'Amboise, Edward Villella, Jillana, Ramon Segarra, Joysann Sidimus, New York City Ballet

Story: A Biblical "spectacle," from the creation to Noah and the ark, performed with orchestra, song, dance, narration and mime. Noah and his human companions in the ark are introduced wearing neo-troglodytic two-dimensional expressionless masks and the paired animals are portrayed by artfully artless toys. The spectacle is prefaced by a "preamble" discussing flood myths in various cultures, and is followed by a tribute to Stravinsky and Balanchine.

This work, commissioned by CBS, was Stravinsky's only work written expressly for television. It does not fit neatly into any single show category. The actual presentation lasted only 20–25 minutes, with the additions listed above rounding out the program to an hour. The work was based on the book of Genesis and the York and Chester Miracle Plays (1430–1500). Stravinsky is said to have been inspired by a visit to flooded Venice. The pre-performance publicity for this work raised expectations and left everyone disappointed. Dutch television (NOS-TV) has produced a video with a modernized studio version of "The Flood," using the original soundtrack; this is combined with Stravinsky's "Oedipus Rex" (Home Vision, 1985).

Reviews: *Time* (June 22, 1962): "Floated into view with strings shimmering, cymbals clanging, horns blaring dissonantly. ... Glimpses of Stravinsky at his best...built Ark with sound...created flood. Dancers moved with agile flowing grace." This reviewer complained that 21 minutes of airtime was too short for the show's varied elements to "demonstrate their virtues."

Musical America (John Ardoin, July 1962): "One of Stravinsky's most accessible in recent years. ... Text too compressed, a strange amalgamation. ... Dance distracted from the music ... a hybrid work based on trick photography."

Music (Peter Jacobs, Aug. 1962): "A badly organized and even pretentious bore. ... Noah as presented on television—despite the good intentions of network and sponsor—was a blow to the progress of the performing arts. Music was acceptable."

149. *O'Halloran's Luck* 60 minutes. Musical. *Dinah Shore Chevy Show.* Broadcast March 12, 1961 (Sunday, 9:00–10:00 P.M.) NBC

Executive Producer Henry Jaffe; *Producer* Perry Cross; *Director* Marc Daniels; *Writer* A. J. Russell; *Lyricists* Diane Lampert, Peter Farrow; *Composer* David Saxon; *Music Director* Henri René; *Choreographer* Ted Cappy; *Art Director* Herb Andrews; *Costumes* Guy Kent; *Sheet Music* Sam Fox (6).

Cast: Art Carney, Bil Baird's Marionettes, Barbara Cook, Ward Donovan, Dan Keyes, John McGovern, Pat Harrington, Sr., Granice O'Malley

Songs: "Cheeks for My Roses," "Every Little Boy Can Be President," "Whatcha Do on Sunday?," "Hoo Boo," "Shenanigans," "Goin' Green."

Story: Fresh off the boat from Ireland, O'Halloran discovers his girl working as a servant in Boston, and being courted by an Orangeman. O'Halloran heads west to find his fame and fortune, and goes to work on the railroad. After a toot one night, he rescues a leprechaun from wolves. The leprechaun begs for his assistance, so O'Halloran passes him off as his nephew and gets him a job with the railroad. The leprechaun is obstreperous and causes O'Halloran many headaches, but he also makes valuable suggestions on the work. O'Halloran passes these suggestions on, and gets himself promoted. He ultimately wins his girl and becomes president of the railroad, while the leprechaun attains human state and goes into business for himself.

Art Carney and Barbara Cook in *O'Halloran's Luck* **(1961). Photofest.**

This musical was based on the short story written by Stephen Vincent Benét in 1938. The story had previously been performed as a television play in 1949.

Review: *Variety* (March 15, 1961): "Failed to emulate the warmth or capture the mood of a *Finian's Rainbow* ... mawkish operetta-like scenes. ... Worthy tunes with professional lyrics."

150. *Oliver and the Artful Dodger*
2 hours. Animated Musical. *ABC Saturday Superstar Movie.* Broadcast October 21 & 28, 1972 (Saturday, 9:30–10:30 A.M.) ABC

Executive Producers/Directors William Hanna, Joseph Barbera; *Story Directors* Alex Lovy, Lew Marshall, Jan Green, George Singer; *Animation Director*

Peter Luschwitz; *Writer* Blanche Hanalis; *Songs* Denby Williams, Joseph Roland, Hoyt Curtin, Richard Bowden; *Music* Hoyt Curtin, Paul De Korte; *Music Director* Richard Bowden; *Video* Hanna-Barbera Home Video.

Cast (voices): Gary Marsh, Michael Bell, John Walmsley, Darryl Pollack, Pam Ferdin, Richard Dawson, Joan Gerber, Ronald Long, Anna Lee, John Stephenson, Bernard Fox, Don Messick, Lucille Bliss, Barbara Frawley, Ngaire Thompson

Songs: "He's a Proper Bad One," "I'm Mean," "We Got Us," "If You'll Come Stay with Me," "Grub," "The Country Is the Place for Me," "The City Is the Place for Me."

Story: In this sequel to *Oliver Twist*, the Dodger has given up his criminal ways and works as an ironmonger. He spends his spare time rescuing orphans from the clutches of Mr. Bumble and cares for his charges as best he can. Oliver, adopted by Mr. Brownlow, is cared for by the housekeeper, Mrs. Putty. As Mr. Brownlow is dying he tells Oliver he has made a will leaving his fortune to Oliver, but the will is hidden, and Brownlow dies before he can reveal the location. Mr. Brownlow's nephew Sam Sniperly, better known as "Snipe," hears about the death, and as the only living relative, sells all the furniture and puts the house up for sale. Oliver, having nowhere to go, is on the streets when he runs across Dodger. When he explains about the missing will, Dodger agrees to help Oliver search for the missing document. They track the furniture to a country dealer at Dreadly House, but Snipe has heard about the will and hastens to the country house also. Oliver and Dodger find the will, but Snipe follows the boys on their way back to London and tries to

steal the will. When he is unsuccessful, he arranges to have Bumble capture the lot on their arrival in London but after a merry chase, the policeman arrests Snipe and leaves the orphans in their hideout. Oliver gets a barrister to handle his will, receives his inheritance and opens his house to other orphans. Dodger goes back to his work.

Shown in two parts, this two-hour animated children's special kicked off ABC's *Saturday Superstar* movie. The film has above-average animation.

Review: *Variety* (Aug. 21, 1985): "The characters are engaging and the story line should be well received by children."

151. *Olympus 7-0000* 60 minutes. Musical. *ABC Stage 67.* Broadcast September 28, 1966 (Wednesday, 10:00–11:00 P.M.) ABC

Producers Willard Levitas, Richard Adler; *Directors* Stanley Prager, Gordon Rigsby; *Writers* Jerome Chodorov, Richard Adler; *Lyricist/Composer* Richard Adler; *Conductor* Philip Della Penna; *Record* LP Command 3307; *Sheet Music* Richcrisand Music.

Cast: Donald O'Connor, Larry Blyden, Phyllis Newman, Eddie Foy, Jr., Lou Jacobi, The New York Jets with Joe Namath

Songs: "Olympus 7-0000," "I've Got Feelings," "We're Gonna Win," "For You," "What I Mean," "The Three of Us," "I Get Around," "Better Things to Do."

Story: New England College has a losing football team. Todd, a young architecture student at the college, takes on the job as coach to earn enough money to marry Mary, the dean's daughter. He finds his sheer determination isn't enough to win games. Meantime, Mary finds an ancient Greek prayer bowl and

Donald O'Connor is a sprightly Hermes, showing off for Phyllis Newman in *Olympus 7-0000* **(1966). © 1996 Capital Cities/ABC.**

summons Hermes, messenger of the Gods. Hermes agrees to help the team, but has his eye on Mary as his reward. After spectacular wins by his team, Todd is offered a high-paying job as coach at a big-time school and decides to give up architecture. Mary is dismayed at his choice and keeps Hermes away from the game. When Todd's team loses, the job offer disappears. Todd resumes his architecture studies, and he and Mary live happily ever after.

This show was based on a story by George Bradshaw. The title is Hermes' telephone number. (Hermes is also known as Mercury.)

A befuddled Rick Nelson plays a has-been rock singer in *On the Flip Side* (1966). © 1996 Capital Cities/ABC.

Review: *Variety* (Sept. 28, 1966): "A lightweight effort that didn't advance the cause of original tuners on TV.... The songs threw brambles into the potentially enjoyable plot, slowing the action and making for an all-too-speedy finish."

152. *On the Flip Side* 60 minutes. Musical. *ABC Stage 67*. Broadcast

December 7, 1966 (Wednesday, 10:00–11:00 P.M.) ABC

Producer Richard Lewine; *Director* Joe Layton; *Writer* Robert Emmett; *Lyricist* Hal David; *Composer* Burt Bacharach; *Conductor/Arranger* Peter Matz; *Record* LP Decca DL 4836; *Sheet Music* Blue Seas Music (3), Jac Music.

Cast: Rick Nelson, Joanie Sommers, Donna Jean Young, Will MacKenzie, Lada Edmund, Jr., Murray Roman, Anthony Holland, Evelyn Russell

Songs: "It Doesn't Matter Any More," "Juanita's Place Montage," "Fender Mender," "Take a Broken Heart," "They Don't Give Medals," "They're Gonna Love It," "Try to See It My Way."

Story: Young rock-and-roll singer Carlos O'Conner at 21 finds himself almost a has-been. His bookings have fallen off, his recording contract has been canceled, and fan clubs have dropped him in favor of newer stars. To save him, Angie and her sister angels form a group calling themselves "The Celestials" and go AWOL from up there to come to his aid. From Carlos' hotel to a Greenwich Village inn, a bankrupt night spot, a cafe and finally a record company, the quartet and their protégé explore the strange underworld of New York nightlife. The Celestials return to their world, leaving Carlos with a hit record and his career on the rebound.

The show was built around Rick Nelson, who coincidentally had hit a slump in his own singing career. *The Adventures of Ozzie and Harriet*, the Nelson family TV sitcom on which Rick had played since 1952, had just ended, and Rick lost his showcase, but he hadn't hit the big time for a while even with program exposure. He experienced a later comeback as a more mature singer. Songwriters Bacharach and David had written songs together and separately, but became better known later, and had a hit Broadway show with *Promises, Promises* in 1968.

Reviews: *Variety* (Dec. 14, 1966): "[Nelson] played a has-been ... though not with anything like impressive conviction. ... Satire too often either lacked edge or was crowded out by such trite tuner conventions as a boy-girl plot." Despite his dissatisfaction, this critic singled out one segment for praise, saying that Anthony Holland (in the role of a recording executive) and Evelyn Russell (playing his mother) provided "some of the snappiest fun of the season."

Joe Selvin, *Ricky Nelson: Idol for a Generation*: "Rick proved woefully inadequate to the demanding sweep of the Bacharach melody line ... robot Rick simply plodded through the paces."

153. *On the Road to Broadway*   60 minutes. Musical. Broadcast April 26, 1982 (Monday, 10:00–11:00 P.M.) NBC

Producer/Director Steve Binder; *Writers* Norman Martin, Lois Weldon, Steve Binder; *Music* Peter Matz.

Cast: Debby Boone, James Low, Dionne Warwick, Jeff Calhoun, Linda Hoxit, Wendy Hutton, Sha Newman, Michael Ragan, Jeffrey Reynolds, Lara Teeter, Carmen Willingham

Songs: "Take a Bow," "Shoe Business or Show Business," "Sleep, Sleep, Sleep," "When You Wish Upon a Star."

Story: A company of singers and dancers, getting ready to open on Broadway, express their hopes and fears, and the problems of life on the road.

This show (also listed as *Debby Boone ... One Step Closer*) was taped at a theater and other locales in Detroit, where the cast was actually appearing in another pre–Broadway show.

154. *Once Upon a Brothers Grimm*
2 hours. Musical. Broadcast November 23, 1977 (Wednesday, 8:00–10:00 P.M.) CBS

Producers Bernard Rothman, Jack Wohl; *Director* Norman Campbell; *Writer* Jean Holloway; *Lyricist* Sammy Cahn; *Composer* Mitch Leigh; *Musical Director* Jerry Toth; *Choral Director* Dick Williams; *Choreographer* Ron Field; *Art Director* Ken Johnson; *Set Decorator* Robert Checci; *Costumes* Bill Hargate; *Video* Heartland.

Cast: Dean Jones, Paul Sand, Betsy Beard, Sorrell Booke, Arte Johnson, Ruth Buzzi, Teri Garr, Clive Revill, Chita Rivera, Cleavon Little, Mia Bendixsen, Corine Conley, Gordon Connell, Dora Correia, Joe Giamalva, Todd Lookinland, Edie McClurg, John McCook, Gary Morgan, Ken Olfson, Maria Pogee, Susan Silo, Dan Tobin, Byron Webster, Stephanie Steele, Julia Rinker, Joanna Kirkland, John Clifford, Los Angeles Ballet Company

Songs: "The Brothers Grimm," "Happily Married Wolf," "I'm Rotten," "Once Upon a Time," "Life Is Not a Fairy Tale," "Don't Tell Me I'm Flying," "Day of Days," "My Name Is Rumpelstiltskin," "The Only Way to Go Is Up," "Schlaf Mein Kind," "Bremen Town Musicians," "Names, Names, Names," "I Love a Fat Man," "Life Can Be a Fairy Tale."

Story: Brothers Jacob and Wilhelm Grimm are riding in their carriage to present a book of their stories to the king when they find themselves in the woods, where they separately and together encounter their fairy tale heroes and villains. Some are seen only in passing, but with others the brothers play active roles. The well-known stories include "Tom Thumb," "The Frog Prince," "Sleeping Beauty," "Hansel and Gretel," "Little Red Riding Hood," "The Swan Princes," "The Twelve Dancing Princesses," "Rumpelstiltskin" and "Cinderella." Various hags, witches and fairies also appear.

Based on the legends the Brothers Grimm collected and recorded in 1812–1815, this show was nominated for Emmys for outstanding children's special (evening) and for art, costumes, taping and makeup. Composer Mitch Leigh is best known for the Broadway show *Man of La Mancha*; lyricist Sammy Cahn has contributed to songs for stage, screen and television (including the TV musical *Our Town*). The show had excellent dance and ballet numbers.

Reviews: *TV Guide* (Nov. 23, 1977): "Elaborate sets and costumes, imaginative special effects, tuneful score."

Variety (Nov. 30, 1977): "Dull writing, leaden humor, tuneless songs with unremarkable lyrics, uninspired performances. ... Handsome physical production. ... None of the mystery, none of the subtext of the true fairy tale."

155. *Once Upon a Christmas Time*
60 minutes. Musical. Broadcast December 9, 1959 (Wednesday, 7:30–8:30 P.M.) NBC

Producer Jack Philbin; *Director* Kirk Browning; *Writer* A. J. Russell; *Lyricist* Al Stillman; *Composer* Robert Allen; *Music Director* Kenyon Hopkins; *Choral Director* Harry Simeone.

Cast: Claude Rains, Margaret Hamilton, Charlie Ruggles, Kate Smith, Patty Duke, Pat Henning, Ronnie Robertson, Ruth Harrison, Stanislau Kessel

Songs: "Packages," "O Little Town of Bethlehem," "Cards, Cards, Cards," "Everybody's Got a Heart," "Christmas Spirit," "Santasville Special," "Adeste Fideles."

Story: Residents of a Vermont village invite the local orphans to their homes for Christmas. But mean Miss Scugg doesn't want to let the children leave the orphanage. The townspeople try to convince Miss Scugg to change her mind. The orphans win over the authorities and all ends well.

Based on Paul Gallico's short story *The Thirteenth Orphan*. Claude Rains played a town character and Santa Claus.

Review: *Variety* (Dec. 16, 1969): The reviewer felt that this show rose above the usual sentimental Christmas fare by virtue of its musical and ice-skating numbers. "It was only when the show fell into the telling of the story that the going became arduous. The best portions of the show ... were the songs ... and the flashy blade work of Ronnie Robertson in a dream sequence."

156. *Once Upon a Tune*
60 minutes. Musical Anthology Series. Broadcast March 6, 1951 to May 15, 1951 (Tuesday, 10:00–11:00 P.M.) DuMont

Producer Bob Loewi; *Writer* Sid Frank; *Lyricists/Composers* Coleman Dowell, Reginald Beane.

Cast: Phil Hanna, Holly Harris, Reginald Beane, Bernice Parks, Ed Holmes

Story: In one episode ("Three Little Pigs"), three young ladies named Pigge come to New York to seek their fortune, but find themselves being questioned in a robbery by a Mr. Wolf. Wolf thinks he is in control, but soon finds the three Pigges are after him. Guest Star: Elaine Stritch. Songs: "I Wanna Settle Down," "Three Little Pigs," plus several standard tunes. In the episode "Rapunzel," a young woman meets her "prince," a soldier named Phil, and runs away from home. Her guardian, Phil and friend, the F.B.I. and the National Guard all search for Rapunzel. Guest Star: Charlotte Rae. Songs: "This Is Love," plus standard songs.

This show presented a complete original musical every week, usually a takeoff on a Broadway show or a famous story or fairy tale.

157. *Once Upon an Eastertime* 60 minutes. Musical. Broadcast April 18, 1954 (Sunday, 5:00–6:00 P.M.) CBS

Producers William Dozier, Martin Manulis, Leon Leonidoff; *Director* Byron Paul; *Writers* Leon Leonidoff, Reginald Lawrence, Arnold Horwitt; *Composer/Conductor/Arranger* Victor Young; *Choreographer* Eugene Loring.

Cast: Gwen Verdon, Bobby Clark, Doretta Morrow, Pud Flanagan, Pat Harrington, Ruth McDevitt, Bobby May, Cameron Prud'homme, Glen Buris

Songs: Not found

Story: A young boy lives in a small town with his grandparents and his sister, and the story revolves around the family, a town character and a visiting friend, with much dancing and singing to celebrate spring. Then the boy eats a forbidden Easter egg and is transported to a world of fantasy with a wicked king and his evil prime minister, a lovely princess and a magic glowworm.

Review: *Variety* (April 21, 1954): "Excellent dancing, singing, clowning ... but slow-paced and meaningless first half. ... In the story department the show fell apart ... Overall the program was a dismal failure." The reviewer hoped the

networks would learn something from the experience—namely, to begin with a story and a consistent point of view, rather than beginning with the stars and trying to build a story around them.

158. *The Original Top Ten* see *Kingdom Chums: The Original Top Ten*

159. *Our Town* 90 minutes. Musical. *Producer's Showcase.* Broadcast September 19, 1955 (Monday, 8:00–9:30 P.M.) NBC

Producers Fred Coe, Henry Jaffe; *Director* Delbert Mann; *Writer* David Shaw; *Lyricist* Sammy Cahn; *Music* James Van Heusen; *Music Director* Nelson Riddle; *Sheet Music* Barton Music (6).

Cast: Paul Newman, Eva Marie Saint, Frank Sinatra, Ernest Truex, Sylvia Field, Peg Hillias, Carol Venzie

Songs: "Our Town," "Love and Marriage," "The Impatient Years," "A Perfect Married Life," "Look to Your Heart," "Wasn't It a Wonderful Wedding?"

Story: A story of family life in the fictional town of Grover's Corners, New Hampshire. The stage manager narrates the story of two families, those of Editor Webb and Dr. Gibbs. The first act presents "The Daily Life," where George Gibbs and Emily Webb are classmates and neighbors. The second act, "Love and Marriage," portrays their courtship and marriage. The third act, "Death and the Meaning of Life," shows Emily's death in childbirth, and her conversations with other dead in the cemetery.

Based on Thornton Wilder's Pulitzer Prize–winning play of 1938. Frank Sinatra suggested Cahn and Van Heusen for the songs, and lyricist Cahn thought

Paul Newman

these the best songs he ever wrote
(though he credited Wilder's words
with being his inspiration).

This live production had a cast of
30, with an orchestra of 40 in a room
across the hall, watching the show on a
monitor. Saint and Newman played the
romantic leads, but Frank Sinatra did
the most singing. Paul Newman and
Eva Marie Saint had received acclaim
for their 1953 Broadway debuts, Newman in *Picnic* and Saint in *A Trip to
Bountiful.*

This show was nominated for six

Emmys, and the song "Love and Marriage" (now used as theme for the TV
series *Married ... With Children*) won
an Emmy as best song. Sinatra's recording of "Love and Marriage" reached #5
on the charts and remained in the Top
40 for 15 weeks.

Author Wilder asked that this version of his play not be used again. A
1977 television version of *Our Town* is
available on video, as is the 1940 movie.
More recently, a different musical version called *Grover's Corners* has been in
production for the stage.

Review: *Variety* (Sept. 21, 1955): "Warm and finely wrought…. The music and lyrics are so deftly integrated into the play's continuity that the viewer is never aware of a song's intrusion."

160. *Owen Wingrave* 2 hours. Opera. *NET Opera Theater.* Broadcast May 16, 1971 (Sunday, 10:00–12:00 P.M.) PBS

Directors Brian Large, Colin Graham; *Librettist* Myfanwy Piper; *Composer/ Conductor* Benjamin Britten; *Sets* David Myers and Cough Jones; *Music* Faber, London.

Cast: Benjamin Luxon, Peter Pears, John Shirley Quirk, Janet Baker, Heather Harper

Story: Young Owen Wingrave is being coached before he is sent up to Sandhurst, the British military academy, but after much thought decides he is morally opposed to war and cannot in good conscience become a career military man. He confesses his feelings to his coach, and though the teacher admires the young man's determination, he does his best to convince Owen to change his mind. The Wingate family has been career military for 300 years, and even the maiden aunt was once affianced to a military man, and the widow and daughter of another lost in battle live with her. At a family conference the relatives hear the news and express their disapproval and disappointment at Owen's decision, and accuse him of cowardice. The young lady challenges him to stay the night in a room haunted by an ancestor who accidentally killed his son and was found dead there; Owen is found dead on the same spot the next morning.

This opera was commissioned for television by the BBC, and was pre-mièred simultaneously by the BBC, EBU and NET. Composer Britten looked for a story more suited to the small screen and selected this short story by Henry James (1909). Britten is cited by Ewen as England's most significant composer of operas in the 20th century; his other works include *Peter Grimes* and *Turn of the Screw.*

Reviews: *Time* (May 24, 1971): "Something less than Britten's best. … Vocal writing showed little warmth or melodic appeal…. A fine cast of acting singers could not quite breathe passion into dialogue that often consisted of abstract arguments for war or peace." The reviewer was, however, impressed with the use of television technology and its contribution to the story.

Opera News (Speight Jenkins, June 12, 1971): "Billed as a pacifist work, this opera does make an anti-war statement—but one relevant only to the British gentry at the end of Empire." For this the reviewer faulted librettist Piper for failing to update James' language. The reviewer went on to note that Britten's music failed to save the work, calling it "angular and unmelodic."

161. *Paris in the Springtime* 90 minutes. Musical. *Max Liebman Presents.* Broadcast January 21, 1956 (Saturday, 9:00–10:30 P.M.) NBC

Producers Max Liebman, Bill Hobin; *Director* Max Liebman; *Writers* Neil Simon, William Friedberg; *Music Director* Charles Sanford.

Cast: Dan Dailey, Gale Sherwood, Helen Gallagher, Jack Whiting, Carleton Carpenter, Marcel Hillaire

Songs: "Sunshine," "Stung," "Down with Love," "Mme. de Paris," "Delicado," "Old Routine," "Can't Be Bothered," "From Another World," "Paris, Paree," "Nobody's Chasing Me," "Marie Antoinette," "Un Coin de France."

Story: A former night club dancer who dreams of performing on the concert stage goes to Paris where he reunites with his former dancing partner and meets a woman leading a group of Bohemian down-and-out American actors. His misadventures with the two women make up the story.

This show was a last-minute substitution for an unavailable musical; writers patched together an original story, and tunes of Gershwin, Porter, Arlen and Rodgers were thrown in.

Review: *Variety* (Jan. 25, 1956): "A more dismal display couldn't have been conjured up ... too much libretto. ... The story [got] in everybody's way."

162. *The Parrot* 30 minutes. Opera. *Armstrong Circle Theater*. Broadcast March 24, 1953 (Tuesday, 9:30–10:00 P.M.) NBC

Director Garry Simpson; *Librettist* Frank P. De Felitta; *Composer* Darrell Peter.

Cast: Josephine Schillig, Shannon Bolin, Chester Watson

Story: A rich and eccentric widow dies and leaves her entire fortune to her pet parrot.

A work written for six solo voices with piano accompaniment, this show has the distinction of being the first television opera commissioned by a commercial sponsor.

Review: *America* (W.A. Coleman, May 16, 1953): "A unique, if not exactly a history-making work of musical art."

163. *La Pastorela* 90 minutes. Musical. *Great Performances*. Broadcast

December 23, 1991 (Monday, 9:00–10:00 P.M.) PBS

Executive Producers Phillip Esparga, Kimberly Myers; *Producer* Richard D. Soto; *Director/Writer* Luiz Valdez; *Music* Joseph Julian Gonzalez; *Art Director* Joe Cardinalli; *Costumes* Gail Russell.

Cast: Linda Ronstadt, Cheech Marin, Don Novello, Freddy Fender, Paul Rodriguez, Karla Montana, Kinan Valdez, Robert Beltran, Anahuac Valdez, Los Lobos.

Songs: Not found

Story: A teenager names Gila goes to church with her family on Christmas Eve to view the pageant. Knocked unconscious by falling scenery, Gila becomes part of the story as she leads a hermit and shepherds on a trip to Bethlehem to see the baby. Lucifer and his demons try to interfere with their trip by many tricks, but archangel San Miguel undoes the tricks. There is a final battle between San Miguel and Lucifer.

Luis Valdez developed this contemporary version of the legendary Spanish morality play.

Review: *New York Times* (Jon Pareles, Dec. 23, 1991): "Mr. Valdez revels in incongruities and anachronisms.... The pageant flips tradition on its ear ... the wackiest Christmas pageant of them all."

164. *Peter Pan* 2 hours. Musical. *Hallmark Hall of Fame*. Broadcast December 12, 1976 (Sunday, 7:30–9:30 P.M.) NBC

Producers Gary Smith, Dwight Hemion; *Director* Dwight Hemion; *Writers* Jack Burns, Andrew Birkin; *Songs* Anthony Newley, Leslie Bricusse; *Music Director*

Mia Farrow and Danny Kaye as Peter Pan and Captain Hook in *Peter Pan* **(1976). Courtesy Hallmark Hall of Fame.**

Ian Fraser; *Conductors* Ian Fraser, Jack Parnell; *Costume Designer* Sue Le Cash; *Art Director* David Chandler.

Cast: Sir John Gielgud (narrator), Mia Farrow, Danny Kaye, Virginia McKenna, Paula Kelly, Briony McRoberts, Tony Sympson, Ian Sharrock, Adam Stafford, Peter O'Farrell, Jerome Watts, Nicky Lyndhurst, Adam Richens,

Michael Deeks, Simon Mooney, Andrew Mooney, Joe Melia, Jill Gascoine, Linsey Baxter, Oscar James, George Harris, Michael Crane, Max Latimer, Fred Evans, Peppi Borza

Songs: "I'm Better with You," "They Don't Make 'Em Like Me Any More," "By Hook or by Crook," "Rotter's Hall of Fame," "A Song Called Love," "The House on Happiness Hill," "I'll Teach You to Fly," "Peter Pan," "Friendly Light Burning Bright," "Never Never Land," "Love Is a House," "If I Could Build a World of My Own," "Pretending," "Mothers," "Growing Up."

Story: Wendy, John and Michael Darling are looked after by a dog called Nana. Peter Pan, a boy who doesn't want to grow up, and Tinker Bell, a fairy, have been listening at the Darlings' window to stories told the children by their mother. One night, hearing a noise, Nana slams the window and catches Peter's shadow. Peter comes to look for his shadow and is seen by Wendy, so he tells her his story, and persuades Wendy and her brothers to come back to Never Land with him. He teaches them to fly and off they go. Wendy looks after all the Lost Boys and tells them stories. Tiger Lily and her Indians guard the boys, but Captain Hook and his pirates are after Peter. Tinker Bell is jealous of Wendy but looks after Peter, and drinks poison left for him by Captain Hook. While she is dying, Peter asks all children who believe in fairies to clap, and their belief keeps Tinker Bell alive. The Darling children and the Lost Boys are captured by Hook and taken to the pirate ship where Hook means to dispose of them, but after a severe fight Peter bests Hook and the children escape. Wendy, John and Michael return home. Mrs. Darling adopts all the Lost Boys except

Peter, who stubbornly refuses to grow up, but Wendy visits him every year to clean his house. When she is grown, with a family of her own, Wendy's daughter visits Peter.

This story is based on the 1904 play by James M. Barrie. Julie Andrews sang the theme "Once Upon a Bedtime" over the credits. The show was nominated for an Emmy as outstanding children's special, but won only for the videoanimation by Jean De Joux and Elizabeth Savel. (Tinker Bell and Peter Pan's shadow were done by animation.) The show was, of course, compared with the earlier successful stage and TV version with Mary Martin, but reviewers had some good things to say. Various versions of the story refer to Never Land, Never Never Land and Never, Never, Never Land.

Songwriters Newley and Bricusse had written the Broadway show *Stop the World—I Want to Get Off* together, and Bricusse had written songs for films *Scrooge* and *Doctor Dolittle*.

Mia Farrow had previously played in the TV series *Peyton Place* and the movie *Rosemary's Baby*. Danny Kaye specialized in tongue-twister songs, performed on stage and in films, and had his own TV variety show.

Reviews: *New York Times* (Dec. 10, 1976): Critic John J. O'Conner despaired over the uninspired songs with their "tendency to gurgle into soppiness," but he praised the script for sticking closely to the original Barrie play and found the production "done to a generally splendid turn. ... Sets and costumes are lavish and attractive ... a visual delight. ... Manages to capture Captain Hook as something more than a bumbling clown."

Bruce K. Hanson (*Peter Pan Chronicles*): "The teleplay ... was a beautiful presentation that had one prob-

lem—the songs! For reasons unknown, an intelligent script ... was
allowed to be cluttered with an
undistinguished score that just got
in the way."

165. *The Pied Piper of Hamelin*
90 minutes. Musical. Broadcast
November 26, 1957 (Tuesday, 7:30–
9:00 P.M.) NBC

Producer Hal Stanley; *Songs* Hal
Stanley, Irving Taylor; *Music Direc-
tor* Pete King; *Choreographer* Ward
Ellis; *Wardrobe* Berman; *Set Decora-
tor* G. W. Berntsen; *Record* LP RCA
LPM 1563; *Video* United American
Video.

Cast: Van Johnson, Claude Rains,
Kay Starr, Lori Nelson, Jim Backus,
Doodles Weaver, Stanley Adams,
René Kroper

Van Johnson

Songs: "Work Song," "Flim Flam
Floo," "How Can I Tell You," "Fools
Gold," "Prestige," "Welcome Song,"
"Feats of Piper," "Mothers' Lament."

Story: The town of Hamelin is besieged
by rats, driven out of the town of
Hamelout by flooding. The people of
Hamelout ask for help from the corrupt
mayor of Hamelin, but he brushes them
off. He is only interested in having
chimes made for the new town clock,
and children are put to work to build
the chimes. A piper with a magic flute
appears and offers to rid the town of rats
for 50,000 guilders, the entire sum in
the town treasury. The mayor agrees,
but after the rats are lured away refuses
to pay. So the piper entices all the children to follow him out of town to a cave
containing a magical land. At the end
the mayor is deposed, the townsfolk
look for change, the children are returned
and the new chimes ring out.

Claude Rains plays the mayor; Van
Johnson plays both the piper and a

townsman. The dialogue is in rhyme.
The story is based on an old West-
phalian legend made famous by Robert
Browning's poem. Songs and instru-
mentals are based on the music of
Edward Grieg.

Review: *Variety* (Dec. 4, 1957): "...
trying for an epic instead of a delicate
fantasy and therefore lost the crucial
ingredient, charm. ... Attractive wardrobe, excellent color photography,
imaginative sets." On the down side,
the reviewer saw wooden direction,
found vocal performances "passable at
best," Kay Starr's song "dreary" and
rhymes "sing-songy." The reviewer
thought Johnson looked more "sinister
than spritely," though Rains was "properly menacing."

166. *Pinocchio*   60 minutes. Musical. Broadcast October 13, 1957 (Sunday, 5:30–6:30 P.M.) NBC

Executive Producer David Susskind; *Director* Paul Bogart; *Writer* Yasha Frank; *Lyricist* William Engvick; *Composer* Alec Wilder; *Conductor* Glenn Osser; *Record* LP Columbia CL 1055; *Sheet Music* Devon Music.

Cast: Mickey Rooney, Fran Allison, Jerry Colonna, Walter Slezak, Stubby Kaye, Martyn Green, Gordon Clarke, dance team of Mata & Hari

Songs: "Listen to Your Heart," "The Fox's Pitch," "Happy News," "The Jolly Coachman," "Pinocchio's Song," "The Birthday Party," "Lullaby," "Underseas Ballet."

Story: Gepetto, the wood carver, makes himself a boy puppet and names him Pinocchio. The wooden boy comes to life and is sent off to school, but runs away and gets involved in a variety of escapades. Taken home, Pinocchio lies about what happened and his nose grows. His guardian angel tells him he has a year and a day to conquer his greed and if he does, he will become a real boy. Once again led astray by his schoolmates, Pinocchio runs off to the Island of Fun, where the boys are all turned into donkeys. Pinocchio escapes but falls into the water and is eaten by a whale where he finds Gepetto. Eventually they get free, Pinocchio learns to behave and becomes a real boy.

This version of the Carlo Collodi story of 1883 was done as a verse play with music.

Reviews: *Time* (Oct. 28, 1957): "Worth the price of transmission. ... A rollicking production, full of style and striking images, a bouncy score.... First rate cast. ... Mickey Rooney gave a remarkably apt performance."

New York Times (Jack Gould, Oct. 14, 1957): "Thoroughly unsuccessful attempt to reproduce the classic children's story. The narrative is confusing in the extreme and could only have baffled and disappointed a child. ... Score and lyrics were routine."

167. *Pinocchio* 60 minutes. Musical. Broadcast February 13, 1967 (Monday, 7:30–8:30 P.M.) CBS

Executive Producer Richard R. Rector; *Producer* Ethel Burns; *Directors* Jim Eiler, Nick Havinga; *Songs* Jim Eiler, Jeanne Bargy; *Conductor* Alfredo Antonini; *Arranger* Richard Hayman; *Record* LP Entertainment Media 999.

Cast: John Joy, David Lile, Will B. Able, Fred Grades, Jodi Williams, Robert Dagny, Hal Holden, Bob Lussier, Marcie Stringer

Songs: "A Real Little Boy," "The Coach Is Coming," "That's a Show," "You Can Sing," "I Don't Want to Go to School," "How Will I Ever Get Along?," "Land of the Toys."

Story: Pinocchio, Gepetto's talking puppet, wants desperately to be a real boy, but must prove himself worthy to the Blue Fairy. He gets himself into many scrapes on his own and by listening to others who lead him astray, but he finally learns his lessons and makes the grade.

Produced by New York's Prince Street Players, Ltd., for CBS. This show was originally presented in December 1965 (exact date unknown) but was shown again on above date as one of four productions by the group. The *Variety* review below was from the 1965 broadcast.

Reviews: *Variety* (Dec. 29, 1965): "A spirited, disciplined and highly talented group.... Songs were bright and infectious."

168. *Pinocchio* 90 minutes. Musical. *Hallmark Hall of Fame*. Broadcast

Con artist Jim Luisi (far left) tricks the innocent Peter Noone in *Pinocchio* (1968). Courtesy of Hallmark Hall of Fame.

December 8, 1968 (Sunday, 7:00–8:30 P.M.) NBC

Producer Richard Lewine; *Director* Sid Smith; *Writer* Ernest Kinoy; *Lyricist/ Composer* Walter Marks; *Conductor/ Arranger* Mort Lindsey; *Choreographer* Michael Bennett; *Costumes* Miles White; *Makeup* Lee Baygan.

Cast: Burl Ives, Peter Noone, Anita Gilette, Mort Marshall, Charlotte Rae, Pierre Epstein, Jack Fletcher, Ned Wertimer, Edwin Steffe, Jim Luisi, James Beard, John Miranda, Bil Baird

Songs: "Chip Off the Old Block," "Walk with Him," "Wonderful World, Hello," "You Could Get to Like It," "Beautiful People," "It's a Dog's Life," "Little Bad Habits," "Too Soon."

Story: Gepetto carves a wooden puppet which comes to life, and names his companion Pinocchio. Pinocchio goes off to school but gets caught for a marionette show, is tricked by some shysters, and otherwise gets in trouble. When he lies to his father his nose grows long. The fairy tells him he must learn to behave if he wants to become a real boy. But he is led astray by the other boys and runs off to the Isle of Fun, where the boys do anything they want to, but are soon turned into donkeys. Pinocchio escapes but falls into the sea and is swallowed by a whale. There he finds Gepetto who had been searching for him. They escape, and Pinocchio, who has learned his lesson, is turned into a real boy.

Peter Noone, who played Pinocchio, was leader of the rock group Herman's Hermits. Songwriter Walter Marks had worked with writer Kinoy on the show *Golden Rainbow,* then running on Broadway.

Reviews: *TV Guide* (Dec. 8, 1968): "Remains true to the tale of Pinocchio."

Variety (Dec. 11, 1968): "This live version punched up morals and messages. ... Plushly mounted, engagingly performed ... an eye filler. ... Noone played the puppet with a zest beyond the call. ... Music and lyrics only serviceable."

169. ***Pinocchio***   90 minutes. Musical. Broadcast March 27, 1976 (Saturday, 8:00–9:30 P.M.) CBS

Executive Producers Bernard Rothman, Jack Wohl; *Directors* Sid Smith, Ron Field; *Writer* Herbert Baker; *Lyricist/Composer* Billy Barnes; *Music Director* Edward Karam; *Choral Director* Alan Copeland; *Choreographer* Ron Field; *Set Decorator* Rick Franke; *Art Directors* Romain Johnson, John Dapper; *Costumes* Bill Hargate; *Makeup* Stan Winston; *Video* Heartland.

Cast: Sandy Duncan, Danny Kaye, Flip Wilson, Liz Torres, Gary Morgan, Clive Revill, Don Corriea, Roy Smith

Songs: "I'm a Talkin' to Myself," "Fun," "That's What," "If I Could Start Again," "I Like It!," "We Wanna Go Home," "More," "This Little Boy of Mine," "I'm Not Worried—Yes I Am," "Look at Us Now," "Look at Me Now," "Pinocchio."

Story: Traveling showman Collodi's daughter Teresa tells him she wants to leave the show and settle down; he tells her she can play Pinocchio forever, but she agrees to only one last night. The curtain opens on the production of *Pinocchio.* Gepetto is talking to his puppets and is surprised when Pinocchio comes to life and answers. The wooden boy wants to know all about everything, and the next morning is sent off to school. Pinocchio comes upon a marionette show. Exploring the stage, he is taken for one of the marionettes and is pleased with the applause. The owner captures him but he escapes, only to be swindled and left on a woodpile to burn by the fox and the cat. Gepetto finds him but Pinocchio lies about what has happened and his nose grows. The next day he leaves for school but is led astray by the other boys and goes off to the Isle of Fun where he cavorts with the other boys until they all turn into donkeys. The coachman says he will sell them. Pinocchio gets away, but falls in the water. He is swallowed by a whale, where he finds Gepetto who had been searching for him and gotten swallowed himself. Together they get free of the whale and Pinocchio saves Gepetto but is exhausted by the effort. At home Gepetto pleads for his boy, and Pinocchio is at last turned into a real boy. After the performance we see Collodi saying goodbye to his daughter.

Sandy Duncan appeared in *The Boyfriend* on Broadway in 1970 and had two TV series, *Funny Face* in 1971 and *The Sandy Duncan Show* in 1972, but both were short-lived. She later played *Peter Pan* on Broadway. Composer/lyricist Billy Barnes wrote musical revues and "special material" for many well-known singers.

170. ***Pinocchio's Christmas***   60 minutes. Animated Musical. Broadcast December 3, 1980 (Wednesday, 8:00–9:00 P.M.) ABC

Producers/Directors Arthur Rankin, Jr., Jules Bass; *Writer* Romeo Muller; *Lyricist* Julian P. Gardner; *Composer* Maury Laws.

Cast (voices): Todd Porter, George S. Irving, Alan King, Pat Bright, Diane Leslie, Tiffany Blake, Carl Tramon, Alice Gayle, Gerry Matthews, Robert McFadden, Ray Owens, Allen Swift

Songs: "What Gifts to Buy," "The Perfect Gift," "Knock on Wood," "The Very Best Friend I Ever Had," "Let 'Em Laugh," "Let's Go Dancin'," "The Whole Truth," "Wicked Glee."

Story: Gepetto and Pinocchio are getting ready for the holidays. Pinocchio gets a job with a puppet show to earn money for a gift for Gepetto, but is once again conned out of his money as he elopes with Julietta. The magical Lady Azura rescues the puppets from angry Maestro Fire-Eater, and Pinocchio is reunited with Gepetto.

171. *The Point* 90 minutes. Animated Musical. Broadcast February 2, 1971 (Tuesday, 7:30–9:00 P.M.) ABC

Producers Jerry Good, Larry Gordon, Harry Nilsson, Fred Wolf; *Director/Animator* Fred Wolf; *Writer* Norman Lenzer; *Lyricist/Composer* Harry Nilsson; *Conductor/Arranger* George Tipton; *Record* LP RCA LSPX 1003; *Video* Vestron 4415; *Sheet Music* Unichappell.

Cast (voices): Dustin Hoffman (narrator), Michael Lookinland, Paul Frees, Lennie Weinrib, Bill Martin, Joan Gerber, Buddy Foster

Songs: "Everything's Got 'Em," "Life Line," "Me and My Arrow," "P.O.V. Waltz," "Think About Your Troubles," "Are You Sleeping?"

Story: A father reads the story to his son. Far away there is a town where everything is pointed, even the people. Their business is making points. A boy named Oblio is born, healthy but with a round head, and word spreads through-

out the town. His mother makes him a pointed hat, but the other boys taunt him, especially the count's son. When Oblio beats the boy in a game (with the help of his pointy dog, Arrow), the count persuades the council that the boy is in violation of the law and must be banished. Even though the king, a decent fellow, and the townspeople are reluctant, Oblio is banished and to the Pointless Forest. He meets a man who points in all directions and says everything is pointless, but Oblio and his dog meet Rock Man, Leaf Man, some dancing fat ladies and others, and these people set Oblio to thinking that each has a point. He returns to the town, where he is welcomed, and tells the king that all people have a point. The townsfolk agree that the law was a bad one, and modify their ways.

Songwriter Harry Nilsson wrote the original story and the songs; he also sings the songs. The song "Me and My Arrow" (recorded by Nilsson) became a pop hit, reaching #34 in the Top 40. This show was the first U.S. made-for-television animated movie. The home video is narrated by Ringo Starr.

Reviews: *Variety* (March 10, 1971): Noting that this show had nearly every element in its favor, including "imagination, originality, seven new songs and the good intentions of making a valid social point," the *Variety* reviewer nevertheless concluded (with evident regret) that the overall product was not quite a success. "The satirical slant of the narrative became muddled when Oblio and his faithful dog encountered the Pointed Man. ... Consistently clever visual images."

Steven H. Scheuer, *Movies on TV & Video*: "Charming animated feature musical fantasy. ... The images are superb, and the musical score by Harry Nilsson creates the appropriate mood."

VideoHound: "Charming and sincere feature. ... Excellent score."

Mark Satern, *Video's Best:* "Something special. This is a thoroughly engaging animated story for children. ... Thoughtful, entertaining and can be genuinely enjoyed by the whole family."

172. Polly 2 hours. Musical. *The Magical World of Disney.* Broadcast November 12, 1989 (Sunday, 7:00–9:00 P.M.) NBC

Director Debbie Allen; *Writer* William Blinn; *Songs/Score* Joel McNeely; *Song* "Stand Up" by Debbie Allen, Norm Nixon; *Choreographer* Debbie Allen; *Record* CD Disney CD 019.

Cast: Keshia Knight Pulliam, Phylicia Rashad, Celeste Holm, Brock Peters, Dorian Harewood, Butterfly McQueen, Larry Riley, Ken Page

Songs: "Stand Up," "Shine a Light," "By Your Side," "Honey Ain't Got Nothin' on You," "Something More."

Story: Polly, a recently orphaned preteen from Detroit, goes to live with her wealthy and autocratic Aunt Polly in the small town of Harrington, Alabama, in 1955. A cheerful child, she makes friends with the local recluses, plays Cupid to Aunt Polly, makes fast friends with orphan Jimmy Bean and brings sunshine to all.

An (almost) all-black remake of Eleanor H. Porter's 1913 story *Pollyanna*, this film was followed by a 1990 sequel, *Polly—Comin' Home!*

Reviews: *Los Angeles Times* (Howard Rosenberg, Nov. 11, 1989): "An ambitious but inferior musical. The story is flat, maudlin and without passion, the characters cardboard and the songs mostly forgettable."

Leonard Maltin *Movie & Video Guide:* "Splashy choreography by director Allen (Rashad's sister) and hand-clapping original score by Joel McNeely."

173. Polly—Comin' Home! 2 hours. Musical. Broadcast November 18, 1990 (Sunday, 7:00–9:00 P.M.) NBC

Executive Producer William Blinn; *Producer* Frank Fischer; *Director* Debbie Allen; *Writer* William Blinn; *Songs* Joel McNeely, Andrew Gold, Michael Cruz, Larry Riley.

Cast: Keshia Knight Pulliam, Phylicia Rashad, Dorian Harewood, Celeste Holm, Anthony Newley, Brandon Adams, Ken Page, Barbara Montgomery, Vanessa Bell Calloway, T. K. Carer, George Anthony Bell, Larry Riley, Vickilyn Reynolds, Bilal, Geraldine Decker, Clark Johnson, Barbara Perry, Matthew Dickens, Paul Kennedy, Ernie Lee Banks

Songs: "What a Gentleman Does," "I Can't Hear My Heart," "Hot 'Lanta, Ga."

Story: Polly returns from a hospital stay. Dr. Shannon has left town, and Polly tries to foster a romance between Aunt Polly and the handsome minister. She has to deal with a stuffy new headmaster running the orphanage and a mayoral race in which Miss Snow decides to run. Polly conquers all.

A sequel to "Polly," 1989.

Reviews: *Variety* (Nov. 16, 1990): "It's pretty hokey stuff that only the little ones may like. ... Allen has ... assembled a professional entourage that handles song and sap equally well. ... Director Allen keeps the pace moving and has staged some nice dance work."

Leonard Maltin *Movie & Video Guide:* "A relatively sappy sequel to [the] 1989

Polly...enhanced by another toe-tapping, hand-clapping score."

Steven H. Scheuer *Movies on TV & Video:* "It's a thin story, but Director Allen has everyone bursting into song; Anthony Newley comes off best in that department."

174. *Queen of the Stardust Ballroom*

2 hours. Musical. Broadcast February 13, 1975 (Thursday, 9:00–11:00 P.M.) CBS

Producers Robert W. Christiansen, Rick Rosenberg; *Director* Sam O'Steen; *Writer* Jerome Kass; *Lyricists* Alan & Marilyn Bergman; *Composer* Billy Goldenberg; *Choreographer* Marge Champion; *Costume Designer* Bruce Walkup; *Record* LP Columbia 35762; *Video* Tomorrow Entertainment.

Cast: Maureen Stapleton, Charles Durning, Michael Brandon, Elizabeth Berger, Lewis Charles, Natalie Core, Charlotte Rae, Michael Strong, Jacquelyn Hyde, Beverly Manners, Alan Fudge, Martha Tilton, Orrin Tucker

Songs: "Who Gave You Permission?," "Call Me a Fool," "Pennies and Dreams," "Suddenly There's You," "A Big Mistake," "I Love to Dance."

Story: Bea Asher is a lonely widow who lives in the Bronx. Despite having a small shop to keep her busy, and attempts by her family to cheer her, she feels that her life is empty. A friend suggests she visit the local dance hall. Reluctant at first, she finally attends a dance session and enjoys the friendly middle-aged people she meets. She dances with and falls in love with a shy but pleasant mailman, Al Rossi, who makes her feel good about herself. Soon Bea and Al are a regular couple on the dance floor, much to the concern of Bea's disapproving family members. It

turns out that Al is married and will stay that way, but after getting over the shock of this revelation, Bea continues to enjoy Al's company and that of her other friends at the dance hall. She is elected "Queen of the Stardust Ballroom." She dies at the end.

The dance hall sequences for this story were filmed at Myron's, a Los Angeles spot for the older crowd. Composer Billy Goldenberg had written many TV and movie themes and soundtracks; lyricists Alan and Marilyn Bergman wrote words to many songs for film and television. This show was nominated for 11 Emmys and won for choreography and cinematography. Additionally, writer Jerome Kass won the Writers Guild of America award for best original anthology drama, and director Sam O'Steen won a Directors Guild of America award for best direction in specials.

The show was expanded (with revisions) into the Broadway musical *Ballroom* which opened December 14, 1978. The show ran for just over three months, but was nominated for eight Tony awards.

Review: *Variety* (Feb. 19, 1975): "The real co-stars (with Stapleton and Durning) were writer Jerome Kass, choreographer Marge Champion, composer Billy Goldenberg, lyricists Alan and Marilyn Bergman, photographer David Walsh, and director Sam O'Steen. ... Brilliant portrayals by Stapleton and Durning."

Leonard Maltin, *Video Movie Guide:* "Beautifully realized love story. ... A filmed song of joy by Jerome Kass, with sensitive performances by the two leads."

Steven H. Scheuer, *Movies on TV & Video:* "...evokes moments of warmth and sympathy. The over-the-hill couple have much to offer, and their moments together, dancing old '30s steps in a ballroom jammed with lively peers, simply lift one's spirits."

175. *Quillow and the Giant* 60 minutes. Musical. *NBC Children's Theater.* Broadcast November 3, 1963 (Sunday, 6:00–7:00 P.M.) NBC

Executive Producer George H. Heinemann; *Director* David Barnhizer; *Lyricist* Ralph Blane; *Composer* Wade Barnes; *Conductor* Joseph Gallicchio.

Cast: Win Strache, The George Latshaw Puppets. Tom Williams sings for Quillo

Songs: "Full Moon Street," "How Many Stars?," "I Hunder," "It's a Serious Situation," "No Such Word as Can't," "I Believe in Something," "Nothing Is the Hardest Thing to Do," "The Chimneys Are Black."

Story: In a far country lives a terrible giant named Hunder. This giant roves the land, terrifying the people and demanding food, clothing and supplies, leaving the towns impoverished. No one is able to stop him. When the giant makes his way to Quillow's quiet town he demands his usual booty and also wants to be told a story a day. The town council meets to discuss what they might do about the giant, but decides their ideas would only annoy the monster. Quillow, the local toymaker, volunteers to be storyteller to the giant. While townspeople feed and supply the giant, Quillow tells him an ingenious tale which, with the cooperation of the townspeople, finally convinces the giant that he is seriously ill and that he must run and jump into the Yellow Sea to be cured. He is never seen again, though a traveler tells a tale of a giant walking into the sea until he sinks to the bottom.

This charming fantasy is based on a 1944 James Thurber story, *The Great Quillow.* The program was taped in Chicago. Actor Win Strache as the giant worked well with the puppets. Lyricist Ralph Blane wrote words to songs for *Meet Me in St. Louis* and other films; composer Barnes was also an actor, announcer and media executive.

Review: *New York Times* (Jack Gould, Nov. 4, 1963): "A number of tunes of engaging delicacy. ... Started a little slowly ... but once the giant ... and little Quillow met face to face, the fantasy came alive. ... A program of tuneful make-believe."

Variety (Nov. 6, 1963): "A fine combination of talent made *Quillow* a delightful and charming hour for children—and adults. *Quillow* had all the elements going for it—fetching music and lyrics, puppets of extraordinary human traits, a real life-menacing giant, humor and wisdom."

176. *Rachel, La Cubana* 90 minutes. Opera. *NET Opera Theater.* Broadcast March 4, 1974 (Monday, 8:00–9:00 P.M.) PBS

Executive Producer Peter Herman Adler; *Producer* David Griffiths; *Director* Kirk Browning; *Librettist* Hans Magnus Enzenberger; *English Adaptation/Lyrics* Mel Mandel; *Composer* Hans Werner Henze; *Choreographer* Bob Herget; *Costume Designer/Scenic Designer* Rouben Ter-Artunian; *Music* Belwyn Mills.

Cast: Lili Darvas, Lee Venora, Alan Titus, Robert Rounseville, Susanne Marsee, Ronald Young, David Rae Smith

Story: The history of Cuba up to the 1959 revolution is seen through the rise and fall of one of Havana's great music hall stars, Amalia Vorg, called Rachel.

Five retrospective scenes from her life of lovers, broken hearts, glitter, a fading career and a final fantasy life are played out, with riots and killings backing the musical comedy works and behind the closed shutters.

This opera was based on a 1969 novel, *La Canción de Rachel* by Miguel Barnet. Darvas plays Rachel as an old woman, Venora as a young and brassy girl. Alan Titus plays three men in Rachel's life.

Reviews: *TV Guide* (March 4, 1974): "Politics blends with flamboyant tongue-in-cheek acting and salty dialog in this vaudeville with music."

Opera News (Robert Jacobson, March 16, 1974): "Henze's score comes across as a put-on, his characters mere caricatures. Rachel herself is shallow, oblivious to social currents around her."

Musical America (Patrick J. Smith, May 1974): "A thudding dud. ... close to musical bankruptcy.... Its weakness is in its pathetic predictability, hand-me-downs from the 1920s German music hall of Kurt Weill. The production was television oriented and quite fluid."

177. *Really Rosie* 30 minutes. Animated Musical. Broadcast February 19, 1975 (Wednesday, 8:30–9:00 P.M.) CBS

Producer Sheldon Riss; *Director/Writer/Creator* Maurice Sendak; *Lyricists* Lou Adler, Maurice Sendak; *Composer* Carole King; *Record* LP Epic 34955; *Video* CC Studios; *Sheet Music* Colgems.

Cast (voices): Carole King, Baille Gerstein, Mark Hampton, Alice Playten, Dale Soules

Vocals: Carole King, Louise Goffin, Sherry Goffin

Songs: "Really Rosie," "Chicken Soup with Rice," "One Was Johnny," "Avenue P," "Alligators All Around," "My Simple Humble Neighborhood," "Pierre," "The Awful Truth," "Screaming and Yelling," "Such Sufferin'," "Ballad of Chicken Soup."

Story: Rosie, a bossy little girl, wants to direct a movie of her life, and screen tests her little friends in tryouts.

Based on Maurice Sendak's Nutshell Library. The record was nominated for a Grammy for best children's recording. The musical was done as a live off–Broadway production in 1980–81 and ran for 274 performances.

Review: *Variety* (Feb. 26, 1975): "Sendak's appreciation of the sense of irony in children was neatly complemented by Carole King's fey lyrics and nifty vocal interpretations. The results of pairing this duo are stunningly successful."

178. *Return of the King* 2 hours. Animated Musical. Broadcast May 11, 1980 (Sunday, 7:00–9:00 P.M.) ABC

Executive Producers/Producers/Directors Arthur Rankin, Jr., Jules Bass; *Associate Producer* Musaki Iizuka; *Writer* Romeo Muller; *Lyricist* Jules Bass; *Composer* Maury Laws; *Record* LP Disneyland 3822; *Video* Lorimar.

Cast (voices): John Huston (narrator), Orson Bean, Roddy McDowall, Theodore Bikel, William Conrad, Glenn Yarbrough, Nellie Bellflower, Paul Frees, Casey Kasem, Sonny Melendrez, Don Messick, John Stephenson, Theodore

Songs: "Frodo of the Nine Fingers," "Where There's a Whip," "It's So Easy Not to Try," "Leave Tomorrow 'Till It Comes," "Bearer of the Ring," "The Cracks of Doom," "Less Can Be More," "Choice of Evils," "Roads," "The Return of the King."

Story: Frodo, a nephew to Hobbit Bilbo Baggins, and his servant Sam, head for Mount Doom to return the evil magic ring to its source. The two run into fearsome obstacles and do battle with demons of various kinds, but finally complete the mission.

This story was based on J. R. R. Tolkien's *Lord of the Rings*. A 1978 theatrical movie, *Lord of the Rings*, was made by a different producer.

Review: Mark Satern *Video's Best:* "J. R. R. Tolkien's ever popular tale about an epic battle between good and evil is greatly diminished in scope and scale. ... However, it is still worthy of watching."

179. *Return to Oz* 60 minutes. Animated Musical. Broadcast February 9, 1964 (Sunday, 5:00–6:00 P.M.) NBC

Producers Arthur Rankin, Jr., Jules Bass; *Directors* F. R. Crawley, Thomas Glynn, Larry Roemer; *Writer* Romeo Muller; *Lyricists/Composers* Gene Farrell, Edward Thomas, James Polack, George Wilkins; *Video* Prism.

Cast (voices): Susan Conway, Carl Banas, Alfie Scopp, Larry Mann, Susan Morse, Pegi Loder

Songs: "I Wanna Go Back," "Wickedest, Wicked Old Witch," "Moonbeam," "I'm Heartless, Through and Through," "We're Munchkins, Naturally," "Dan, Dan, Dandy Lion," "You Can't Buy a Brain."

Story: Dorothy returns to Oz and finds her friends the Scarecrow, the Lion and the Tin Man are in trouble. The Wicked Witch of the West is still alive and threatening them all, as well as holding the Wizard captive. Dorothy and her friends free the Wizard and regain their lost qualities again.

This was the first television production of Rankin-Bass, who made many more. This story (based on the L. Frank Baum book) was later made into a feature film.

Review: *Variety* (Feb. 12, 1964): "Seemed a rather heavy rendition of the classic. The predominating sound was the witch's cackle. There was music, and some of it was quite catching, but the renditions seemed devoid of spirit."

180. *The Road to Lebanon* 60 minutes. Musical. *The Danny Thomas Special.* Broadcast April 20, 1966 (Wednesday, 9:00–10:00 P.M.) NBC

Executive Producer Danny Thomas; *Producers* Alan Handley, Bob Wynn; *Writers* Garry Marshall, Jerry Belson; *Music* Earl Hagen; *Orchestra* Harper MacKay; *Video* Video Yesteryear.

Cast: Danny Thomas, Bing Crosby, Claudine Auger, Sheldon Leonard, Bob Hope, Hugh Downs

Songs: "The Road to Lebanon," "You'll Enjoy Being a Girl," "Oh Moon," "Tea for Two" (dance), "Together," "The Last Roundup."

Story: The story is told by Hamid the Storyteller. In Hollywood, Bing sings the title song, then tells reporter Hugh Downs that he doesn't want to team up with Bob Hope again for another "Road" picture, but he hopes to get Danny Thomas, who has gone to Lebanon to judge a beauty contest. In the meantime we see Sheik Ali-Ali, who treats his daughter as a son, and says the "son" must avenge the family honor by killing Danny Thomas. In Beirut Danny is kidnapped, not by the Sheik, but by men hired by Bing so that he can talk to Danny alone about pairing up. The "son," Lawrence of Lebanon, finds them and tells them of her mission. Bing convinces her she would do better as a girl, but the sheik's men capture them. Danny asks the captors what his crime is, and is told it had to do with a "nose job." When he says he never had a nose job, he is told his great grandfather did when he went to America, and that someone has to pay. Bing and Danny do the "patty cake" routine, and while their captors are fighting and girls dancing they attempt to escape but are caught and buried in sand up to their necks. Bob Hope comes flying to the rescue in a golf cart; he just happens to have a picture of Danny's great grandfather and is able to show that he had his nose enlarged. All is forgiven. Back in Beirut, Danny picks the beauty contest winner: Lawrence Ali.

This show is lean on original music, but is great fun. Its writers won the Writers Guild award for best comedy or variety show. Danny's nose was a running joke in his comedy skits and his television series. Bing Crosby and Bob Hope had made seven "Road" pictures from 1940 to 1962, and used certain standard comedy routines throughout.

Danny Thomas had a number of television specials in addition to his several series, but most of the specials could best be characterized as variety shows.

Review: *Variety* (April 29, 1966): "A single skit that encompassed the full hour. ... Full of whimsey and studded with one-liners that could have made the *Reader's Digest.* Overall it was pleasant if unmemorable."

181. *The Royal Follies of 1933* 60 minutes. Musical. *The Danny Thomas Hour.* Broadcast December 11, 1967 (Monday, 9:00–10:00 P.M.) NBC

Producer/Director Alan Handley; *Music Director* Earl Hagen.

Cast: Johnny Carson (narrator), Danny Thomas, Shirley Jones, Ken Berry, Gale Gordon, Jackie Joseph, Hans Conried, Eve Arden, Kurt Kasznar, Bob Hope

Songs: "All the World's a Stage," "Million Dollar Baby," "I'm Cyrano of Hackensack," "The Cream in My Coffee," "I'll Take Romance," "My Lucky Star."

Story: To escape a husband-hunting heiress, a bachelor prince joins a Broadway show that is threatened by gangsters.

A light-hearted spoof of 1930s movie musicals, with standard songs.

Review: *Variety* (Dec. 13, 1967): "Second-rate stuff unworthy of a primetime hour. Scripting and direction so banal that the talent was ... almost entirely wasted."

182. *Rudolph and Frosty's Christmas in July* 90 minutes. Animated Musical. Broadcast November 25, 1979 (Sunday, 7:00–8:30 P.M.) ABC

Producers/Directors Arthur Rankin, Jr., Jules Bass; *Writer* Romeo Muller; *Lyricist/Composer* Johnny Marks; *Other Music* Maury Laws, Michael Colicchio; *Video* Lightning Video.

Cast (voices): Mickey Rooney (narrator), Billy Richards, Jackie Vernon, Shelley Winters, Red Buttons, Ethel Merman, Alan Sues, Harold Peary, Cynthia Adler, Nellie Bellflower, Steffi Calli, Darlene Conley, Shelby Flint, Paul Frees, Eric Hines, Robert McFadden, Don Messick, Howard Shapiro

Songs: "Rudolph the Red-Nosed Reindeer," "Everything I've Always Wanted," "Christmas in July," "Chicken Today and Feathers Tomorrow," "I See Rainbows," "Don't Let the Parade Pass You By," "I Heard the Bells on Christmas Day," "Rockin' Around the Christmas

Tree," "No Bed of Roses," "Frosty the Snowman," "Now and Then," "We're a Couple of Misfits."

Story: The evil Winterbolt wants to take over the North Pole. Rudolph is asked by his friend Milton, ice-cream man at a failing circus, to come help out the circus. Frosty—and his family— have never seen a circus and want to go, but are afraid they will melt in the summer sun. Winterbolt, as part of his scheme to get rid of the Pole's inhabitants, encourages the trip, and gives the snow people magic amulets that will keep them from melting as long as they return before the last fireworks. Santa agrees to pick them up for the return trip. Winterbolt finds a bad reindeer, Scratcher, and sends him to the circus. All goes well at first, and Rudolph is the highlight of the show, but then Scratcher talks Rudolph into taking the circus money and giving it to a crook dressed as a policeman. Lady Borealis has told Rudolph his nose will only glow as long as he thinks good thoughts, so after his theft his nose does not glow. Rudolph confesses to the theft to save Frosty, and Frosty gives his magic hat to Winterbolt to help Rudolph, but Winterbolt has tricked them both. Frosty and family melt, but Big Ben, the whale, brings a winter wind and Jack Frost from South America to revive the snow people. Rudolph chases Winterbolt and gets the hat back; circus manager Lily shoots Winterbolt and he turns into a tree. Santa and his wife, who had been lost in a storm, arrive and take the snow people back to the Pole, while Rudolph stays to help the circus.

The longest of the Rudolph specials, this one had an all-star cast, an intricate plot and mostly new songs. Ethel Merman as Lily (the circus manager) was a standout.

183. *Rudolph the Red-Nosed Reindeer* see *The Story of Rudolph the Red-Nosed Reindeer*

184. *Rudolph's Shiny New Year* 60 minutes. Animated Musical. Broadcast December 10, 1976 (Friday, 8:00–9:00 P.M.) ABC

Producers/Directors Arthur Rankin, Jr., Jules Bass; *Writer* Romeo Muller; *Lyricist/Composer* Johnny Marks; *Musical Director* Maury Laws; *Video* Lightning Video; *Music* Columbia (Vocal Selections).

Cast (voices): Red Skelton (narrator), Billy Richards, Frank Gorshin, Morey Amsterdam, Paul Frees, Hal Peary

Songs: "Rudolph, the Red-Nosed Reindeer," "Have a Little Faith in Me," "Have a Happy," "It's Raining Sunshine," "Turn Back the Years," "The Moving Finger Writes," "The 4th of July Parade," "What a Wonderful World."

Story: Happy, the Baby New Year, has run away from Father Time, and if he is not found, there will be no New Year. Rudolph sets out to find him, and after many adventures, does so, but finds Happy is ashamed of his big ears. Rudolph tells him about his own problem nose, and convinces the baby that ears are not a problem. Santa arrives to take Happy back just in time to start the New Year.

Review: *Variety* (Dec. 15, 1976): "A rather imaginative story line ... old-fashioned melodic songs meshed with mood and content."

185. *Ruggles of Red Gap* 90 minutes. Musical. *Showcase Productions.* Broadcast February 3, 1957 (Sunday, 7:30–9:00 P.M.) NBC

Producer Charles Friedman; *Director*

Clark Jones; *Writer* David Shaw; *Lyricist* Leo Robin; *Composer* Jule Styne; *Conductor/Arranger* Buddy Bregman; *Vocal Arranger* Buster Davis; *Record* LP Verve 15000/DRG 15007; *Sheet Music* Chappell/Shapiro.

Cast: Michael Redgrave, Peter Lawford, Imogene Coca, Jane Powell, David Wayne, Paul Lynde, Hal Linden, Joan Holloway, Buster Davis Choir

Songs: "Oh, Those Americans," "The Way to a Family's Heart," "I Have You to Thank," "It's a Glorious Fourth," "I'm in Pursuit of Happiness," "When You Dance in Paris, France," "Welcome Home," "A Ride on a Rainbow," "Kickapoo Kick," "I Don't Want to Be a Gentleman," "It's Terribly, Horribly, Frightfully Nice."

Story: A western cattleman on a trip to Europe wins a stuffy English valet in a poker game. To his social-climbing wife's delight, they take the valet to their home in Red Gap, Washington. Valet Ruggles writes his former owner Lord Brinstad of his fears and unhappiness in this strange environment. But by the time the Lord arrives in Red Gap, Ruggles has gotten used to American ways, has a business of his own and a girlfriend, and is thoroughly enjoying himself. Lord Brinstad finds his own fun there.

Based on the 1915 book by Harry Leon Wilson, this story was previously on stage in 1915 with "incidental music" by Sigmund Romberg. The 1935 movie starred Charles Laughton in a delightfully comedic portrayal. The 1950 film *Fancy Pants*, with Bob Hope, was also based on this story and had music by Livingston and Evans (including "Home Cookin'"). This show had new, original music. The tune to "I'm in Pursuit of Happiness" later became "You'll Never Get Away from Me" in *Gypsy*, with new

words by Stephen Sondheim. Robin and Styne had earlier collaborated on the Broadway musical *Gentlemen Prefer Blondes.*

Review: *Variety* (Feb. 6, 1957) opined that television had wasted its potential by using such an "outdated" property. "In converting it to TV they lost the comedy and created a framework for half a dozen musical comedy love songs." The reviewer found the adaptation neither clever, fresh or ingenious. The reviewer commented favorably on Michael Redgrave's "surprisingly melodious" voice, but was not as enthused over Peter Lawford's efforts.

186. *The Saga of Sonora* 60 minutes. Musical. Broadcast May 3, 1973 (Tuesday, 10:00–11:00 P.M.) NBC

Producers Burt Rosen, David Winters; *Director* Marty Pasetta; *Writers* Bernard Rothman, Jack Wohl; *Musical Director* Larry Cansler.

Cast: Dale Evans and Roy Rogers (hosts), Don Adams (cowboy narrator), Zero Mostel, Vince Edwards, Sam Jaffe, Lesley Ann Warren, Jill St. John, George Gobel, Frankie Avalon, Cass Elliott, George Kirby, Carl Ballentine, Kenny Rogers and the First Edition

Songs: "I Want to Be Rich," "What Would We Do Without You," "Belly Up to the Bar, Boys," "You and Me Babe," "A Cowboy's Work Is Never Done," "Ballad of Sonora," "How Could You Believe Me When I Said I Loved You When You Know I've Been a Liar All My Life?"

Story: Sam is transported back to the 19th century and finds he is the town sheriff. He is met by an old prospector and his daughter who buy him a drink to celebrate their finding a gold mine. The saloon dancer, Molly, snuggles up to Sam. But the prospector is murdered for his map and the evil town boss Harry (a singing villain) plots to steal the gold. Sam and Harry shoot it out. As he is leaving town, Sam says goodbye to little Jesse James and his mother. A musical spoof of Westerns. Though the review mentions new songs, it appears standard songs were used.

Review: *Variety* (May 16, 1973): According to the reviewer, this show's "sophisticated sophomoric humor" succeeds on the strength of an enthusiastic cast. "Part of the fey charm of this Western spoof came from a batch of funny and forgettable original tunes mixed with Anthony Newley tunes from his shows. ... Inspired silliness."

187. St. George and the Dragon 30 minutes. Operetta. Broadcast June 7, 1953 (Sunday afternoon) NBC

Producer/Director Burr Tillstrom; *Lyricists* John Fascinato, Burr Tillstrom; *Composer* John Fascinato.

Cast: Fran Allison, Oliver J. Dragon, Kukla, Arthur Fiedler and the Boston Pops. Special Guest: Boston Mayor John B. Hines.

Songs: "Beware, Dragon," "I Feel a Tear."

Story: The traditional legend of St. George and the Dragon relates that St. George is asked to come and subdue an evil dragon who is eating people in its neighborhood. St. George comes, rescues a princess from the dragon's clutches, then slays the dragon. But with Ollie playing the dragon, the storyline had to be revised to favor Ollie.

This show was broadcast from Symphony Hall in Boston. It was the first network telecast in compatible color; it was seen in color in Washington, D.C., black and white elsewhere.

Reviews: *Variety* (June 10, 1953): "A pleasant, tuneful confection for children.... The battle between knight and dragon was an awesome thing. Fran made a lovely looking princess, and Kukla a handsome Sir George. But it was Ollie's show."

Max Wilk, *The Golden Age of Television*: "Ollie spent a considerable amount of time disposing of his typecast prey, Kukla, whose death scene was a classic piece of overacting."

188. Sam Found Out see Liza Minnelli in Sam Found Out: A Triple Play

189. Santa Claus Is Comin' to Town 60 minutes. Animated Musical. Broadcast December 13, 1970 (Sunday, 7:00–8:00 P.M.) ABC

Producers/Directors Arthur Rankin, Jr., Jules Bass; *Writer* Romeo Muller; *Music & Lyrics, Title Song* J. Fred Coots, Haven Gillespie; *Other Lyrics* Jules Bass; *Other Music* Maury Laws; *Orchestrator* Maury Laws; *Design* Paul Coker; *Record* LP MGM SE 4732; *Video* Viacom; *Music, Title Song* Leo Feist.

Cast: Fred Astaire (narrator), Mickey Rooney, Robie Lester, Keenan Wynn, Joan Gardner, Paul Frees, Dida Lydd, Greg Thomas, Anazea Sacido, Gary White, Westminster Children's Choir

Songs: "Santa Claus Is Comin' to Town," "First Toymaker to the King," "Be Prepared to Pay," "Put One Foot in Front of the Other," "My World Is Beginning Today," "What Better Way to Tell You."

Story: The mailman (played by a Fred

Astaire look-alike) gets letters asking questions about Santa Claus. He tells the children the story of how the Kringles acquire an abandoned baby, name him Kris and raise him among the toy-making elves. The elves are afraid to deliver the toys to Sombertown because of the winter Warlock on the mountain, so a grown-up Kris takes on the job. Mrs. Kringle makes him a red suit for his trip; Kris goes to Sombertown and passes out the toys with the help of Miss Jessica, the local schoolteacher. But the Burgermeister hates toys and has banned them; he confiscates the toys given out by Kris. Kris and his penguin run away and are captured by the Warlock but make friends with him. Jessica brings letters from the town's children, and Kris says to leave their doors open so he can deliver toys. The Burgermeister orders townsfolk to lock their doors, so Kris goes down the chimneys and leaves the toys in stockings. The Burgermeister arrests Kris and his family, but they escape on flying reindeer. Now an outlaw, Kris grows a beard, changes his name to Claus and marries Jessica. Since he is still hunted, the family moves to the North Pole, and Kris decides to deliver toys only once a year, on Christmas Eve.

The song "Santa Claus Is Comin' to Town" was written in 1934. Other than its use as a title, the song has little to do with this fanciful story, which purports to explain how Santa and the various Christmas customs we observe got started.

Review: *New York Times* (Howard Thompson, Dec. 1, 1972): "A cute, perky bundle for the romper set. ... Pleasant tunes. ... The voice of Fred Astaire ... adds a definite patina of charm and verve. ... Nicely pitched and sustained on a level of simple diversion and fun. The overall tone is saucy-sweet."

190. Sarah   30 minutes. Opera. *Look Up and Live.* Broadcast November 30, 1958 (Sunday, 10:30–11:00 A.M.) CBS

Executive Producer Pamela Ilott; *Producer (series)* Jack Kuney; *Director* Roger Englander; *Librettist* Clair Roskam; *Composer* Ezra Laderman.

Cast: Patricia Neway, Mildred Allen, Ara Berberian, Alan Baker

Story: Abraham and his wife Sarah are, in their later years, concerned about Sarah's barrenness. Sarah decides to provide a son for Abraham by giving him her slave/servant girl Hagar. This triangle creates difficult feelings and conflicts.

Look Up and Live was a CBS nondenominational religious program that ran for 24 years on Sunday mornings and explored different religious and cultural themes. The story of Sarah, Abraham and Hagar is found in Genesis, Chapter 16. This opera was one of the earliest works of composer Laderman.

Reviews: *Opera News:* Reviewer Allen Hughes praised the librettist for her sympathetic exploration of the characters' relationships, and the composer for an "admirable score" that intensified the emotional impact of the story. He went on: "Textually as well as musically lines are eminently singable; the orchestral substructure is consistently vibrant, glowing and colorful."

New York Times (Eric Salzman): "The unusual quality of the product was emphasized by the complete seriousness of the work and its presentation. ... The dark and compact score contains harmonic and melodic patterns used insistently to suggest the East." Salzman complained that the work lacked an identifiable point of view.

191. Satins and Spurs   90 minutes. Musical. *Max Liebman Presents.* Broadcast September 12, 1954 (Sunday, 7:30–9:00 P.M.) NBC

Producers Max Liebman, Bill Hobin; *Director/Choreographer* Charles O'Curran; *Writers* William Friedberg, Max Liebman, Neil Simon, William Glickman, Fred Saidy; *Lyricist* Ray Evans; *Composer* Jay Livingston; *Conductor/Orchestrator* Nelson Riddle; *Musical Director* Charles Sanford; *Arrangers* Nelson Riddle, Irwin Kostel, Henry Mancini; *Choral Director* Clay Warnick; *Costumes* Paul du Pont; *Set Designer* Frederick Fox; *Record* LP Capitol 547 (10").

Cast: Betty Hutton, Kevin McCarthy, Genevieve, Guy Raymond, Josh Wheeler, Edwin Phillips, Neva Patterson, Maggie McNellis, Ray Drakely, Joe Ross, Mary Ellen Moylan

Songs: "Whoop Diddy Ay," "I've Had Enough," "Wildcat Smathers," "Nobody Cares," "Satins and Spurs," "Back Home," "The Little Rock Roll," "You're Right for Me."

Story: Pretty cowgirl Cindy Smathers goes to New York to ride in a Madison Square Garden rodeo. A magazine sends a writer/photographer to do a picture story on a western girl in the big city. This embarrasses Cindy, and she decides to leave town. At the last minute, the reporter convinces her to stay and wins her affections, and the photographs win the girl a job on the stage.

This show was the first NBC 90-minute color spectacular. Sylvester (Pat) Weaver, NBC network president, envisioned a series of such shows and put Max Liebman in charge of production. Despite a lavish color production (the show cost $300,000) and Betty Hutton as the heroine, things did not go well for this show. Hutton insisted that husband O'Curran direct, and apparently he did

not work well with the network people. The show ran seven minutes short, and Steve Allen hastily gave viewers a tour of the new NBC studio. Nelson Riddle's orchestration received an Emmy nomination, but the show got mixed reviews, and Hutton, who had had vocal problems, retired for a while. Songwriters Livingston and Evans were well known for their work together at Paramount, where they had written Oscar-winning tunes; Hutton had starred in MGM's *Annie Get Your Gun* and a number of Paramount musicals.

There was an extravagant publicity buildup for this show, and perhaps no program could have lived up to the hype. Most viewers didn't yet have color, so couldn't truly appreciate the spectacle.

Reviews: *Variety* (Sept. 15, 1954): "Miss Hutton was the standout element of the show as she bounced into TV ... with an explosive gusto. ... The book was only a springboard for the songs. ... The show was definitely short on humor."

New York Times (Sept. 13, 1954): "Musical had its good moments when tunes were lively and action imaginative. ... Miss Hutton did her best. ... More help from music and lyrics than from book [which was] unusually weak and short on comedy."

Newsweek: "A $300,000 letdown! ... The book smacks of *Annie Get Your Gun* or any other saga about a cowpoke in the big city."

Hollywood Reporter: "A big, beautiful hodge-podge ... a lot of perspiration but no inspiration."

Time (Sept. 20, 1954): "First rate ... big and tuneful ... a fine vehicle for Hutton. ... Music astonishingly good."

192. *The Secret Garden*　90 minutes. Animated Musical. Broadcast

November 5, 1994 (Saturday, 11:30 A.M.–1:00 P.M.) ABC

Producers Mike Young, Ellen Freyer; *Director* Dave Edwards; *Writer* Libby Hinson; *Songs* Misha Segal, Harriet Schlock; *Music Director* Misha Segal; *Video* Capital Cities/ABC Video.

Cast (voices): Honor Blackman, Sir Derek Jacobi, Glynis Johns, Victor Spinetti, Anndi McAfee, Joe Baker, Felix Bell, Naomi Bell, Richard Stuart, Frank Welker

Songs: "Home," "If You Listen to the Meaning, Not the Word," "Growing, Growing, Grown," "The Manor Will Be Mine."

Story: Young Mary Lennox, orphaned in India, is sent to her Uncle Archibald's gloomy estate in Yorkshire. Mrs. Medlock, the mean housekeeper, tells Mary to keep to her room, but with the help of Martha, the maid, and Darjeeling, the cat, she explores the house and grounds. She meets Ben Weatherstuff, the gardener, who explains that nothing is blooming because it is winter, and English gardens bloom in the spring. Mary finds a secret walled garden and takes Dickens, Martha's brother, to see the garden. The two work to bring the garden back to life. Mary discovers Colin, her cousin, who has been kept an invalid by the housekeeper and Dr. Craven, brother to Archibald. Mary and Dickens take Colin to the garden and inspire him to enjoy life and to walk.

This animated film is based on the book by Frances Hodgson Burnett, written in 1911.

193. *Sextuplets* 60 minutes. Musical. *Kraft Television Theatre.* Broadcast August 7, 1957 (Wednesday, 9:00–10:00 P.M.) NBC

Director William Graham; *Writer* John J. Morrin; *Additional Dialogue* Robert Emmett.

Cast: Tammy Grimes, Ferlin Husky, Fred Gwynne, William Redfield, Ruth White, Mike Kellin, Kenny Delmar, Jack Weston, John Cameron Swayze, William Sheidy, Olin Howl, Dwight Marfield, James Tapp, William Duell, Don P. Smith, Frank Bolger, William Culpepper, Ed Wagner, Pete Gumeny, Jan Lieghton, William Drew

Songs: "Pickanickin," "I Feel Better All Over."

Story: Set in the Ozark Mountains, this is a tale about some gallant hillbillies, more sensible and genuine than city folk. News has spread across the nation that sextuplets have been born to this backwoods family. A television engineer who discovered them wants the big story, and the governor tries to give them help, but they don't want the publicity or the aid. As it turns out, there are no sextuplets, only two sets of triplets with some family complications. This was Ferlin Husky's acting debut.

Review: *Variety* (Aug. 14, 1957): "Morrin expertly dictated a broadly humorous tale ... a clever backwoodsy yarn. ... Husky tops ... his acting debut on a par with his singing."

194. *Sing a Sign* 30 minutes. Musical. Broadcast May 20, 1978 (Saturday, 9:00–9:30 P.M.) PBS

Producer/Writer Susan Smith; *Director* Sterling Smith; *Lyricists* Susan Davidoff, Vince Di Zebba, Susan Smith; *Composer* Steve Swab; *Choreographer* Vince Di Zebba.

Cast: Bernard Braff, Rita Corey, Vince Di Zebba, Donna Gadling, Rodney Johnson, Ogden Whitehead, Martin

Stephens, Tracy Tuttle, David McFarlane

Story: A joyful celebration of dance, music, poetry and mime.

Though listed as a revue, this program is included because it is the first nationally televised musical in sign language, with a cast of young deaf and hearing performers. Miss Deaf America wrote the lyrics to the title song.

195. *Singin' Idol* 60 minutes. Drama with Music. *Kraft Television Theatre*. Broadcast January 30, 1957 (Wednesday, 9:00–10:00 P.M.) NBC

Director Paul Bogart; *Writer* Paul Monash; *Songs* Joe & Audrey Allison; *Sheet Music* Central Songs.

Cast: Tommy Sands, Fred Clark, Jamie Smith, Vaughn Taylor, Don Briggs, Ray Boyle, Jane McArthur, Doreen Lang and 24 others

Song: "Teenage Crush."

Story: Ewell Walker, a naive country boy, becomes a rock star with the help of a fast-talking, ruthless manager. Successful but lonely, he returns home when his preacher grandfather has a stroke and makes a death-bed promise to become a preacher.

Not really a musical, this show is included here because of the success of the song. Discussed previously (see entry on *Let Me Go, Lover*) was the success of ballads strategically placed in TV dramas, but this show fed into the rock-and-roll generation. The story was written to star Elvis Presley, but when he turned it down, his manager Col. Tom Parker recommended young Tommy Sands, already a performing singer and guitarist, for the part. Sands' recording of "Teenage Crush" reached #2 on the charts in a very short time. On the tenth anniversary of *Kraft Television Theatre*,

company ads proclaimed, "It can make a new star overnight, as it did this year with *The Singin' Idol*. The story was filmed by 20th Century–Fox in 1958 as *Sing Boy Sing*, also with Sands. Reviews of the movie also commented favorably on Sands' singing and his acting ability. Sands went on to a number of acting roles on television and in movies.

Review: *Variety* (Feb. 6, 1957): "Old-hat story, but excellent performances sustained interest. Sands was completely persuasive.... The denouement was somewhat ambiguous; at the curtain the boy surrenders his ideals, but there's a suggestion he will yet be redeemed."

196. *Skinflint* 2 hours. Musical. Broadcast December 18, 1979 (Tuesday, 9:00–11:00 P.M.) NBC

Executive Producers Joseph & Gilbert Cates; *Producers* Marc Daniels, Joseph Cates; *Director* Marc Daniels; *Writer* Mel Mandel; *Songs* Mel Mandel, Norman Sachs, Aaron Schroeder.

Cast: Hoyt Axton, Mel Tillis, Lynn Anderson, Barbara Mandrell, Larry Gatlin, Tom T. Hall, Martha Raye, Daniel Davis, Dottie West, Julie Gregg, The Statler Brothers

Story: It is Christmas in a small Tennessee town, where Scrooge-like banker Cyrus Flint begrudges his employees' salaries, turns down charity requests and thinks Christmas is humbug. He is visited by the ghostly three who show him the sad effects of his miserly ways and cause him to find the holiday spirit.

An all-star, updated country-and-western version of Dickens' *A Christmas Carol*.

Reviews: *TV Guide* (Dec. 18, 1979): "The ghostly visitations [are] enlivened by rousing choreography, lavish production values, and songs blending Broadway rhythms with a down-home beat."

197. *A Snow White Christmas* 60
minutes. Animated Musical. Broadcast November 19, 1980 (Wednesday, 8:00–9:00 P.M.) CBS

Executive Producers Lou Scheimer, Norm Prescott; *Producer* Don Christensen; *Director* Kay Wright; *Writer* Marc Richards; *Songs* Jeff Michael, Dean Andre; *Other Music* Yvette Blais, Jeff Michael; *Video* Prism; *Sheet Music* Shermley Music.

Cast (voices): Erika Scheimer, Arte Johnson, Melendy Britt, Diane Pershing, Charlie Dell, Larry Mann, Clinton Sundberg

Songs: "A Snow White Christmas," "The Perfect Christmas," "It's Christmas," "The Darker Side," "She's Sleeping," "Seven Friendly Giants."

Story: Queen Snow White and King Charming, now living "happily ever after," have a lovely daughter, also named Snow White. The young princess hopes to make the old, gloomy, boarded-up castle into a Christmas castle for the children and animals of the land. But the wicked-stepmother queen has escaped her imprisonment, and vows to do away with the whole family of Charmings. With her magic, she freezes the king, queen and people of the town, but Princess Snow White and Grunion escape and find sanctuary on a farm run by seven kindly giants. The evil queen tries many schemes to get rid of the giants and kill Snow White. She is finally defeated by the giants, but not until she has put Snow White into a coma. When Snow White awakens, there is a fine Christmas celebration, and since the old castle has been destroyed, the giants build Snow White a new castle.

198. *So Help Me, Aphrodite* 60
minutes. Musical. *Ford Startime.* Broadcast May 31, 1960 (Tuesday, 9:30–10:30 P.M.) NBC

Producer Larry Burns; *Director* Bob Henry; *Writer* Danny Arnold; *Lyricists* Danny Arnold, Jack Brooks; *Composer* Jack Brooks; *Musical Director* Axel Stordahl.

Cast: Nanette Fabray, Tony Randall, Jean-Pierre Aumont, Stubby Kaye, Robert Strauss, Peter Leeds

Songs: "Save a Place on the Wall," "Who Needs It," "Po-Po-Pocahontas," "You've Got to Keep a Woman in the Right-Hand Lane."

Story: Sally, a waitress in a roadside diner, daydreams of becoming famous while truck-driver customers become impatient. She keeps her job only because her boss is in love with her, but she refuses to marry him. In her fantasies, she imagines she is Pocahontas and Marie Antoinette, and the diner patrons become figures in Sally's dreams. In the end she agrees to a partnership and a wedding.

Review: *Variety* (June 8, 1960): "A cut above the average of musicals presented in this season. Fairly good book for the musical [and] sets of exceedingly clever lyrics."

199. *The Sojourner and Mollie Sinclair* 60 minutes. Opera. Broadcast December 15, 1963 (Sunday, 6:00–7:00 P.M.) NBC

Producer Gene Strassler; *Director* Edgar R. Loessin; *Librettist/Composer* Carlisle Floyd; *Conductor* Julius Rudel; *Set Design* John A. Sneden; *Choreographer*

Norman Treigle (in kilt, center) expounds on a musical point while Patricia Neway (right, arms folded) listens skeptically in *The Sojourner and Mollie Sinclair* (1963). Courtesy Gary Faircloth, East Carolina University, Department of Theatre Arts.

Betty Rose Griffith; *Music* Boosey and Hawkes.

Cast: Patricia Neway, Norman Treigle, Alison Hearne Moss, William Newberry, Jerold Teachey, Opera Workshop of East Carolina College

Story: Set in the Cape Fear River Valley in the 18th century. A Scottish laird, Dougald MacDougald, is loyal to the Crown and raises a British flag daily on his eastern Carolina plantation. This day, in full clan regalia, he awaits the arrival of his clansmen to celebrate his birthday. His daughter Jenny and her boyfriend, Lachlan Sinclair, are quarreling. Dougald tells Lachlan to leave until he returns properly dressed, but Lachlan remembers he is to help his mother organize a brigade to march on Wilmington to protest the Stamp Act, and goes. The kinsmen arrive and perform a Scottish dance. Suddenly Mol-

lie Sinclair and her brigade appear, and she asks Dougald and his kin to join her in her march. Dougald is upset by the request, but furious when he learns the British have blockaded Wilmington Harbor. Dougald and Molly have a long talk in which she urges him to become loyal to his new country. He ultimately decides to join the rebellion, and replaces his British flag with another.

This opera was commissioned for television by the Carolina Charter Tercentenary Commission. It was produced by the School of Music and the Department of Drama, East Carolina College, with guest conductor Julius Rudel of the New York City Opera. The drama was staged at the Raleigh Little Theater on December 2, 3 and 4, 1963, and was then taped for broadcast.

Reviews: *The New York Times* and local papers said only that the show was "well received."

200. *A Special London Bridge Special* 60 minutes. Musical. Broadcast May 7, 1972 (Sunday, 9:00–10:00 P.M.) NBC

Producers Burt Rosen, David Winters; *Director* David Winters; *Writers* Marty Farrell, Marc Ray, Ronnie Cass, David Ross; *Musical Directors* Marvin Hamlisch, Johnnie Spence.

Cast: Tom Jones, Jennifer O'Neill; **Guests:** The Carpenters, Kirk Douglas, Hermione Gingold, Elliott Gould, Rudolf Nureyev

Songs: "London Is London," "We've Only Just Begun," "She's a Lady," "For All We Know," "You've Got a Friend," "Love Is Surrender," "He Loves Me," "Style," "Consider Yourself," "If," "Got to Get You Into My Life."

Story: The tale follows the meeting and courtship of a couple from London to Lake Havasu City, Arizona (site of the rebuilt London Bridge).

Listed as a "musical fantasy," this show has a thin storyline and enough guest stars to be considered a variety show, but the attempt at a plot makes it a borderline musical with mostly standard songs.

Review: *Variety* (May 10, 1972): "Results were good on the rock musical and terps side of the ledger, not-so-hot on the continuity level. Musical direction, along with the choreography, was top notch."

201. *The Stingiest Man in Town* 90 minutes. Musical. *Alcoa Hour.* Broadcast December 23, 1956 (Sunday, 9:00–10:30 P.M.) NBC

Producer Joel Spector; *Director* Dan Petrie; *Writer/Lyricist* Janice Torre; *Composer* Fred Spielman; *Conductor* Camarata; *Choreographer* John Heawood; *Costumes* Motley *Set Design* Kim Swados; *Choral Director* Jerry Packer; *Record* LP Columbia CL 950; *Video* See below; *Music* Harms (8), Warner (Score).

Cast: Vic Damone, Johnny Desmond, The Four Lads, Patrice Munsel, Basil Rathbone, Robert Weede, Betty Madigan, Martyn Green, Robert Wright, John McGiver, Alcie Frost, Dennis Kohler, Olive Dunbar, Bryan Herbert, Philippa Bevans, Ian Martin, Keith Harrington, Richard Morse, Karol Ann Trauman, Karson Woods, Karin Wolfe, John Heawood

Songs: "A Christmas Carol," "It Might Have Been," "An Old Fashioned Christmas," "The Christmas Spirit," "Humbug," "Yes, There Is a Santa Claus," "The Stingiest Man in Town," "One Little Boy," "I Wear a Chain," "Birthday Party of the King," "Golden Dreams," "Mankind Should Be My Business."

Story: After an Overture, carolers introduce us to Scrooge in song. Scrooge's nephew Fred and chorus portray an old-fashioned Christmas street scene with song and dance. Fred visits his Uncle Scrooge. Scrooge scorns his nephew's gift, turns down gentlemen soliciting for charity, and reluctantly gives Bob Cratchit Christmas Day off. Scrooge's cleaning lady, a ragpicker and a group of beggars discuss Scrooge's stinginess. The carolers return to narrate the story of Marley's ghost, followed by the visit. Scrooge is then visited by the Ghost of Christmas-Past who takes Scrooge to visit his old school and to Fezziwig's office, where young Scrooge and his sweetheart Belle dream of their future together, with song and dance. But young Scrooge becomes obsessed with making money, and the golden dreams sour. The Ghost of Christmas-Present (introduced by carolers) tells Scrooge about the Christmas spirit as the toys dance Scrooge around, then the Ghost takes Scrooge to visit the Cratchit family and nephew Fred's home. Carolers bring on the Ghost of Christmas-Yet-to-Come, who comes accompanied by sounds of devils and lost souls; the Ghost takes Scrooge to the cemetery to view his own tombstone while devils dance around. Scrooge at last realizes that mankind is his business. Next morning he hops about, runs into his cleaning lady and sends her to buy a turkey. He leaves the turkey on the Cratchits' doorstep, then rings again with armfuls of presents. He promises Bob Cratchit a raise and says he will help Tiny Tim. He doesn't accept their dinner invitation because he says he is going to his nephew's, but this version ends at the Cratchits.

Narrator-carolers introduce this musical version of Charles Dickens' *A Christmas Carol*. The cast, which includes opera singers and pop singers of the day as well as actors, does ample justice to the many songs which follow the traditional plot. There is also a toy ballet, and a piano "Concerto Inferno" played by composer Spielman in the cemetery scene. The production is an embarrassment of riches, perhaps too much for one show, with added scenes, characters and (especially) dance numbers.

Basil Rathbone had played Marley's ghost in the 1954 *Christmas Carol*. Songwriters Spielman and Torre worked as a team to write many songs for films. This show was later redone as a 60-minute animated feature (see separate entry) which is available on video.

Reviews: *Variety* (Dec. 26, 1956): "Any resemblance ... to *A Christmas Carol* is purely coincidental.... Too many stars ... came out like Ed Sullivan show with Christmas plot. Torres' story was sketchy and unmoving and lyrics seldom helped. ... Melodious."

New York Times (Jack Gould, Dec. 24, 1956): "Sought to interpolate modernistic songs and dances within the framework of the classic. To make room for these elaborations much of the Dickens narrative had to be sacrificed." Here and there, said Gould, the music "had body," but he found it lacking in originality, not to mention "tenderness or feeling."

202. The Stingiest Man in Town

60 minutes. Animated Musical. Broadcast December 23, 1978 (Saturday, 8:00–9:00 P.M.) NBC

Producers/Directors Arthur Rankin, Jr., Jules Bass; *Writers* Romeo Muller, Janice Torre; *Lyricist* Janice Torre; *Composer* Fred Spielman; *Conductor/Arranger* Bernard Hoffer; *Animation Coordinator* Toru Hara; *Design* Paul Coker, Jr.; *Vocal Arrangements* Jerry Raff; *Video* Warner Home Video; *Music* Warner Bros. (Score).

Cast (voices): Tom Bosley (narrator), Walter Matthau, Theodore Bikel, Robert Morse, Dennis Day, Paul Frees, Charles Matthau, Eric Hines, Steffanie Calli, Darlene Conley, Debra Clinger, Robert Rolofson

Songs: "A Christmas Carol," "It Might Have Been," "An Old Fashioned Christmas," "The Christmas Spirit," "Humbug," "Yes, There Is a Santa Claus," "The Stingiest Man in Town," "One Little Boy," "I Wear a Chain," "Birthday Party of the King," "Golden Dreams," "Mankind Should Be My Business."

Story: As carolers sing, B. A. H. Humbug, Esq., introduces Scrooge. In his office, Scrooge bawls out Bob Cratchit, then grumbles at his cheerful nephew come to wish him a Merry Christmas. At home in bed, Scrooge is visited by the ghost of his former partner, Jacob Marley, who announces that Scrooge will be visited by three spirits. The Ghost of Christmas-Past takes him to Fezziwig's, where he sees his old love Belle, and once again hears her break off their engagement. The Ghost of Christmas-Present causes the toys to dance around Scrooge, takes Scrooge to the Cratchit home, then to his nephew's house. The Ghost of Christmas-Yet-to-Come shows him the ragpickers with his goods, and his tombstone. Scrooge realizes the error of his ways, and in the morning is a new man. He has a turkey sent to the Cratchits, buys presents for the Cratchits and his nephew, and enjoys Christmas with both. The next day he catches Cratchit coming in late and gives him a raise, goes about helping others with his generosity and spends time with Tiny Tim.

This is a shorter, animated version of the show that had been broadcast in 1956. With an entirely different cast, the songs are retained, and well sung. B. A. H. Humbug is a small winged bug who narrates the tale.

Reviews: *VideoHound*: "Dickens tale inspires celebrity voices to break into frequent musical numbers."

Variety (Dec. 27, 1978): "Songs were functional and satisfactory ... the animation slick and effective."

203. *The Story of Rudolph the Red-Nosed Reindeer*   60 minutes. Animated Musical. *General Electric Fantasy Hour*. Broadcast December 6, 1964 (Sunday, 5:30–6:30 P.M.) NBC

Producers/Directors Arthur Rankin, Jr., Jules Bass; *Director* Larry Roemer; *Associate Director* Kizo Nagashima; *Writer* Romeo Muller; *Lyricist/Composer* Johnny

Marks; *Conductor* Maury Laws; *Records* Decca, MCA; *Video* Viacom; *Sheet Music* St. Nicholas Music (vocal selections and songs).

Cast (voices): Burl Ives (narrator), Billy Richards, Paul Soles, Larry Mann, Stan Francis, Janis Orenstein, Corine Conley, Peg Dixon, Paul Kligman, Alfie Scopp, Carl Banas

Songs: "Rudolph, the Red Nosed-Reindeer," "Jingle, Jingle, Jingle," "There's Always Tomorrow," "Silver and Gold," "We Are Santa's Elves," "Most Wonderful Day of the Year," "Fame and Fortune," "A Holly, Jolly Christmas."

Story: Rudolph, born with a shiny nose, is teased by the other reindeer and grows up feeling like a misfit. Hermy, one of Santa's elves, really wants to be a dentist. Rudolph and Hermy run away, encounter the Abominable Snowmonster, and are rescued by prospector Yukon Cornelius. They visit the Island of Lost Toys, but cannot stay. Rudolph and Hermy return to Christmasville and find that Rudolph's parents have gone to look for him. Rudolph and Hermy search and find the parents have been captured by the monster. Cornelius reappears and hatches a scheme where he stuns the monster and Hermy pulls its teeth. Thus tamed, the monster lets his prisoners go free. They return to Christmasville only to find there may be no Christmas because of a bad storm. Santa realizes Rudolph can light the way, and Christmas is saved. Hermy gets to be a dentist, and the monster comes to help the elves.

The story of Rudolph was written in 1939 (in rhyme) by Montgomery Ward employee Robert L. May as a Christmas giveaway for the company. Johnny Marks wrote the song in 1949, and Gene Autry's recording was a best seller; many others recorded the song.

Ad for the first broadcast of *The Story of Rudolph the Red-Nosed Reindeer*. Reproduced by permission of the General Electric Company.

Johnny Marks specialized in writing Christmas songs, and many of his other songs are used as background music in this feature. An earlier cartoon version of *Rudolph* was made by Max Fleischer in 1944.

Rudolph, the Red-Nosed Reindeer is the longest consecutively aired special, having been shown every year since its 1964 introduction. The show was the first to use "Animagic," the stop-motion photography of three-dimensional figures used in most subsequent Rankin-Bass specials. This show took a year to make and cost $500,000.

Review: *Variety* (Dec. 9, 1964): "Johnny Marks wrapped a confection of new tunes and lyrics. The hour came off winningly, full of charm, occasional wit, and tunes which caught the spirit of the piece."

204. *Stover at Yale* 90 minutes. Musical. *Omnibus*. Broadcast October 20, 1957 (Sunday, 4:00–5:30 P.M.) NBC

Producer Robert Saudek; *Director* Richard Dunlap; *Writer* Douglas Wallop; *Choreographer* John Butler; *Drama Consultant* Walter Kerr; *Orchestrator* Phillip Lang.

Cast: Bradford Dillman, Peter Benzoni, Wayne Maxwell, Wynn Pearce, Larry Hagman, Jim Congdon, Rory Harrity, Berkeley Harris, Jim Costigan, Isabelle Hoopes, Ted Patterson, Bob Manders, Wallace Rooney, Evans Evans, Richard Striker, Suzanne Storrs

Story: Around the turn of the century, Dink Stover, a graduate of Lawrenceville Prep School, looks forward to his years at Yale: knowing the right people, joining the preferred organizations, becoming a campus leader. Naive but eager, he makes friends and receives advice from upper classmen. Only later does he begin to find out that he can learn much from others who come from different backgrounds and more worldly experiences. He becomes interested in the world of ideas and matures into a fine young man. Along the way, he participates in a movement to overthrow the secret societies and run the campus democratically. His classmates include a young maverick working his way through school, a campus reformer and a snob. Aside from their campus activ-

ities, the boys make the rounds of Mory's and lesser saloons, dance the turkey trot, ragtime and jagtime, and fool around with the naughty dancing girls. Dink does his share of carousing, but learns to control his impulses, also part of growing up, and meets a lovely young woman who gives him incentive to follow his heart.

From the novel by Owen Johnson, published in 1911. Actor Bradford Dillman was a Yale graduate; director/writer Wallop wrote the novel *The Year the Yankees Lost the Pennant*.

Little information was available about the music in this show. Actor Dillman remembers this as more of a drama with music, and it appears musical numbers include dancing girls and old Yale standards. Nevertheless, since two of the reviews refer to the show as a musical, and in recognition of the highly varied and unusual works of *Omnibus*, this show is included here.

Reviews: *Time* (Nov. 4, 1957): "A tongue-in-dimpled cheek musical adaptation. ... Much of the play lived up to Alastair Cooke's introduction of it as a 'gentle thing both odd and funny' which sometimes came to life."

Variety (Oct. 23, 1957): "A thoroughly enjoyable period piece ... Dillman was the perfect Stover.... Butler's period choreography was delightful and the college music was perfectly orchestrated and executed in the old rah-rah style."

New York Times (Jack Gould, Oct. 27, 1957): "Was done in a stilted, old-fashioned way of the Nineteen Hundreds. Caught the flavor of the period as well as the spirit of the campus.... As a whole the experiment had a sustained attractiveness."

Newsweek (Nov. 4, 1957): "*Omnibus* returned for its sixth season with a musical version of Stover at Yale. ... An offbeat mixture of sense and nonsense, scholarship and sentimentality."

205. *Strawberry Blonde* 60 minutes. Musical. Broadcast October 18, 1959 (Sunday, 10:00–11:00 P.M.) NBC

Producer David Susskind; *Director* William Corrigan; *Writer* George Baxter.

Cast: Janet Blair, David Wayne, Eddie Bracken, Dolores Dorn-Heft, Iggie Wolfington

Songs: Not found

Story: A small-town dentist is framed and sent to jail by an ambitious contractor, who also steals the dentist's girl. The dentist plots his revenge when the contractor needs emergency dental work.

Sources list this show as a musical adaptation of the Broadway play *One Sunday Afternoon* by James Hagan. However, there was a 1933 movie, *One Sunday Afternoon*, a 1941 movie, *The Strawberry Blonde* and a 1948 musical film, *One Sunday Afternoon*. The story had also been done as a TV drama at least five times. One wonders whether the original play or one of the many adaptations was used. Further, since no information about the songs/music was found, this may have been borrowed from the musical film or from other sources. In any event, this appears to have been one time too many.

Review: *Variety* (Oct. 21, 1959): "Overworked ... same story as '41 movie. ... Slight story, good music."

206. *Svengali and the Blonde* 90 minutes. Musical. Broadcast July 30, 1955 (Saturday, 9:00–10:30 P.M.) NBC

Producer/Director Alan Handley; *Lyricists/Composers* Alan Handley, Charles Gaynor; *Music Director* Vic Schoen; *Choreographer* Tony Charmoli; *Set Designer* Ed Stephenson; *Costume Designer* Grady Hunt.

Cast: Ethel Barrymore (narrator), Carol Channing, Basil Rathbone, Russell Arms, William Meigs, Franklin Pangborn, Nancy Kulp, Mitzi McCall, Edit Angold, Charlotte Knight, Hal Smith, Bea Benadaret, Harry Varteresian, Jack Nestle, Alice Armbruster

Songs: "Vive La Vie," "Disenchanted Blues," "The Last Rose of Summer," "Le Fiacre," "Marie," "Hypnotism Ballet," "I Looked at Love," "Scarf Dance."

Story: Trilby O'Ferrall, a Parisian artist's model, is loved by three artists, but becomes engaged to Billee. A mysterious Austrian musician who calls himself Svengali lures Trilby away, hypnotizes her and keeps her under his spell. He teaches her to sing and the couple tour Europe with Trilby giving concerts and gaining fame. When she performs in Paris the artists attend and recognize their old friend. Svengali has a heart attack and dies; Trilby cannot sing once the spell is broken, but Billee and Trilby are reunited and spend their lives happily together.

Based on George Du Maurier's novel *Trilby* (1894), this show attempted to spoof the classic and much-done story.

Reviews: *Variety* (Aug. 3, 1955): According to *Variety's* reviewer, this show was "on its way to becoming one of the most satisfying musicals written for television" until "someone remembered there was a story," which evidently deflated the show's "buoyant spirit of sophisticated buffoonery." The reviewer called the songs "interesting" and praised the dances. In all, it was "fun when they let themselves go."

New York Times (Jack Gould, Aug. 1, 1955): "Too much pedestrian book, too many conventional TV production numbers. Played too much as a love story, not enough for laughs. Only Miss Barrymore was tongue-in-cheek."

207. *The Swing*   15 minutes. Opera. *The Home Show.* Broadcast June 11, 1956 (Monday) NBC

Producer Lewis Ames; *Director* Garth Dietrick; *Librettist/Composer* Leonard Kastle.

Cast: Norman Atkins, Edith Gordon, Marguerite Lewis

Story: A very simple show, with two singing roles, one speaking role, and a single set. A young bride-to-be sits in the swing in her family's garden, both happy and sad. Her father pushes her in the swing for the last time, reminiscing about her childhood, and calms her fears by telling her he loves her, her mother loves her and everyone wishes her well. Her mother arrives and they all leave happily for the wedding.

An unusual feature of the *Home* show, this opera was commissioned for a program with a June bride theme. Twenty-six-year-old composer Leonard Kastle provided the piano accompaniment. Arlene Francis hosted the show. *The Home Show* was called a "woman's magazine of the air."

Review: *New York Times* (June 12, 1956): "The music is tuneful ... everything flows easily ... with a charmingly rhymed text. ... All just a touch too pretty, like an Easter greeting ... impersonal and unreal."

208. *Tell Me on a Sunday*   60 minutes. Musical. Broadcast: April 16, 1980 (Wednesday, 8:00–9:00 P.M.) Metromedia

Musical Director Harry Rabinowitz; *Lyricist* Don Black; *Composer* Andrew

Lloyd Webber; *Record* LP Polydor POLD 5031 and see below; *Video* See below; *Music* Hal Leonard (Vocal Selections).

Cast: Marti Webb

Songs: "Take That Look Off Your Face," "Let Me Finish," "It's Not the End of the World," "Letter Home to England," "Sheldon Bloom," "Capped Teeth and Caesar Salad," "You Made Me Think You Were in Love," "Second Letter Home," "Come Back with the Same Look in Your Eyes," "Let's Talk About You," "Tell Me on a Sunday," "I'm Very You, You're Very Me," "Nothing Like You've Ever Known."

Story: A young English girl living in New York City recounts her bittersweet love affairs through song.

This one-woman concert was written for television by Andrew Lloyd Webber and Don Black, and was shown first in the United Kingdom. It was later produced on the London stage as *Song and Dance* (with dance added) in 1982, and with revised book and lyrics by Don Black and Richard Maltby, *Song and Dance* opened on Broadway in 1985. There is a British video of *Song and Dance* with Sarah Brightman, and an LP/CD/Cass of the New York *Song and Dance* with Bernadette Peters. Marti Webb, who starred in this show, was then playing the lead in *Evita* in London.

Review: *New York Times* (Tom Buckley, April 16, 1980): "In many respects praiseworthy.... The direction, cinematography, set design, lighting and sound are work of a standard seldom attained or even aspired to in this country."

209. *That's Life*   60 minutes. Musical/Comedy Series. Broadcast Septem-

Robert Morse and E. J. Peaker are the young lovers starring in the musical series *That's Life* (1968–1969). Photofest.

ber 24, 1968 to May 20, 1969 (Tuesday, 10:00–11:00 P.M.) ABC

Executive Producer Marvin Marx; *Director* Stan Harris; *Musical Director* Elliot Lawrence; *Choreographer* Tony Mordente.

Cast: Robert Morse, E. J. Peaker, Shelley Berman, Kay Medford, Tony Mordente Dancers

Story: The weekly episodes of this series follow a young couple from their first meeting through courtship, marriage, buying a house, having a baby and further adventures of married life in the town of Ridgeville. There were half a dozen songs in each episode.

This is one of only two tries at musical series documented herein. (The other is *Cop Rock*.) While many show songs relating to the week's theme were used (often sung by guest stars), there also appear to be some new songs centered around the themes. In any event,

this one lasted a whole season, and was lively musical fun. Robert Morse had played the lead in the original Broadway production of *How to Succeed in Business Without Really Trying*.

Review: *Women's Wear Daily* (Rex Reed, Oct. 4, 1968): "A Broadway musical every Tuesday night at least tries to be fresh and original…. A pleasant way to kill an hour."

210. *The Thief and the Hangman*
30 minutes. Opera. *Directions '62.* Broadcast October 15, 1961 (Sunday) ABC

Executive Producer (series) Sid Darion; *Production (series)* Wiler Hance; *Librettist* Morton Wishengrad; *Composer* Abraham Ellstein; *Conductor* Sylvan Levan.

Cast: Frank Poretta, Norman Atkins, Rosalind Elias, Ralph Herbert, John Macurdy, Robert Trehy, Elaine Bonazzi, Mark Chalat

Story: A thief who stole because he was hungry and who has been convicted asks to plant the seed of the Tree of Life. But he finds no one, especially those who judge and execute him, has clean hands.

Reviews: *Musical America* (Wriston Locklair, Dec. 1961): "Mr. Ellstein's vocal writing is uncomplicated…. But the music, over all, was not sufficiently dramatic to underline the seriousness of the opera's subject matter."

Opera News (Dec. 23, 1961): "Began disastrously when the audio signal evaporated. … Turned out to be an ion-plated [sic] bore due to an inadequate libretto. … A sociological allegory in a traditional medieval morality play plot. … Raucous shrieking orchestration…."

New York Times (Oct. 16, 1961): Critic Eric Salzman said this opera deserved respect as a "serious and ambitious" work for television but concluded that good intentions could not transform "a well-intentioned musical morality play into a work of art." He called the libretto "a strange mixture of a Biblical parable, Kafka, *Alice in Wonderland* and Walter Mitty" and the music "a basically post–Puccini score with added measures of dissonance and modernity."

All reviewers highly praised Frank Poretta's acting and singing.

211. *Think Pretty*   60 minutes. Musical. *Bob Hope Presents The Chrysler Theatre.* Broadcast October 2, 1964 (Friday, 8:30–9:30 P.M.) NBC

Producer Richard Lewis; *Director* Jack Arnold; *Writers* Garry Marshall, Jerry Belson.

Cast: Fred Astaire, Reta Shaw, Louis Nye, Barrie Chase, Jean Hersholt, Roger Perry, Linda Foster, Edward Mallory, Eddie Ryder, Jack Bernardi

Songs: "Think Pretty," "Watusi Dance."

Story: A former dancer and record company owner, Fred Adams, is trying to sign comedian Mickey Marshall as a client, but a rival company owner wants to sign up the same comedian.

Listed as a "musical comedy," this show was apparently an excuse for Fred Astaire and Barrie Chase to dance again, but it was not as well received as the earlier (1958 and 1959) *Evening with Fred Astaire* specials, which were done as variety shows.

Review: *New York Times* (Jack Gould): "A long hour of ridiculous sitcom. Hopelessly intricate and pedestrian story about an absurd adventure in the record business."

212. *The Thirteen Clocks*   60 minutes. Musical. *Motorola TV Hour.* Broadcast December 29, 1953 (Tuesday, 9:30–10:30 P.M.) ABC

Producer Herbert Brodkin; *Directors* Donald Richardson, Ralph Nelson; *Writers* Fred Sadoff, John Crilly; *Lyricists* Mark Bucci, James Thurber; *Composer* Mark Bucci; *Costumes* Al Lehman; *Settings* Fred Stover.

Cast: Basil Rathbone, John Raitt, Sir Cedric Hardwicke, Roberta Peters, Russell Nype, Alice Pearce

Story: In a gloomy castle lives an evil duke who takes great delight in thinking up fiendish deeds to amuse himself. He is always cold, and has even frozen the hands of all the clocks in the castle. The natives say, "Time lies frozen there." With him lives his lovely niece, Princess Saralinda, who is sweet and warm. Many princes have tried to earn her hand, but the duke devised impossible feats, and slew them when they failed, if they hadn't already disappeared. Young Prince Zorn of Zorna, disguised as a minstrel, comes to town and hears about the beautiful princess. The natives tell him horror stories about the duke and what he has done to previous suitors, but prince Zorn is determined to win the princess. With the help of an addle-headed Golux, the minstrel gets taken to the castle, but the duke has spies and knows who he really is. The prince, through various tricks and with the help of his friend, meets the duke's challenges and wins the princess who was previously enchanted. They leave happily together, while the duke gets his comeuppance at the hands of the Todal. The clocks are restarted and time moves forward again.

Based on the book of the same name by James Thurber, which was published in 1944, this early holiday show was one of the most favorably received musicals.

Reviews: *Time* (Jan. 11, 1954): "Seldom have characters leaped as brilliantly from the printed page to TV life." The reviewer praised Basil Rathbone in the role of the duke (he "hammed magnificently"); Roberta Peters as the princess ("appealing visually and vocally"); John Raitt as Prince Charming; and Sir Cedric Hardwicke as the Golux. ... Donald Richardson directed this "fragile nonsense" with a hand "both light and steady... with an air of intelligent good humor."

Billboard (June Bundy, Jan. 9, 1954): "Raitt and Miss Peters were defeated by a rather dull musical score, but Rathbone and Hardwicke were perfect in their roles. ...Costumes and sets were strikingly right."

New York Times (Jack Gould, Jan. 3, 1954): "A complete and joyous delight, a romp in nonsense that was staged with both spirit and appreciation. ...The performance of Sir Cedric Hardwicke as the Golux was simply superb. ... It was enchanting fun for the holiday season."

213. Three for the Girls 90 minutes. Drama/Musical. *Carroll O'Connor Special.* Broadcast November 5, 1973 (Monday, 9:30–11:00 P.M.) CBS

Producer Robert H. Precht; *Directors* Bob La Hedro, Ron Field; *Writers* Fred Ebb, John Kander; *Lyricist* Fred Ebb; *Composer* John Kander.

Cast: Carroll O'Connor, Barbara Sharma, Nancy Walker, T. J. Sullivan

Songs: "Clothes Make the Girl," "Step by Step," "It's a Man's World," "In the Same Boat."

Story: A man from a small town is shocked to see his daughter acting in an off–Broadway nudie show. This segment includes musical dream montages of show girls, sailors and mermaids.

This mini-musical is part of a trio of plays starring O'Connor as father, son and husband. The cast, credits and story above relate only to the musical segment, titled "Clothes Make the Girl."

Review: *New York Times* (Howard Thompson, Nov. 5, 1973): "Some intelligent planning and taste have gone into the *Carroll O'Connor Special.* Fred Ebb's lines are often genuinely amusing."

214. The Tiny Tree 30 minutes. Animated Musical. Broadcast December 14, 1975 (Sunday, 7:30–8:00 P.M.) NBC

Executive Producers David H. De Patie, Friz Freleng; *Producer/Director* Chuck Couch; *Writers* Chuck Couch, Bob Ogle, Lewis Marshall; *Lyricist/Composer* Johnny Marks; *Musical Director* Dean Elliott.

Cast (voices): Buddy Ebsen (narrator),

Allan Melvin, Paul Winchell, Janet Waldo, Stephen Manley, Frank Welker. Vocalist: Roberta Flack

Songs: "The Tiny Tree," "When Autumn Comes," "To Love and Be Loved," "Tell It to a Turtle," "ACaroling We Go."

Story: A crippled farm girl is friends with the animals in the meadow, and they rescue her when she falls out of her wheelchair. Later, when a winter blizzard threatens to keep the girl's father from getting home for Christmas, the little tree decides to become a Christmas tree, and the animals move the tree to the girl's window and decorate it, cheering the girl.

Review: *Variety* (Dec. 17, 1975): "Strictly for tots. Bland story ... bumbled along rather coyly, its only distinction being two fine songs."

215. *Tippy Top* 30 minutes. Musical. *General Electric Theater.* Broadcast December 17, 1961 (Sunday, 9:00–9:30 P.M.) CBS

Director Sherman Marks; *Writers* Sidney Michaels, Mark Sandrich; *Songs* Sidney Michaels, Mark Sandrich.

Cast: Red Buttons, Ronny Howard, Joan O'Brien, Frank Aletter

Songs: "Tippy Top," "Isn't It Nice?," "What Do You Suppose?," "You Can't Run Away from a Problem," "When We're Created."

Story: A fatherless boy would be lonely except for his grown-up friend Tippy Top; he gets upset when told his friend is imaginary.
   Little Ronny Howard had only recently debuted as "Opie" on *The Andy Griffith Show,* and was the right age for a fantasy tale of this type.

216. *Tom Sawyer* 60 minutes. Musical. *U. S. Steel Hour.* Broadcast November 21, 1956 (Wednesday, 10:00–11:00 P.M.) CBS

Writer/Lyricist/Composer Frank Luther; *Conductor* Ralph Norman Wilkinson; *Record* LP Decca 8432.

Cast: John Sharpe, Jimmy Boyd, Ross Bampton, Clarence Cooper, Bennye Gatteys, The Song Spinners

Songs: "In the Spring," "You Can't Teach an Old Dog New Tricks," "My Friend Huckleberry Finn," "I Gotta Whitewash the Fence," "The Big Missouri," "That Lucky Boy Is Me," "There's a New Girl in Town," "Why Would You Want to Kiss Me?," "Girls Can't Lie," "What Do You Kiss For?," "That's the Life for Me," "My Love Has Gone Away," "He Wasn't a Bad Boy," "Aunt Polly's Prayer," "Storm Come A'Risin'," "I Want to Go Home," "The Time Has Come to Say Goodbye," "We'll All Shout Together in the Mornin'," "It Ain't fer Me," "Please Make Up," "McDougal's Cave," "Have a Happy Holiday."

Story: A series of adventures in the life of Tom Sawyer include a schoolroom scene where, despite having fought with Becky earlier, Tom confesses to tearing a page in the teacher's anatomy book and takes the punishment to save Becky (which naturally brings about their reconciliation); Tom whitewashing the fence as punishment for his truancy, where he cons his friends into doing most of the work; Tom and Huck witnessing their own funeral after running off to play pirates and being thought dead; Tom testifying in the trial of Muff Potter that Injun Joe did the crime; and Tom and Becky's scary time in the caves, where they get lost from the others and cannot find their way out for several days and Tom once encounters Injun Joe.

Based on the Mark Twain novel of 1876, this show was carried along by the narrative ballads, dance numbers and an incredible number of songs. Jimmy Boyd who played Huck in this show also starred in the later production of *Huck Finn.*

Review: *Variety* (Nov. 28, 1956): "A captivating musical stanza.... The main credit goes to Frank Luther whose adaptation succeeded in evoking the essential Americana qualities of the novel."

217. *The Trial at Rouen*   90 minutes. Opera. *NBC Opera Theater.* Broadcast April 8, 1956 (Sunday, 4:00–5:30 P.M.) NBC

Producer Samuel Chotzinoff; *Director* Kirk Browning; *Librettist/Composer* Norman Dello Joio; *Musical Director* Peter Herman Adler; *Sets* Trew Hocker; *Costumes* Noel Taylor.

Cast: Elaine Malbin, Hugh Thompson, Chester Watson, Paul Ukena, R. W. Barry, Francis Monachino, James Norbert, David Smith, William Wolff, Marvin Worden, Leon Driscoll, Carole O'Hara, Francis Paige

Story: This two-act opera centers around Joan of Arc's trial and her personal struggles. Friar Julien is partial to Joan and urges her to submit to the authority of the church; Bishop Cauchon wants to destroy her. In her cell, Joan weighs her options. During the trial Joan reviews her military achievements, is condemned to die, and is ultimately burned at the stake. The opera has a triple chorus: inquisitors, populace and heavenly voices.

Composer Dello Joio wrote his opera *The Triumph of St. Joan* in 1950, but was not satisfied with his work and withdrew the earlier opera. This version is entirely different in text and music.

Reviews: *Variety* (April 11, 1956): The reviewer complained that oversimplification of the story and elimination of characters resulted in a "single-dimension Joan who is torn and tense." Nevertheless the reviewer found much to praise, writing that the music "carries intense fire ... has depth and some coloration." He called Elaine Malbin "ideal" and said that except for the flawed conception of the main character, "all concerned are worthy of tremendous kudos."

New York Times (Howard Taubman, April 9, 1956): "A brilliant performance. ... The simple allusive sets ... were a strong dramatic factor, and Kirk Browning's direction had the fluidity of a musical score."

Musical America (April 1956): "[Elaine Malbin] made the character of Joan come vividly and sympathetically to life."

Time (April 16, 1956): "A 75-minute work of massive and somber effect, full of vocal know-how and modern coloration, but weak in dramatic contrast. ... One of the composer's finest works." The reviewer praised Elaine Malbin both as a singer and as "an actress of imposing ability."

218. *The Trial of Mary Lincoln*   60 minutes. Opera. *NET Opera Theater.* Broadcast February 14, 1972 (Monday, 8:00–9:00 P.M.) PBS

Producer Peter Herman Adler; *Director* Kirk Browning; *Librettist* Anne Howard Bailey; *Composer* Thomas Pasatieri; *Music Director* Peter Herman Adler.

Cast: Elaine Bonazzi, Wayne Turnage, Chester Watson, Louise Parker, Carole Bogarde, Mark Howard, Lizabeth

Pritchett, Julian Patrick, Alan Titus, Robert Owen Jones, Fred Stuthman

Story: In 1875 Mary Todd Lincoln, widow of President Abraham Lincoln, is on trial. Brought to court by her son on charges of insanity, she conjures up the past as she recalls it. Being a Southerner, she saw events of the Civil War through her own perspective, and recalls with her own unique vision events which have now become parts of a tragic whole. The President's voice is heard offstage.

Reviews: *Musical America* (April 1972): Critic Patrick J. Smith felt that this opera succeeded as a television production at least partly on the strength of the libretto; he praised Bailey's structure as "canny and effective." Smith was less impressed with the music: "[It] keeps the drama moving ahead, but contains little of real interest. The idiom is conservative but not very melodious." He praised Elaine Bonazzi for an "incisive and moving portrayal of a strong-minded woman."

Saturday Review (March 4, 1972): Like *Musical America*'s Smith, reviewer Irving Kolodin found much to admire in the "dramatic interest of the text," but he also praised the composer: "It is a mark of exceptional talent that Pasatieri is able to sustain a largely intellectual discussion for nearly an hour. ... Pasatieri brings together a variety of compositional elements to result in an outcome distinctly his own."

219. *Trouble in Tahiti*   60 minutes. Opera. Broadcast November 16, 1952 (Sunday, 3:00–4:00 P.M.) NBC

Librettist/Composer Leonard Bernstein; *Record* LP Polydor 827845 (also CD, Cassette); *Music* Amsterdam Enterprises (Vocal Selections).

Cast: Beverly Wolff, David Atkinson, Miriam Workman, Earl Rogers, Robert Bollinger

Story: One day in the life of a typical American suburban couple. Sam and Dinah bicker at breakfast. Sam goes to work, then to his gym, while Dinah visits her psychiatrist, then goes to see a movie called *Trouble in Tahiti*. The couple quarrel again at dinner, but decide to go together to see *Trouble in Tahiti*.

This opera had premiered earlier in the year, but received its first professional production on television. The opera had a short Broadway run in 1955 as part of a triple-play *All in One*. In the 1980s Bernstein and his colleagues developed a sequel called *A Quiet Place* to explain what happened to the family afterwards. Portions of *Trouble in Tahiti* were inserted as flashbacks in the second act.

While the score does not list individual songs, the following numbers have been identified as being from this show: "I Was Standing in a Garden," "What a Movie!", "A Quiet Place" and Island Magic."

Review: *Musical America* (James Lyons, Dec. 1, 1952): "As an opera it is at best a slender offering, but as an adventure, as a viscera-visual experience and as an expedition into the terra incognito of the TV medium, it is a rewarding sample."

Other critics recognized Bernstein's music as "ingenious," "inventive," "clever" and "skillful," but had some reservations about the storyline.

220. *'Twas the Night Before Christmas*   30 minutes. Animated Musical. Broadcast December 8, 1974 (Sunday, 8:00–8:30 P.M.) CBS

Producers/Directors Arthur Rankin, Jr., Jules Bass; *Writer* Jerome Coopersmith;

Lyricist Jules Bass; *Composer* Maury Laws.

Cast (voices): Joel Grey (narrator), Tammy Grimes, John McGiver, George Gobel, Patricia Bright, Scott Firestone, Robert McFadden, Allen Swift, Christine Winter, The Wee Winter Singers

Songs: "Even a Miracle Needs a Hand," "Give Your Heart a Try," "Silent Night," "'Twas the Night Before Christmas," "Christmas Chimes."

Story: The story of the Trundle family, living above their clock shop, and a mouse family living down below. All is not well this Christmas Eve; Santa has canceled his trip because of an anonymous letter in the newspaper saying he is a phony. Misunderstandings are resolved and the families settle down to await Santa, then celebrate his visit.

This frequently shown Christmas special is loosely based on Clement Moore's Christmas poem.

221. *Uncle Sam Magoo* 60 minutes. Animated Musical. Broadcast February 15, 1970 (Sunday, 6:30–7:30 P.M.) NBC

Executive Producer Henry G. Saperstein; *Producer* Lee Orgel; *Director* Abe Levitow; *Writer* Larry Markes; *Music Director/Arranger* Walter Scharf; *Choral Director/Additional Lyrics* Eliot Daniel; *Video* Paramount Home Video.

Cast (voices): Jim Backus, Lennie Weinrib, Barney Phillips, Bob Holt, Dave Shelley, Patti Gilbert, John Himes, Bill Clayton, Sid Grossfeld, Sam Rosen

Songs: "The Magic of Hollywood," "Johnny Appleseed" (to the tune of "Blue Tailed Fly"), "Inventions."

A large number of traditional folk songs were used, many with additional verses or new words. Some of these were "Yankee Doodle Dandy," "Sailing, Sailing," "Blow the Man Down," "We Gather Together," "My Sally Ann," "The Star Spangled Banner," "Red River Valley," "Let My People Go," "Battle Hymn of the Republic," "Dixie," "She Wore a Yellow Ribbon," "When Johnny Comes Marching Home," "Sound Off," "Home on the Range," "I've Been Working on the Railroad," "Shenandoah," "Camptown Races," "Oh Susannah," "Clementine," and "America the Beautiful."

Story: Mr. Magoo heads for the UPA studios and bumbles into a costume room, where he dons the Uncle Sam costume. He then wanders through American history where he encounters great men, legends and heroes, and visits significant events and places.

The film used a variety of graphic styles and some live photography. The lively music score was cited as an asset.

Reviews: *Variety* (Feb. 18, 1970): "A nicely written hour, with oodles of traditional songs, it played off as very pleasant fare.... A tastefully strong meshing of song and storyline continuity."

VideoHound: "Mr. Magoo provides a history lesson in his own unmatchable style."

222. *A Waltz Dream* 30 minutes. Musical. *Nash Airflyte Theater*. Broadcast January 4, 1951 (Thursday, 10:30–11:00 P.M.) CBS

Cast: Kitty Carlisle, Jimmy Carroll, Marcia Van Dyke

Sounds like a musical, but no details could be found.

223. *What Day Is It?* 30 minutes. Musical. *Screen Directors' Playhouse*. Broadcast June 6, 1956 (Wednesday, 8:00–8:30 P.M.) NBC

Director Gower Champion; *Writer* Jean Holloway; *Songs* Jeff Barley, Jack Latimer; *Music Director* Leon Klotzkin; *Arrangers* Walter Sheets, Russ Garcia.

Cast: Marge & Gower Champion, Bob Dixon, Pinky Jackson, Cheeta & Chico (chimps)

Songs: "Yankee Doodle Boy," "Mary's a Grand Old Name," "When You're a Clown."

Story: A married nightclub dance team are bickering backstage. The wife is planning a celebration, but the husband can't remember important dates, so he doesn't know what the celebration is for. The day turns out to be his birthday, and they kiss and make up.

Review: *Daily Variety* (June 8, 1956): "Three song and dance numbers are interspersed to best effect. Two, based on [George M.] Cohan standards, are ably used to take neatly satirical digs at prosaic nitery presentations. The third … is a wonderful airy bit of nonsense and the highpoint of the half hour."

224. *Who's Afraid of Mother Goose?* 60 minutes. Musical. *Off to See the Wizard.* Broadcast October 13, 1967 (Friday, 7:30–8:30 P.M.) ABC

Executive Producer Hubbell Robinson; *Writer/Producer* Frank Peppiatt; *Directors* Bill Davis, Peter Gennaro; *Lyricist* Ruth Batchelor; *Composer* Sherman Edwards; *Choreographer* Peter Gennaro.

Cast: Maureen O'Hara, Peter Gennaro, Nancy Sinatra, Frankie Avalon, Fred Clark, Margaret Hamilton, Dick Martin, Dan Rowan, Dick Shawn, Joanie Sommers, Stuart Getz, Scooter Jolley

Songs: "Jack Be Nimble," "Put a Penny By," "After the Fall," "Lovenberry Tree."

Story: Schoolboard head William H. Berry wants to ban Mother Goose from the schools; he says all the characters are losers and set a bad example to children. Mother Goose turns him into a young boy and takes him to visit her family, including Jack and Jill, Simple Simon, Old King Cole, Mother Hubbard, Little Bo Peep and others, and convinces him her stories are not a bad influence.

ABC's *Off to See the Wizard* series was a melange of films and nature documentaries; only this show was an original musical.

Review: *Variety* (Oct. 18, 1967): "It was either an unimaginative idea done blandly or a bland idea done unimaginatively…intended to be fanciful but only silly. The original score and lyrics were undistinguished."

225. *Who's Earnest?* 60 minutes. Musical. *U.S. Steel Hour.* Broadcast October 9, 1957 (Wednesday, 10:00–11:00 P.M.) CBS

Director David Alexander; *Writer/Lyricist* Anne Croswell; *Composer* Lee Pockriss; *Conductor* Ralph Norman Wilkinson; *Record* See below; *Sheet Music* Edwin H. Morris.

Cast: Edward Mulhare, Dorothy Collins, Martyn Green

Songs: "Mr. Bunbury," "Metaphorically Speaking," "Perfection," "Lost," "My Eternal Devotion," "My Very First Impression," "A Wicked Man."

Story: This is a comedy of manners, in which young Jack Worthing and his friend Algernon Moncrieff are both posing as "Ernest" for different reasons. Jack proposes to Gwendolen Fairfax, Algernon to Cecily Cardew. Both girls love the name "Ernest" and so do not wish to hear the boys' true names.

Gwendolen's aunt, Lady Bracknell, questions Jack's suitability when she discovers he was a foundling. After many complications, the mystery is resolved when Miss Prism, the nursemaid who left Jack in a handbag at Victoria station, confesses to her misdeed. This connects Jack with an honorable family, and he finds his name is really Ernest. The lovers are united and all ends happily.

Based on Oscar Wilde's play *The Importance of Being Earnest* (1895), this show was expanded by the authors and appeared off–Broadway as *Ernest in Love* in 1960, running for 111 performances. Reviews of the stage show called the music "deft and droll," the book and lyrics "clever," the show "charming." There is an original cast recording of the stage show, Columbia OL5530/OS 2027.

Review: *Variety* (Oct. 16, 1957): "A sprightly score," wrote the reviewer, going on to say that any short comings were largely due to the one-hour running time, which required that the show be reduced to "bare plot and the musical numbers. ... Croswell's sharp and lively lyrics compensated for the Wilde wit left out of the adaptation. Pockriss' tunes were lively and melodic...."

226. The Wind in the Willows 2 hours. Animated Musical. Broadcast July 5, 1987 (Sunday, 7:00–9:00 P.M.) ABC

Producers/Directors Arthur Rankin, Jr., Jules Bass; *Associate Producer* Lee Dannacher; *Director of Animation* Masaki Iizuka; *Writer* Romeo Muller; *Lyricist* Jules Bass; *Composer* Maury Laws; *Video* Family Home Entertainment.

Cast (voices): Charles Nelson Reilly, Roddy McDowall, José Ferrer, Eddie Bracken, Paul Frees, Robert McFad-

den, Jeryl Jagoda, Ron Marshall, Gerry Matthews, Ray Owens, Alice Tweedle

Songs: "Messin' Around in Boats," "We Don't Have Any Pâté De Foie Gras," "I Hate Company," "Benefit of the Doubt," "A Party That Never Ceases," "The Wind in the Willows."

Story: Self-indulgent Mr. Toad wreaks all sorts of havoc piloting his steamboat down the river, disrupting his friends Mole, Ratty and Badger. Then he buys a gypsy caravan and sets out on a trip with his friends until an automobile forces him off the road. Next Mr. Toad buys a Rolls Royce and causes more problems with his erratic driving; finally he is arrested and put in jail. While he is away, wicked animals trash his house. After escaping from prison and a merry chase, Mr. Toad eventually recaptures Toad Hall with the help of his friends.

Based on the 1908 Kenneth Grahame story, this is the first version to present the story in its entirety in full animation.

Review: *TV Guide* (Judith Crist, July 4, 1987): "Offers the pleasures of adventure and song. ... The voices provided are as good as they are familiar. It is beguiling and timeless."

227. The Year Without a Santa Claus 60 minutes. Animated Musical. Broadcast December 10, 1974 (Tuesday, 8:00–9:00 P.M.) ABC

Producers/Directors Arthur Rankin, Jr., Jules Bass; *Writer* William Keenan; *Lyricist* Maury Laws; *Composer* Jules Bass; *Musical Director* Maury Laws; *Video* Lightning Video.

Cast (voices): Shirley Booth (narrator), Mickey Rooney, Dick Shawn, George S. Irving, Robert McFadden,

Bradley Bolke, Rhoda Mann, Ron Marshall, Colin Duffy, Christine Winter, The Wee Winter Singers

Songs: "Year Without a Santa Claus," "Snowmiser," "Anyone Can Be Santa," "Heatmiser," "I Believe in Santa Claus," "Blue Christmas," "It's Gonna Snow," "Here Comes Santa Claus."

Orchestra: "Sleighride"

Story: Santa is tired, has a cold, aches all over and feels miserable. Mrs. Santa calls the doctor who tells Santa to take a vacation and that nobody cares about Christmas any more. Santa announces to his elves that Christmas will be canceled, then takes to his bed. Mrs. Santa thinks about taking his place, but decides to send the elves out to find some Christmas spirit. Elves Jingle and Jangle take Vixen and head for Southtown. Santa hears this and takes off after them. The children there say they don't care about Santa, until Iggy's family says they still believe. Meanwhile, the dog catcher captures Vixen (disguised as a dog). The elves go to see the mayor, who doesn't believe them, but says if they can make it snow in Southtown he will believe. The elves call Mrs. Santa for help, and she takes them to see Heatmiser and Snowmiser. The feuding brothers will not agree, so the party goes to see Mother Nature, who orders the boys to cooperate. Santa takes the ill Vixen back to the North Pole. Southtown gets their snow, and the mayor proclaims the day off to honor Santa. Children around the world are sad hearing that Christmas has been canceled and make gifts for Santa. Santa is convinced that the Christmas spirit still exists, and cheerfully takes off in his sleigh.

Based loosely on Phyllis McGinley's book of the same name. The "Heatmiser" and "Snowmiser" numbers

(sung by George S. Irving and Dick Shawn) were particularly lively, toe-tapping bits.

Review: *VideoHound:* "Really a standout in the children's Christmas parade. Great musical numbers and fun for adults too. Watch for Heatmeiser and Coldmeiser [sic]—pure camp!"

228. *The Young Man from Boston*
60 minutes. Musical. Broadcast July 22, 1965 (Thursday, 10:00–11:00 P.M.) ABC

Producer Allan Jay Friedman; *Writer* Stephen Longstreet; *Lyricist* Paul Francis Webster; *Composer* Allan Jay Friedman; *Research* Jules North; *Sheet Music* Webster Music (1).

Cast: Joseph Cotten (narrator), Gordon MacRae, Kingston Trio, Mormon Tabernacle Choir

Song: "Profile in Courage."

Story: A musical biography of John F. Kennedy, from his ancestry to his death, this program consists of photographs and "never before seen" film clips, with a narrative ballad (sung by the Kingston Trio) describing each stage of Kennedy's public life, and narration filling in the details. Summarizing Kennedy's legacy, Gordon MacRae (backed by the Mormon Tabernacle Choir) sings "Profile in Courage."

A surprising entry among a number of solemn memorials to the late president, though surely intended as an uplifting hour.

Information was obtained from an audio tape of the broadcast.

Review: *Variety* (July 28, 1965): "Treatment of the man and his time was strictly lowercase and as an interpretive piece this was fourth grade history at its worst."

CHRONOLOGY

1944

The Boys from Boise (9/28, DuMont)

1950

The Box Supper (10/19, CBS)

1951

A Waltz Dream (1/4, CBS)
Once Upon a Tune (3/6-5/15, DuMont)
Amahl and the Night Visitors (12/24, NBC)

1952

Autumn in New York (5/16, CBS)
Trouble in Tahiti (11/16, NBC)

1953

The Marriage (2/7, NBC)
The Parrot (3/24, NBC)

St. George and the Dragon (6/7, NBC)
The Mercer Girls (6/28, NBC)
A Bouquet for Millie (12/17, CBS)
Cinderella '53 (12/21, CBS)
Miss Chicken Little (12/27, CBS)
The Thirteen Clocks (12/29, ABC)

1954

Once Upon an Eastertime (4/18, CBS)
Satins and Spurs (9/12, NBC)
Let Me Go, Lover (11/15, CBS)
A Christmas Carol (12/23, CBS)

1955

The Mighty Casey (3/6, CBS)
Burlesque (3/17, CBS)
High Pitch (5/12, CBS)
Svengali and the Blonde (7/30, NBC)
The King and Mrs. Candle (8/22, NBC)
Our Town (9/19, NBC)
Heidi (10/1, NBC)
Griffelkin (11/6 NBC)
A Child Is Born 12/25, CBS)

1956

Paris in the Springtime (1/21, NBC)
High Tor (3/10, CBS)
The Trial at Rouen (4/8, NBC)
The Adventures of Marco Polo (4/14, NBC)
A Bell for Adano (6/2, CBS)
What Day Is It? (6/6, NBC)
Holiday (6/9, NBC)
The Magic Horn (6/10, NBC)
The Swing (6/11, NBC)
It's Sunny Again (7/3, ABC)
The Bachelor (7/15, NBC)
The Lord Don't Play Favorites (9/17, NBC)
Manhattan Tower (10/27, NBC)
Jack and the Beanstalk (11/12, NBC)
Tom Sawyer (11/21, CBS)
The Stingiest Man in Town (12/23, NBC)

1957

The Singin' Idol (1/30, NBC)
Ruggles of Red Gap (2/3, NBC)
La Grande Bretèche (2/10, NBC)
Cinderella (3/31, CBS)
A Man's Game (4/23, NBC)
Drummer Man (5/1, NBC)
A Drum Is a Woman (5/8, CBS)
He's for Me (7/21, NBC)
Sextuplets (8/7, NBC)
Who's Earnest? (10/9, CBS)
Pinocchio (10/13, NBC)
Stover at Yale (10/20, NBC)
The Adventures of Huck Finn (11/20, CBS)
The Pied Piper of Hamelin (11/26, NBC)
Come to Me (12/4, NBC)
Junior Miss (12/20, CBS)

1958

Hans Brinker (2/9, NBC)
Aladdin (2/21, CBS)
The Land of Green Ginger (4/18, NBC)
Hansel and Gretel (4/27, NBC)
Little Women (10/16, CBS)
Art Carney Meets Peter and the Wolf (11/30, ABC)
Sarah (11/30, CBS)
Gift of the Magi (12/9, CBS)
Mother Goose (12/21, NBC)

1959

Keep in Step (1/23, CBS)
No Man Can Tame Me (2/1, CBS)
Maria Golovin (3/8, NBC)
Art Carney Meets the Sorcerer's Apprentice (4/5, ABC)
The Juggler (5/3, NBC)
The Cage (5/10, NBC)
Dolcedo (5/17, NBC)
The Decorator (5/24, NBC)
A Diamond for Carla (9/14, CBS)
Strawberry Blonde (10/18, NBC)
Beatrice (10/23, Local)
Once Upon a Christmas Time (12/9, NBC)
Cindy's Fella (12/15, NBC)

1960

Around the World with Nellie Bly (1/3, NBC)
So Help Me, Aphrodite (5/31, NBC)
Golden Child (12/16, NBC)

1961

Deseret (1/1, NBC)
O'Halloran's Luck (3/12, NBC)
Break of Day (4/2, ABC)
The Happiest Day (4/23, NBC)
The Accused (5/7, CBS)
The Thief and the Hangman (10/15, ABC)
Feathertop (10/19, ABC)
Tippy Top (12/17, CBS)

1962

Cabeza de Vaca (6/10, CBS)
Noah and the Flood (6/14, CBS)
Gallantry (8/30, CBS)
Mr. Magoo's Christmas Carol (12/18, NBC)

1963

Labyrinth (3/3, NBC)
Quillow and the Giant (11/3, NBC)
The Sojourner and Mollie Sinclair (12/15, NBC)

1964

Return to Oz (2/9, NBC)
Think Pretty (10/2, NBC)
The Story of Rudolph, the Red-Nosed Reindeer (12/6, NBC)

1965

Cinderella (2/22, CBS)
The Final Ingredient (4/11, ABC)
Martin's Lie (5/30, CBS)

The Young Man from Boston (7/22, ABC)
The Hero (9/24, PBS)
The Dangerous Christmas of Red Riding Hood (11/28 ABC)
A Charlie Brown Christmas (12/9, CBS)

1966

Alice in Wonderland, or What's a Nice Kid... (3/30, ABC)
The Road to Lebanon (4/20, NBC)
Olympus 7-0000 (9/28, ABC)
The Canterville Ghost (11/2, ABC)
Alice Through the Looking Glass (11/6, NBC)
Evening Primrose (11/16, ABC)
The Ballad of Smokey the Bear (11/24, NBC)
On the Flip Side (12/7, ABC)
Dr. Seuss' How the Grinch Stole Christmas (12/18, CBS)
Jack and the Beanstalk (12/19, CBS)
The Honeymooners (1966-1970, CBS)

1967

Pinocchio (2/13, CBS)
Jack and the Beanstalk (2/26, NBC)
The Danny Kaye Show (3/8, CBS)
I'm Getting Married (3/16, ABC)
Galileo Galilei (5/14, CBS)
The Emperor's New Clothes (9/4, CBS)
Who's Afraid of Mother Goose (10/13, ABC)
Androcles and the Lion (11/15, NBC)
Aladdin (12/6, CBS)

The Royal Follies of 1933 (12/11, NBC)
The Cricket on the Hearth (12/18, NBC)

1968

The Legend of Robin Hood (2/18, NBC)
The Mouse on the Mayflower (11/23, NBC)
Pinocchio (12/8, NBC)
Fenwick (12/8, NBC)
The Little Drummer Boy (12/19 NBC)
That's Life (9/24/68-5/20/69, ABC)

1969

The Littlest Angel (12/6, NBC)
Frosty the Snowman (12/7, CBS)
Hans Brinker (12/14, NBC)

1970

Uncle Sam Magoo (2/15, NBC)
My Heart's in the Highlands (3/18, PBS)
Goldilocks (3/31, NBC)
The Night the Animals Talked (12/9, ABC)
Santa Claus Is Comin' to Town (12/13, ABC)

1971

The Point (2/2, ABC)
Here Comes Peter Cottontail (4/4, ABC)

Li'l Abner (4/26, ABC)
Owen Wingrave (5/16, PBS)

1972

The Trial of Mary Lincoln (2/14, PBS)
The Emperor's New Clothes (2/21, ABC)
A Special London Bridge Special (5/7, NBC)
Oliver and the Artful Dodger (10/21 & 10/28, ABC)

1973

All About Me (1/13, NBC)
The Death Goddess (1/22, PBS)
The Incredible, Indelible, Magical, Physical Mystery Trip (2/7, ABC)
The Great Man's Whiskers (2/13, ABC)
Dr. Jekyll and Mr. Hyde (3/7, NBC)
Myshkin (4/23, PBS)
The Saga of Sonora (5/3, NBC)
Three for the Girls (11/5, CBS)
The Borrowers (12/14, NBC)
The Bear Who Slept Through Christmas (12/17, NBC)

1974

Rachel, La Cubana (3/4, PBS)
In Fashion (3/13, PBS)
The Magical Mystery Trip Through Little Red's Head (5/15, ABC)
'Twas the Night Before Christmas (12/8, CBS)
The Year Without a Santa Claus (12/10, ABC)

1975

Queen of the Stardust Ballroom
  (2/13, CBS)
Really Rosie (2/19, CBS)
The Tiny Tree (12/14, NBC)

1976

The Entertainer (3/10, NBC)
Pinocchio (3/27, CBS)
Freedom Is (Summer, Syn)
Rudolph's Shiny New Year (12/10,
  ABC)
Peter Pan (12/12, NBC)

1977

Minstrel Man (3/2, CBS)
It's a Brand New World (3/8, NBC)
The Easter Bunny Is Comin' to
  Town (4/6, ABC)
Jack: A Flash Fantasy (7/26,
  PBS)
Once Upon a Brothers Grimm
  (11/23, CBS)
Doonesbury (11/27, NBC)
The Hobbit (11/27, NBC)

1978

Hi-Hat (1/8, CBS)
Cindy (3/24, ABC)
Sing a Sign (5/20, PBS)
Li'l Abner in Dogpatch Today (11/9,
  NBC)
The New Adventures of Heidi
  (12/13, NBC)
Gift of the Magi (12/21, NBC)
The Stingiest Man in Town (12/23,
  NBC)

1979

Rudolph and Frosty's Christmas in
  July (11/25, ABC)
Jack Frost (12/13, NBC)
Skinflint (12/18, NBC)

1980

Return of the King (5/11, ABC)
Gnomes (11/11, CBS)
A Snow White Christmas (11/19,
  CBS)
Pinocchio's Christmas (12/3,
  ABC)
Tell Me on a Sunday (Syn, Metro-
  media)

1982

On the Road to Broadway (4/26,
  NBC)

1984

The Night They Saved Christmas
  (12/13, ABC)

1985

Ace Hits the Big Time (4/2,
  CBS)
Happily Ever After (10/21, PBS)
Copacabana (12/3, CBS)
Alice in Wonderland, Part I (12/9,
  CBS)
Alice in Wonderland, Part II (12/10,
  CBS)
The Life and Adventures of Santa
  Claus (12/17, CBS)

1986

Kingdom Chums: Little David's
    Adventure (11/28, ABC)
Babes in Toyland (12/19, NBC)

1987

The Wind in the Willows (7/5,
    ABC)

1988

Liza Minnelli in Sam Found Out
    (5/31, ABC)
Madeline (11/7, HBO)

1989

Polly (11/12, NBC)

1990

Polly—Comin' Home! (11/18, NBC)
Cop Rock (9/26-12-26, ABC)

1991

La Pastorela (12/23, PBS)

1993

Kingdom Chums: The Original Top
    Ten (4/10, ABC)
Charles Dickens' David Copperfield
    (12/10, NBC)

1994

The Secret Garden (11/5, ABC)

1995

Frosty Returns (12/1, CBS)
Mr. Willowby's Christmas Tree
    (12/6, CBS)

1996

Mrs. Santa Claus (12/8, CBS)

BIBLIOGRAPHY

Adler, Richard, with Lee Davis. *You Gotta Have Heart*. New York: Donald I. Fine, 1990.

Andrews, Bart, with Dunning, Brad. *The Worst TV Shows Ever: Those TV Turkeys We Will Never Forget ... (No Matter How Hard We Try)*. New York: Dutton, 1980.

Ardoin, John. *The Stages of Menotti*. New York: Doubleday, 1985.

Bloom, Ken. *American Song: The Complete Musical Theater Companion, 1877–1995*. 2d ed. New York: Schirmer, 1996.

Brooks, Tim, and Marsh, Earle. *The Complete Directory to Prime Time Network and Cable TV Shows, 1946 to Present*. 6th ed. New York: Ballantine, 1995.

Burke, Richard C. *A History of Televised Opera in the United States*. Ph.D. diss., University of Michigan, 1963. Ann Arbor, Mich.: UMI, 1963.

Cahn, Sammy. *I Should Care: The Sammy Cahn Story*. New York: Arbor House, 1974.

Citron, Stephen. *Noël and Cole: The Sophisticates*. New York: Oxford University Press, 1993.

Collier, James Lincoln. *Duke Elling-

ton*. New York: Oxford University Press, 1987.

David, Nina. *TV Season 74–75, 75–76, 76–77, 77–78*. Phoenix, Ariz.: Oryx.

Davis, Jeffrey. *Children's Television, 1947–1990: Over 200 Series, Game and Variety Shows, Cartoons, Educational Programs and Specials*. Jefferson, N.C.: McFarland, 1995.

Eells, George. *The Life That Late He Led: A Biography of Cole Porter*. New York: Putnam, 1967.

Ellington, Duke [Edward Kennedy Ellington]. *Music Is My Mistress*. Garden City, N.Y.: Doubleday, 1973.

Ericson, Hal. *Syndicated Television: The First Forty Years, 1947–1987*. Jefferson, N.C.: McFarland, 1989.

Ewen, David. *The New Encyclopedia of the Opera*. New York: Hill and Wang, 1971.

Fireman, Judy, ed. *TV Book: The Ultimate Television Book*. New York: Workman, 1977.

Fordin, Hugh. *Getting to Know Him: A Biography of Oscar Hammerstein II*. New York: Random House, 1977.

Gardner, Martin, ed. *The Annotated

"Casey at the Bat"; A Collection of Ballads About the Mighty Casey. New York: Dover, 1995.

Gianakos, Larry James. *Television Series Drama Programming: A Comprehensive Chronicle, 1947–1959.* Metuchen, N.J.: Scarecrow, 1980.

Goldstein, Fred, and Goldstein, Sam. *Prime-Time Television: A Pictorial History from Milton Berle to "Falcon Crest."* New York: Crown, 1983.

Green, Stanley. *The Rodgers and Hammerstein Story.* New York: Da Capo, 1963.

Hanson, Bruce K. *The Peter Pan Chronicles: The Nearly 100-Year History of "the Boy Who Wouldn't Grow Up."* New York: Birch Lane, 1993.

Harris, Steve. *Film, Television and Stage Music on Phonograph Records: A Discography.* Jefferson, N.C.: McFarland, 1988.

Hawes, William. *American Television Drama: The Experimental Years.* University, Ala.: University of Alabama Press, 1986.

_____. *A History of Anthology Television Drama Through 1958.* Ph.D. diss., University of Michigan, 1968. Ann Arbor, Mich.: UMI, 1981.

Inman, David. *The TV Encyclopedia.* New York: Perigee, 1991.

Jewell, Derek. *Duke: A Portrait of Duke Ellington.* London: Pavilion, 1977, 1986.

Lenburg, Jeff. *The Encyclopedia of Animated Cartoons.* New York: Facts on File, 1991.

Leonard, William Torbert. *Theatre: Stage to Screen to Television.* 2 vols. Metuchen, N.J.: Scarecrow, 1981.

Lynch, Richard Chigley. *TV and Studio Cast Musicals on Record:*

Discography of Television Musicals and Studio Recordings of Stage and Film Music. Westport, Conn.: Greenwood, 1990.

McNeil, Alex. *Total Television: The Comprehensive Guide to Programming from 1948 to the Present.* 3rd ed. New York: Penguin, 1991.

Maltin, Leonard. *Leonard Maltin's Movie and Video Guide.* New York: Penguin, 1995.

Marill, Alvin H. *Movies Made for Television: The Telefeature and the Mini-Series, 1964–1986.* New York: Zoetrope, 1987.

Martin, Mick, and Porter, Marsha. *Video Movie Guide.* New York: Ballantine, 1992.

Moore, Douglas, and Sundgaard, Arnold. *Gallantry: A Soap Opera in One Act.* New York: Schirmer, 1958.

Nelson, Craig. *Bad TV: The Very Best of the Very Worst.* New York: Delta, 1995.

Nolan, Frederick. *The Sound of Their Music: The Story of Rodgers and Hammerstein.* London: Unwin, 1979.

Parish, James Robert. *Actors' Television Credits, 1950–1972.* Metuchen, N.J.: Scarecrow, 1973.

Rathbone, Basil. *In and Out of Character.* London: Ianmead, 1989.

Raymond, Jack. *Show Music on Record: The First 100 Years.* Washington, D.C.: Smithsonian Institution Press, 1992.

Ritchie, Michael. *Please Stand By: A Prehistory of Television.* Woodstock, N.Y.: Overlook, 1994.

Rodgers, Richard. *Musical Stages: An Autobiography.* New York: Random House, 1975.

Satern, Mark. *Video's Best.* Phoenix, Arizona: Satern, 1994.

Scheuer, Steven H. *Movies on TV and Videocassette, 1993–1994.* New York: Bantam, 1992.

Selvin, Joel. *Ricky Nelson: Idol for a Generation.* Chicago: Contemporary, 1990.

Shulman, Arthur, and Youman, Roger. *How Sweet It Was: Television, a Pictorial Commentary.* New York: Shorecrest, 1966.

Slonimsky, Nicholas. *Music Since 1900.* New York: Scribner, 1971.

Smith, Steven C. *A Heart at Fire's Center: The Life and Music of Bernard Herrmann.* Berkeley, Cal.: University of California Press, 1991.

Steinberg, Cobbett. *TV Facts.* New York: Facts on File, 1980.

Stone, Desmond. *Alec Wilder in Spite of Himself: A Life of the Composer.* New York: Oxford University Press, 1996.

Sturcken, Frank. *Live Television: The Golden Age of 1946–1958 in New York.* Jefferson, N.C.: McFarland, 1990.

Taylor, Theodore. *Jule: The Story of Composer Jule Styne.* New York: Random House, 1979.

Terrace, Vincent. *Encyclopedia of Television: Series, Pilots and Specials 1937–1973.* 3 vols. New York: Zoetrope, 1986.

_____. *Television 1970–1980.* San Diego: Barnes, 1981.

_____. *Television Specials: 3201 Entertainment Spectaculars, 1939–1993.* Jefferson, N.C.: McFarland, 1995.

Trudeau, Garry. *A Doonesbury Special: A Director's Notebook.* Kansas City, Mo.: Sheed, Andrews & McMeel, 1978.

Turck, Mary C. *A Parent's Guide to the Best Children's Videos and Where to Find Them.* New York: Houghton Mifflin, 1994.

VideoHound's Family Video Retriever. Detroit: Visible Ink, 1995.

VideoHound's Golden Movie Retriever. Detroit: Visible Ink, 1993.

Woolery, George W. *Animated TV Specials: The Complete Directory to the First Twenty-five Years, 1962–1987.* Metuchen, N.J.: Scarecrow, 1989.

Zadan, Craig. *Sondheim & Co.* 2d ed. New York: Harper & Row, 1986.

Periodicals

America
Billboard
Boston Herald-Traveler
Hi-Fi/Musical America
Hollywood Reporter
Los Angeles Times
Musical America
Musical Courier
New York Daily News

New York Herald Tribune
New York Times
Newsweek
Opera News
Saturday Review
Time
TV Guide
Variety
Women's Wear Daily

SONG INDEX

References are to entry numbers

NAME INDEX

References are to entry numbers